MINNEAPOLIS
ST. PAUL
STILLWATER
WAYZATA
FERNDALE
WAYZATA BAY
FORT SNELLING
CALHOUN
HARRIET
MINNEHAHA CREEK
BREEZY PT.
DEEPHAVEN
HOPKINS
BROWNDALE
DEEPHAVEN JCT.
LINWOOD
FAIRVIEW
PURGATORY
PURGATORY CREEK
ST. ALBANS BAY
CHRISTMAS LAKE
GLEN MORRIS
CHRISTMAS LAKE

BEAUTIFUL BIG ISLAND PARK AND LAKE MINNETONKA

OSGOOD CO.

By the Waters of Minnetonka

Also by Eric Dregni Published by the University of Minnesota Press

Minnesota Marvels: Roadside Attractions in the Land of Lakes

Midwest Marvels: Roadside Attractions across Iowa, Minnesota, the Dakotas, and Wisconsin

In Cod We Trust: Living the Norwegian Dream

Never Trust a Thin Cook and Other Lessons from Italy's Culinary Capital

Vikings in the Attic: In Search of Nordic America

By the Waters of Minnetonka

ERIC DREGNI

University of Minnesota Press

Minneapolis · London

Portions of this book have been published previously in Lake Minnetonka *magazine.*

"Air-Ship View of Beautiful Big Island Park and Lake Minnetonka," Twin City Rapid Transit Company, 1907. Courtesy of the Hennepin History Museum.

Published by the University of Minnesota Press
111 Third Avenue South, Suite 290
Minneapolis, MN 55401-2520
http://www.upress.umn.edu

Design and production by Mighty Media, Inc.
Interior and text design by Chris Long

Library of Congress Cataloging-in-Publication Data

Dregni, Eric.
By the waters of Minnetonka / Eric Dregni.
Includes bibliographical references.
ISBN 978-0-8166-8315-4 (hc : alk. paper)
Minnetonka, Lake, Region (Minn.)—History.
I. Title. F612.H5D74 2014
977.6'57—dc23

2014023203

Printed in the United States of America on acid-free paper

The University of Minnesota is an equal-opportunity educator and employer.

20 19 18 17 16 15 14 10 9 8 7 6 5 4 3 2 1

To my grandparents, Evie and Al, cottagers on the lake,
and my parents, for moving us to Minnetonka

Contents

By the time this photograph was taken in 1865, the land surrounding Wayzata Bay had already been plowed and cultivated by early settlers. Photograph by Joel E. Whitney. Courtesy of the Minnesota Historical Society.

Preface

Growing up in Minnetonka, I never imagined the area had such a fascinating history behind its suburban shopping malls, but gradually I noticed relics of bygone days. My grandparents showed me photographs of their cottage on the lake in the 1920s, when Lake Minnetonka was still mostly for vacationers. I went to the Cottagewood Store, which harkened back to general stores filled with bizarre contraptions such as whalebone corsets and hernia truss belts. I visited the annual ice cream social at the historic Burwell House in Minnetonka Mills—but wondered where the actual "mills" were. I vaguely remember the last real remnant of the old glory days, the Excelsior Amusement Park, but the park closed in 1973 and the old carousel ended up at Valleyfair in Shakopee. I had heard that devout churchgoers warned there would be hellfire to pay by those who attended the dances in Excelsior, dances that were "the curse of the community" and featured such bands as the Beach Boys and Rolling Stones. These guardians of moral standards wouldn't know what to say about Prince, who famously told his girlfriend in *Purple Rain* that she must be purified in the

My grandparents in front of their Lake Seton cottage, circa 1920. At this time, Lake Minnetonka was considered a long summertime trek from Minneapolis.

waters of Lake Minnetonka—only to tell her, after her dunking, that they were not presently at that lake.

Beyond the mansions, grand hotels, and amusement parks, I knew there was unusual architecture in the area. A Buckminster Fuller geodesic dome popped up near our house, but even stranger was the Mushroom House in Minnetrista, made entirely of foam sprayed over chicken wire. Lake Minnetonka has a grand tradition of getting rid of architectural gems, such as Frank Gehry's guest house in Orono and Frank Lloyd Wright's masterpiece, the Francis Little House, parts of which ended up in the Metropolitan Museum of Art in Manhattan, the Minneapolis Institute of Arts, and the Allentown Art Museum in Pennsylvania. I learned that Wright, my favorite architect, fled his Taliesin workshop when his lover was murdered. Trying to escape his second wife's morphine addiction, he shacked up with a dancer on Lake Minnetonka but was arrested there for "white slavery" and thrown into the slammer at the Hennepin County jail.

The holier-than-thou mind-set that gave Wright trouble apparently has a history on the lake. For example, I read in an old *Minneapolis Tribune* that the antiliquor Reverend Charles Sheldon of Excelsior tried to shoot a saloon owner in the head with his hunting

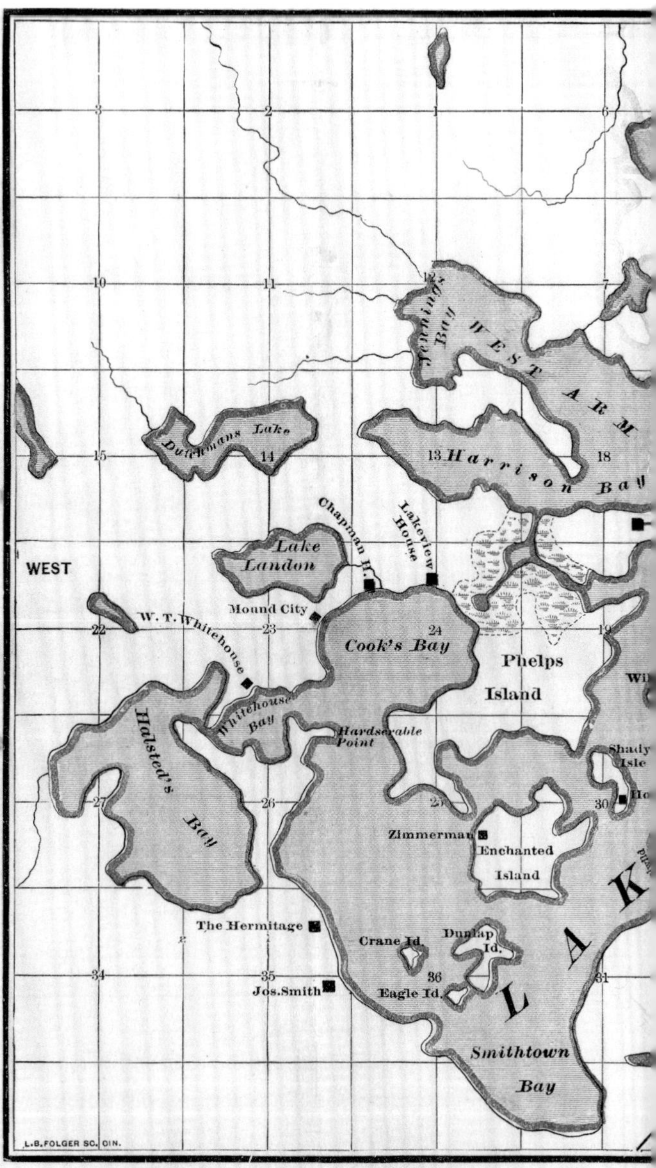

Many bays and inlets gave the lake its early name, Peninsula Lake. By the 1880s, the name had been replaced by Governor Alexander Ramsey's more marketable designation, Minnetonka, from the Dakota words for "great water." Courtesy of the David Rumsey Map Collection, www.davidrumsey.com.

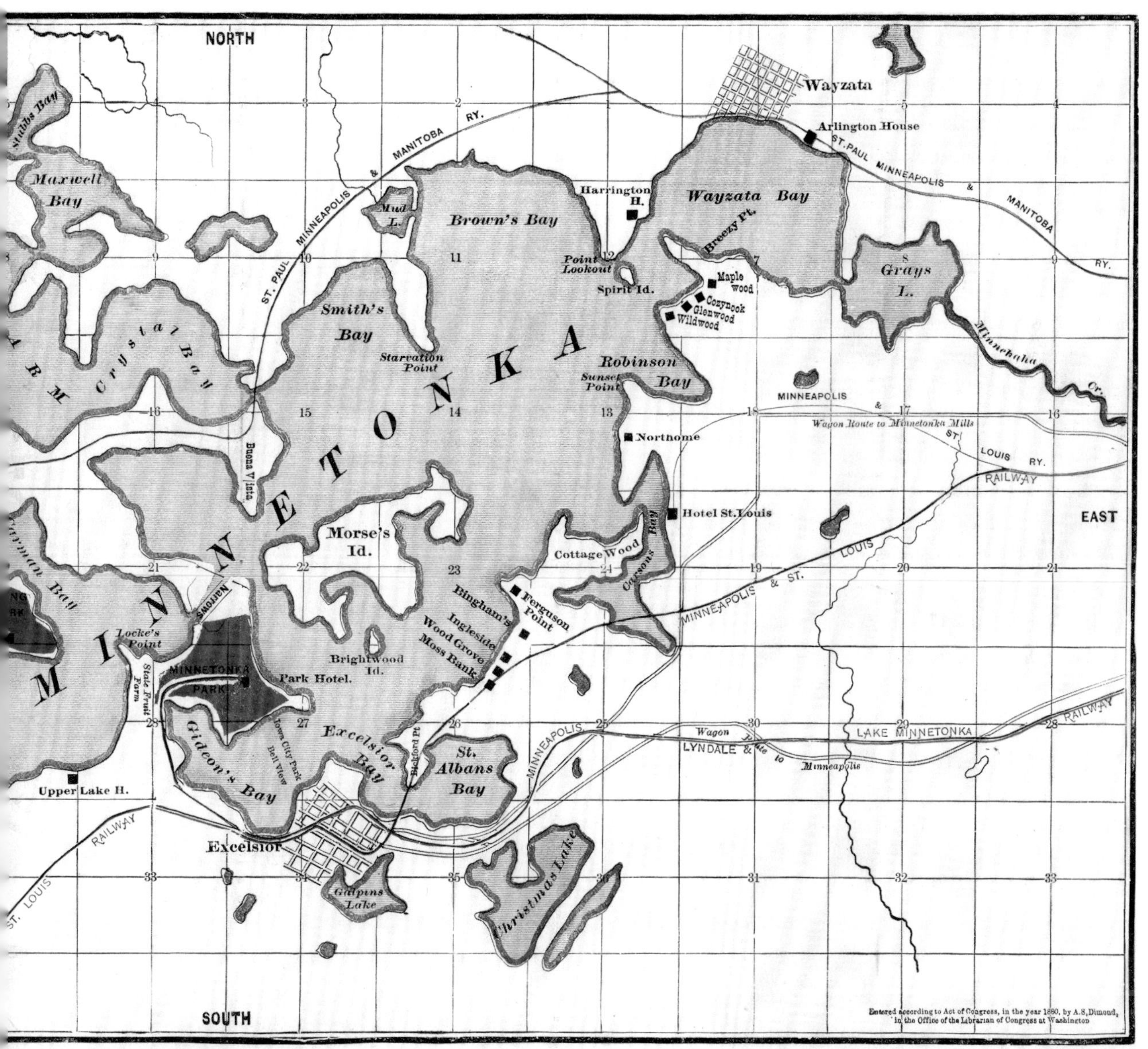

OF LAKE MINNETONKA, MINNESOTA.

D AND CORRECTED FOR 1881.

rifle when the bar owner would not leave town. Sheldon grazed the saloon keeper's head and neatly removed an ear. Don't believe everything you read, though: the *Tribune* was hoaxed, and the story turned out to be bunk.

Not only did the "Wets" and the "Drys" go to battle during Prohibition—when moonshine could make boozers blind, literally—but the area also hosted one of America's most famous outlaws: Jesse James. Minnetonka had a reputation for its hospitality to southerners, including two Confederates from Missouri, Jesse and Frank James.

Gangsters were not the only risk to those on the lake. People died from arson, shipwrecks, tornadoes, and drownings. Some danger was self-imposed: thrill-seeking ice yachters could hit 110 miles per hour zipping from Wayzata to Excelsior over the frozen lake. The lake suddenly seemed less dull and far more exciting. Some of the stories that were difficult to accept came from the earliest history of the area, when Minnesota the territory became Minnesota the state. No one taught the lake's nineteenth-century scandalous history in my classes at Groveland Elementary School. Most histories begin with the "discovery" of Lake Minnetonka in 1822—which of course meant "discovery" by Europeans and wipes away the thousands of years that Native Americans lived here. And what about the French voyageurs, who surely knew of the lake and often intermarried with and learned from the nearby Indian tribes? On my own, I learned about the sacred stone of Lake Minnetonka on Spirit Knob, which was probably stolen by a doctor from St. Louis and never seen again. Most brief histories of the lake tend to gloss over these unsavory moments, but this book attempts to set the record straight.

I had always been fascinated by Purgatory Creek behind our house; I heard that the immigrants thought this area was "worse than hell." The early white settlers had a terrible time; their horses sank out of sight in mud pits and feral pigs ran loose through the villages. Dinner often was squirrel stew, baked raccoon, or dried beaver tail, apparently a delicacy at the time. Far from idyllic, the earliest cabins often had only a blanket for a door and no windows—and the gaps between the rough-hewn logs allowed wolves to try to snatch babies from their cradles. Really. And let's not even talk about the insects.

The destitute settlers learned that men in China would pay thousands of dollars for roots that grew in Minnesota forests. The ginseng boom swept the area as businessmen from Virginia set up shop in Wayzata and even brought slaves to work at the lake. Yes, there were slaves in Wayzata and at Fort Snelling.

After the brutal Civil War and the devastating Dakota War, the 1880s brought elegance to Lake Minnetonka. Trains came, and lavish hotels (some of the most beautiful in the nation) graced the pristine shores of the lake. Wealthy plantation owners escaped the war-ravaged South to visit this lovely lake with their servants—often former slaves—who slept out back with the other "colored folk." Steamboats reminiscent of Mark Twain's *Adventures of Huckleberry Finn* puffed around the lake with big orchestras on deck. The defeated Dakota occasionally danced on them as entertainment. Most histories forget to mention that several of these steamboats blew up, leaving carnage on the beach before at least one Fourth of July celebration. The grandeur of the lakeside hotels was fit for presidents: Ulysses S. Grant and Chester Arthur both vacationed here. Soon trolleys chugged out to the lake, bringing hundreds of "cottagers"; the landed gentry preferred not to mix with these commoners and soon summered further west.

I came to understand that Lake Minnetonka's history is a microcosm of Minnesota's past, and also, to a certain extent, of the country's past. This is not an exhaustive history of the lake but, rather, my compilation of some of its most fascinating and surprising stories. Here is the history that I missed in school and that I wish I had known all along.

Many people supported my research and made this book possible. Thanks to Concordia University's great librarians for help procuring books and the quasi-endowment fund for financial support to complete this project. Paul Hillmer assisted in the search for the sometimes disturbing Indian Guides photographs.

A special thanks goes to the historical societies and museums around the lake for preserving its little-told history. Susan Larson-Fleming helped me find the more unusual photographs within the archives of the excellent Hennepin History Museum. Please support the Minnetonka Historical Society, the Excelsior–Lake Minnetonka Historical Society, the Wayzata Historical Society, the Minnesota Streetcar Museum, the "floating" Museum of Lake Minnetonka, the Westonka Historical Society, and the Minnesota Historical Society; thanks to these organizations and others, Lake Minnetonka's history has remained alive.

Parts of this book were previously published in *Lake Minnetonka* magazine. The staff there, especially Molly Kentala Broman, Nicolle McKinnon, and Laura Haraldson, published my articles over the years: many thanks. The remarkable staff at the University of Minnesota Press, especially Erik Anderson and Heather Skinner, recognized the value of transforming these articles into a book. Thanks to Kathy Delfosse for her incredible editing. A special salute to Kristian Tvedten for digging up all these wonderful illustrations. ☙

This photograph of marshy Halstead's Bay from 1888 shows the lake before the Gray's Bay dam raised the water level. Courtesy of the Minnesota Historical Society.

1

"Big Water"

Mound's Mounds

The Earliest Inhabitants around Lake Minnetonka

The popular history of early Lake Minnetonka is loaded with embellishment. The stories of the Native Americans of the area have been "recorded" by the white settlers—history is written by the victors. The City of Minnetonka Web site states that the first settlement was established in 1852 and makes no reference to earlier "settlements" by the Dakota in the area. Many sources declare that in 1822 the lake was "discovered," a troubling word, considering that people already lived there.

In fact, even early European visitors to the lake noticed lots of conical mounds on high points around the shore and other mounds that were hundreds of feet long. Settlers along the Mississippi River found thousands of mysterious burial mounds in prominent spots overlooking the water. Few believed that ancestors of the Indians could have built such intricate monuments; many thought instead that a long-lost race of "mound builders" had lived here, and that their civilization had disappeared. Others theorized that the Vikings had ventured inland to teach the Native Americans their burial technique, but this theory fell flat when some of the mounds were dated back six thousand years, before the Norsemen set foot on North America in AD 1000. Finally, in 1880, after Indian-made objects were found inside the mounds, the Smithsonian Institution confirmed that the mounds had indeed been built by ancestors of the Native Americans.

Suddenly, the term "New World" did not fit so well. Besides the mounds at Lake Minnetonka, three-thousand-year-old octagonal terraces were found near Epps, Louisiana, measuring four thousand feet across and probably influenced by the Olmec of Mexico. The ancient "Monks Mound" was discovered near the Mississippi River with a base larger than the Great Pyramid of Giza. Among a hundred other mounds, this monument covered sixteen acres and was one of the main attractions of Cahokia, one of the earliest cities in North America with a population of forty thousand and located in what is now southern Illinois.

Not many birch trees grow around Lake Minnetonka, so the Dakota used hollowed-out trees for boats. In 1934 archaeologists pulled this dugout canoe from the lake's waters. Courtesy of the Minnesota Historical Society.

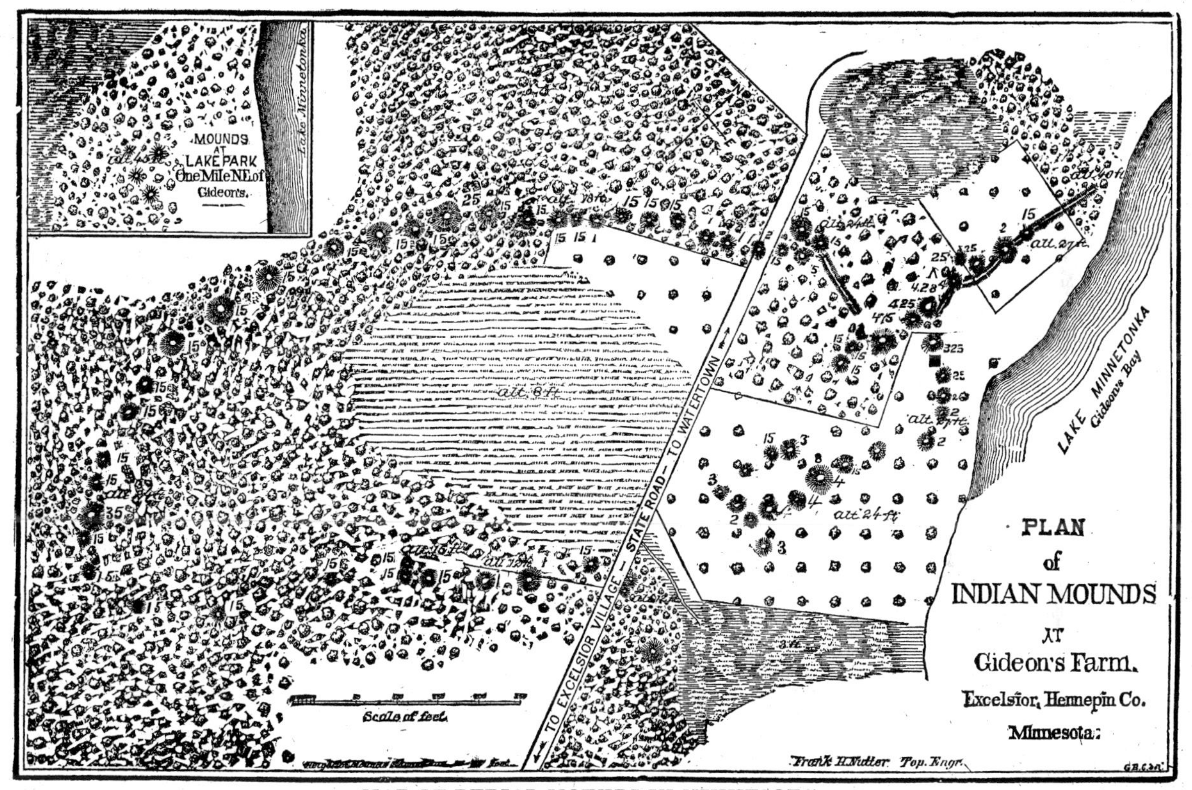

MAP OF BURIAL MOUNDS IN MINNESOTA.

About five hundred Indian burial mounds were discovered near the shores of Lake Minnetonka. This map from 1892 shows the mounds at the Excelsior farm of Peter Gideon, one of the few who actually protected them from plunderers. From Stephen D. Peet, The Mound Builders: Their Works and Relics, *vol. 1 (Chicago: Office of the American Antiquarian, 1892), 59.*

The oldest bones found in Minnesota were discovered about two hundred miles west of Lake Minnetonka. In 1931, road-construction crews paving U.S. Route 59 unearthed the ancient bones of what came to be called the "Minnesota Man," the oldest skeleton in the state—possibly dating back ten thousand to twenty thousand years. Archaeologists determined that the skeleton was so small because it was that of a fifteen-year-old girl. Newspapers renamed her "Eve," "Miss Minnesota," and "Lady of the Lake," since she probably drowned in ancient glacial Lake Agassiz, which covered most of Minnesota during the last ice age. Her hands clutched an elk-antler dagger and a shell from the ocean, meaning that early trade extended far and wide.

Her skeleton is one of the oldest Indian or Eskimo skeletons ever found and is perhaps the oldest female skeleton in America. Her bones were eventually turned over to the Dakota Indians (even though archaeologists doubt she was related to the Dakota tribe). She was reburied in South Dakota.

Some historians claim that the area around Lake Minnetonka was "undoubtedly inhabited" well before 1000 BC because it has one of the largest concentrations of Indian mounds in the state. Many early surveys of the mounds cataloged these burial sites. For example, the "Linwood Mounds," surveyed in 1883, revealed a series of eight mounds just two to three feet high but twenty to twenty-eight feet in diameter. Approximately five hundred mounds were found around the lake, and the largest cluster, the Bartlett group, had eighteen mounds, with one measuring fifty-two feet in diameter.

In Excelsior, a town on the south side of the lake, a circle of mounds was discovered in a low meadow, separated from the shore of the lake by a sort of wall. Sixty-nine burial mounds were charted, and one contained thirty-five skulls arranged in a circular pattern. Considering the number of mounds, this was probably the site of an early village. Inside the mounds, visitors found pottery shards and arrowheads and took them as souvenirs. A diary written by Stephen Denison Peet in 1883 recalls, "On the excursion to the Lake the series of mounds near the Chapman House were again visited. . . . They consist of ordinary tumuli interspersed with oblong mounds, and are situated on the back of the lake overlooking the water, and bordering a stream that empties here." That same year, Theodore Lewis charted all the existing mounds. Many of the mounds that brought fame to the city of Mound (on the west shore of Lake Minnetonka) have since been plowed over for farms.

While simple conical mounds are the most common and oldest, effigy mounds in the shape of animals, usually birds, bears, bison, turtles, or lizards, have been discovered between eastern Iowa and the shores of Lake Michigan. Three special effigy mounds include a 600-foot-long bird-shaped mound near Madison, Wisconsin; a 210-foot-long mound in the form of a standing man near Baraboo, Wisconsin; and a huge lizard-shaped mound near Milwaukee. The largest, however, is the Great Serpent Mound near Hillsboro, Ohio, which measures a quarter mile long. The earth to build these burial mounds was carried entirely by hand, probably in baskets, and valuable artifacts were placed inside. Copper from the Great Lakes, obsidian from the Rocky Mountains, shark teeth from Chesapeake Bay, pearls from the Gulf of Mexico, and mica from the Appalachian Mountains have been found in the mounds, evidence of an extensive trade network.

Little is known about these ancient Native Americans, often called "Woodland Indians," "Mound Builders," or even "Effigy Mounds People," but evidence shows that people have been living in the greater Lake Minnetonka region for about twelve thousand years.

Opening mounds around Lake Minnetonka became an advertised tourist attraction. Self-proclaimed professors and experts would come to discuss the mounds and collect money from visitors. Tourists grabbed a shovel and began digging, with dreams of uncovering hidden treasure. Old bones were tossed aside—ruining the archaeological site—and usually not much more than pottery shards and arrowheads were uncovered.

White immigrants who laid claim to a section of land often were not sure what to do with these burial sites. "Sometimes it was impossible, or at least inconvenient, for a homeowner to avoid building his house or cultivating his garden on one of these historic grave sites," according to *Tales from Tonka: Stories of People around Lake Minnetonka.* The father of early settler Helen Austin bought land on the lake in 1886 to build a large, seven-bedroom house. She recalled her dad putting the house right on the top of the biggest mound.

Peter Gideon, an early apple horticulturalist in the Excelsior region, had ninety-eight mounds on his claim. Originally he opened several of the mounds out of curiosity, but he soon realized he was desecrating burial sites. On July 4, 1872, Gideon refused to let "despoilers set foot on his property," saying they "belonged to a group determined to open an Indian mound. . . . The sparks which flew probably rivaled the evenings fireworks," according to *Happenings around Deephaven: The First Hundred Years.* Years later, when Gideon received a letter from a woman asking whether he had any Indian artifacts from these mounds to display at the 1893 World's Columbian Exposition in Chicago, he wrote back a vicious letter (as quoted in *Tales from Tonka*):

> Dear Madam: I have no Indian relics and don't know of anyone that has, and as to Indian treaties, they can only be had in the National Archives, and for the credit of the American nation it would be well were they burned that future generations should not know the meanness of their ancestors in making fraudulent treaties with them and then, as greed prompted, violate the treaties

Early artistic representations of the lake by Edwin Whitefield show an area he called "South Bay" and the pastoral landscape of early Minnetonka, circa 1850. Many area mounds were later flattened or excavated as tourist spectacles. Courtesy of the Minnesota Historical Society.

Now largely discontinued, the YMCA Indian Guides program brought fathers and sons together to dress up in Native American outfits, with headbands and feathers, for monthly powwows. In this photograph, Minnesota governor Elmer Andersen meets with a group of young guides. Courtesy of YMCA Archives and Paul Hillmer.

> and drive the Indians from place to place as often as the rich wanted their homes and land. Exterminate them, then name rivers, towns and cities in honor of their names.

Most of the mounds have since been spoiled and leveled. An early settler in the north-shore town of Wayzata, Charlie Gibbs, recalled the numerous mounds on Ball Hill. "You could always spot an arrowhead in 'em, it stood out so white," he said in an interview in *Once upon a Lake*. What happened to the mounds? "They hauled them away for fill, a thousand loads of it."

The Legends of the Lake

The Dakota and Ojibwe Come Together

White settlers near this seemingly magical lake began telling stories around their campfires about the Dakota. The erasure of the lake's early history proved convenient for selling the lake and for creating a history that probably never existed as told. Land speculators commodified Native culture and played up tales of beautiful maidens singing along the shores to bring tourists to the lake. These stories could be neither confirmed nor denied, but they obviously served the purpose of opening the land and somehow soothed immigrants' fears.

Once Europeans forced the Native Dakota off the land, some of them were asked back to "perform" for tourists on steamboats or on the verandas of the grand hotels. Sometimes these new immigrants themselves

During the 1920s and '30s, Wisconsin artist Adelaide Hiebel glorified the myth of the "Indian princess" with paintings like By the Waters of Minnetonka, *depicting a maiden who never actually existed (and does not look particularly Native American). Hiebel's paintings helped encourage the overly romantic view of Minnetonka's past that attracted new settlers to this "enchanted" land.*

dressed up in Indian garb and performed Indian plays, written by the white settlers, of course, just as whites donned blackface for minstrel shows at the lake, presenting a skewed version of African American culture.

This tradition of wearing Indian clothes dates back to the Revolutionary War and the Boston Tea Party, when the English colonists set out to distance themselves from their British past and to adopt the indigenous culture, or at least what they envisioned it to be. The Redcoats were not fooled by the disguises since no one imagined that the actual Mohawk Indians would travel hundreds of miles for a dispute that was not theirs.

Appropriation of Indian culture by the white settlers went beyond pageants. In the YMCA Indian Guides program founded in 1926, fathers and sons would wear their interpretation of Native American clothes and face paint, divide into tribes, and perform rituals. The program expanded to include young girls with Indian Princesses and Indian Maidens. It brought hundreds of youngsters out into the wilderness, in spite of the dubious game of dressing up as a member of a culture that had been decimated by many of their forefathers. Author Michael Chabon said this glorification of a vanishing culture conjured "not an imaginary world of Indians, but a world of imaginary Indians." The YMCA finally, in 2003, replaced the name "Indian Guides" with "Adventure Guides" for the few remaining groups.

This wistful and stereotypical vision of Indian culture proved to be a powerful draw. The centerpiece of this massive body of water, Big Island, has had many inhabitants, long before the bandstand and its two-hundred-foot electric tower were erected in the early 1900s. In fact, some of the earliest European settlers supposedly called it "Cottage Island" because, according to the *Northwestern Democrat* from January 19, 1856, "there are upon it numerous Indian cottages—not the common teepees made of poles and covered with skins and canvas, but houses built of timber, and in addition a large fort made of logs, enclosing nearly an acre." The Dakota probably called the island Wetutanka (Big Island), which appeared on some of the earliest maps of the lake from 1860.

Some early settlers viewed the Dakota here as the stereotyped "noble savage" and sought to learn the myths and stories. What we have left are romanticized versions of what might be partly true tales. One such commonly told legend of the lake features Mahpiyata, who was "the most beautiful of the Dakota" and the daughter of Chief Wakanyeya (He Who Towers among Men). Many of the young Dakota braves brought her gifts of deer, buffalo, and bear from their hunts. Her father saw that none of them were worthy of his daughter.

A battle loomed between Mahpiyata's Dakota tribe and the attacking Ojibwe, and she insisted she watch, perhaps to see if one of her suitors was worthy. Her father gave his permission, as long as she stayed in the safety of the forest, unseen and away from the action.

The battle raged on an island near Gale Island. Mahpiyata dutifully hid behind the trees to watch the clash, but witnessed her side losing badly. She could not resist, so she stepped out from the woods to encourage her warriors. She knew she would be a target for the intruders, but the Ojibwe were so impressed by her bravery that their young chief Tayandwada (I Esteem Him Well) ordered that she not be touched. He "claimed" her for himself and dangerously ran by the Dakota warriors and captured her.

He took her back to the Turtle Mountains with his tribe, where she was received, after initial trepidation, with much respect. She lived with them for ten years and eventually taught them many of the ways of the Dakota. She was joined with Tayandwada in marriage and sought peace between the Dakota and Ojibwe people. As the story goes, she convinced her husband and a small group of Ojibwe to return to her village near Lake Minnetonka and the Minnesota River to make peace. She made such a positive impression that messengers went to many tribes from the two nations to summon them to Big Island for a powwow. The dancing, eating, and merrymaking lasted for days and led to more marriages between the Dakota and Ojibwe. When Mahpiyata and Tayandwada died, they were buried side by side on Big Island as a symbol of peace between the two nations.

Stories such as this may have stemmed from actual events, but ultimately they romanticized the lake as a blessed area and conveniently covered up less savory histories of how the land was acquired.

The French Voyageurs

Le Gros Lac *in* Le Grand Bois

Before other Europeans arrived, the French voyageurs traveled far and wide through the *grand bois* (big woods) of Minnesota as part of "the trade" to gather beaver pelts to sell to the lucrative European market. The *coureurs de bois* were "bushrangers," "vagabond fur traders" who often learned Native American languages and sometimes even lived with the tribes. These free agents often came under government scrutiny and scorn, but they were relied on by new settlers for their knowledge of the land, the lakes, and the people who already lived there. The voyageur "liked the woods and the license of Indian villages because they emancipated him from restraint. He was picturesque to say the least," according to *The Old Regime in Canada.*

No confirmation can prove that the voyageurs knew of Lake Minnetonka, but in 1855, J. S. Letford found the remnants of a two-story log house in the town of Carver, just south of Lake Minnetonka. The structure had no doors or windows. Nearby, he found a French pistol, probably from the era of the comte de Frontenac's governorship of Louis XIV's New France.

Long before the St. Anthony Falls were harnessed for energy, Father Hennepin "discovered" them, as seen in this painting by Douglas Volk from 1905. Legend says members of Hennepin's party ventured further, toward Minnetonka. Courtesy of the Minnesota Historical Society.

Another early American writer, Elizabeth Ellet, wrote in her 1853 book *Summer Rambles in the West* about talking to an old trader in St. Paul who already knew of the existence of this beautiful lake. "Heard of it. Yes, to be sure I have; I can't tell you how long. Why, there's a Frenchman at 'Little Six's Village' [Shakopee, which was named for their chief], eighty-one years old . . . says he has known of it since he can remember." This Frenchman was an "old half-breed voyageur, Augustine Rocque, who was in the country long before Napoleon sold it to Jefferson," according to *The Early Background of Minnetonka Beach*. Rocque knew the Dakota language and also worked at Prairie du Chien as an interpreter for Major Stephen Harriman Long on government-approved explorations of Minnesota in 1817 and 1823.

Another far-fetched myth, which was told widely around Lake Minnetonka in the 1870s, describes the "discovery" of Lake Minnetonka by the first Europeans. This unsubstantiated story begins with the group of three voyageurs, led by Belgian-born Father Louis Hennepin, who ventured up the Mississippi River in 1680 into the land of the Dakota at the behest of Louis XIV. They chose a particularly bad time to go, during the late winter, and struggled against ice floes and the swift current. Thirty-three canoes filled with "120 Mdewakanton Dakota warriors . . . in search of hostile Miamis" met them and took them under their wing as half captives, half honored guests. The Dakota probably saved the voyageurs' lives—even though the Europeans might have been terrified—and gave them the first tour of Minnesota. Father Hennepin famously set eyes on the only waterfall on the Mississippi River, which he blessed and named for Saint Anthony of Padua.

Now the story ventures into tall tales. One of the voyageurs, Antoine Auguelle—nicknamed Picard du Gay—stole off one evening in search of another white man the Dakota had supposedly mentioned, even though Auguelle could not understand the Indians' language. As the myth goes, Hennepin scolded Auguelle when he stumbled back into the camp at St. Anthony Falls the next day. Perhaps put on the spot to explain his dangerous side trip, Picard told of a strange hermit, a young Spanish cavalier, who lived on a lake of peninsulas and islands surrounded by mounds just west of St. Anthony Falls, possibly Lake Minnetonka.

When fellow Frenchman Daniel Greysolon du Luth came to "liberate" the supposed prisoners, Auguelle told him his story of the bizarre recluse. This young Spaniard had greeted Auguelle in French. He spoke of traveling with Ponce de Leon in 1512 in search of the fountain of youth. They had bathed in many lakes and fountains, and one of them proved to be the true source of eternal life (perhaps Lake Minnetonka). Unfortunately, they had seen so many springs that he could not say which it was. The young conquistador had returned to Andalusia only to find his wife and children withered and old. His unnatural youth repulsed them, so he returned to the inland seas of the New World, since no hunger or cold could kill him. He only wished to die, but being at Minnetonka was still good.

Hennepin did not believe a word of it, but Du Luth retold the mysterious legend to more French voyageurs, who went in search of the lake. No one ever heard from them again, or so the story goes.

Hennepin, Du Luth, Robert de La Salle, and others wrote their own embellished stories of their travels and sent them to eager audiences back in France and elsewhere; no one could corroborate or correct them

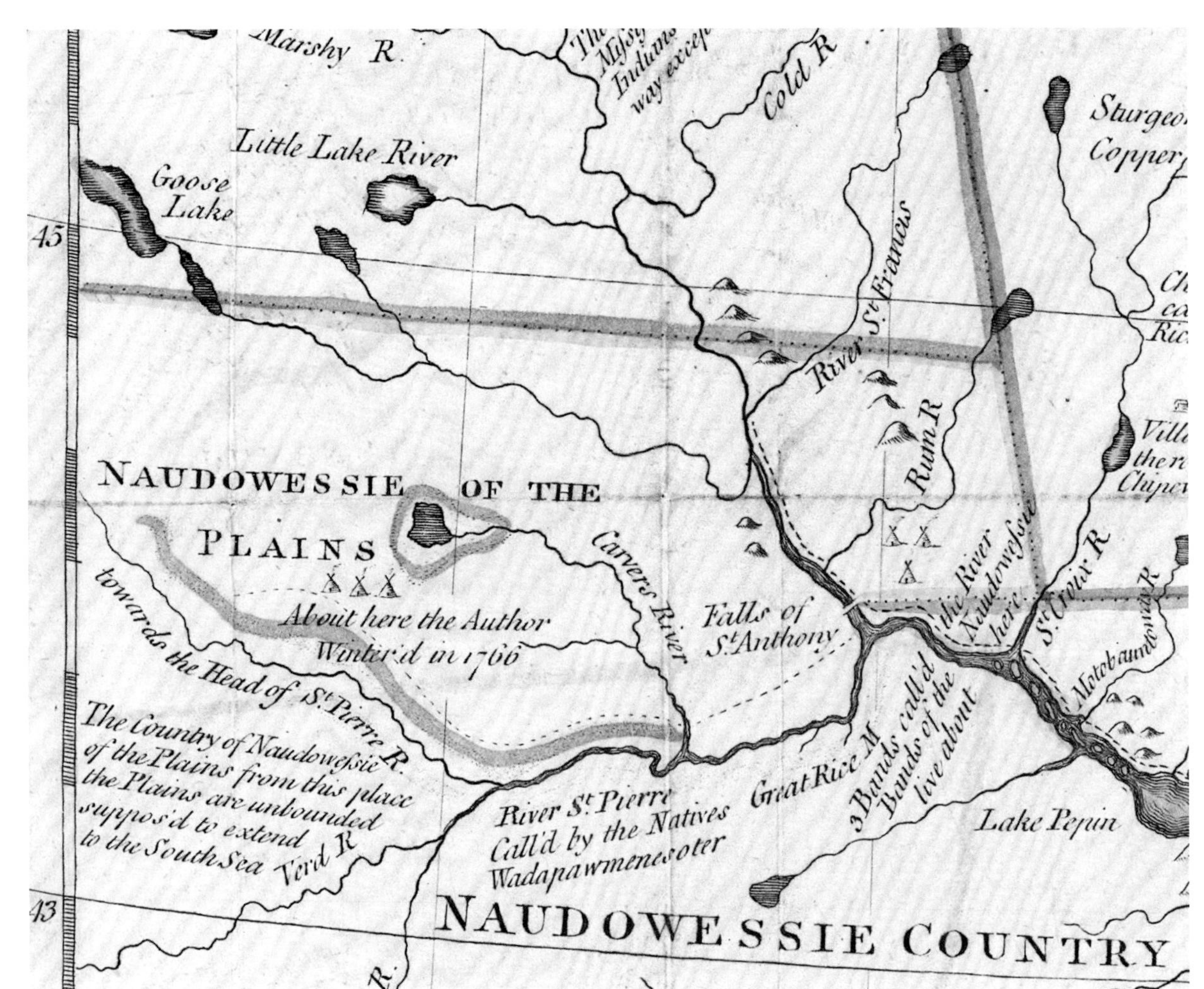

This detail from Jonathan Carver's map shows the location of his winter encampment as well as "Carver's River," possibly Minnehaha Creek. Courtesy of the David Rumsey Map Collection, www.davidrumsey.com.

besides the other voyageurs, who were often illiterate. The myths of the "savage" Indians and the need to tame the frontier made for exciting reading, but they also stirred up unnecessary controversy and tension between the groups, tensions that would later explode.

Jonathan Carver's Travels

On the Paths of the Voyageurs

Before any treaties were signed for the area that included Lake Minnetonka, Europeans claimed the land. France claimed the territory from 1671 to 1762; it was arguably part of Spain from 1762 to 1800; and the United States claimed it after 1803. Lake Minnetonka has been part of six different territories within the United States: Louisiana from 1805 to 1812, Missouri from 1812 to 1821, Michigan from 1834 to 1836, Wisconsin from 1836 to 1838, Iowa from 1838 to 1846, and finally Minnesota since 1849.

During the early years of European presence on these shores, the area saw explorers from various nations. Jonathan Carver came at least close to the lake when he wintered with the Mdewakonton Dakota in 1766–67. Major Robert Rogers, governor of the British outpost on Mackinac Island, had sent Carver inland to explore the territory, looking for a Northwest Passage. He had followed the trails and portages of the French voyageurs from Michigan through Wisconsin into Minnesota, and he chronicled his voyage in *Travels into the Interior Parts of North America.*

Carver spent most of that cold winter downstream on the Mississippi in eastern Iowa, but he wrote about venturing two hundred miles upriver and then to the Minnesota River (or Wadapawmenesoter in Dakota) to a village that was probably present-day Shakopee—just seven miles south of Lake Minnetonka. He probably would have traveled with the Dakota up to the hunting grounds and to go ice fishing on the lake.

Carver also wrote about what was probably Minnehaha Creek, which he called Carver's River: "I arrived at a small branch that fell into [the Mississippi River] from the north; to which, as it had no name to distinguish it by, I gave my own." Accompanying this text is a drawing of the creek, whose source looks suspiciously like Lake Minnetonka, or perhaps Lake Harriet, a few miles farther east in what is now Minneapolis. In *The Aborigines of Minnesota* of 1911, Newton H. Winchell points out that Carver's map was decent, considering he was just passing through the area, and notes, "It has 'Carver's' river from the north draining some lake, apparently lake Minnetonka."

Fur trader Peter Pond, who like Carver hailed from Connecticut, was inspired by Carver's book. Pond followed Carver's footsteps around 1775 and wrote about the voyage in his diary. In 1868, Connecticut governor Charles Pond discovered this document from his forefather in his kitchen, where it was being used

In 1830, Fort St. Anthony (later Fort Snelling) was the first major settlement of Europeans in Minnesota. Courtesy of the Minnesota Historical Society.

as wastepaper. Peter Pond wrote, in his halting English, "As we Past up St. Peter's River about fourteen miles We Stopt to Sea Carvers Hut whare he Past his Wintar when in that Countrey. It was a Log House about Sixteen feet long Covered With Bark—With a Fireplace But one Room and no flore." Could this have been part of the mysterious two-story log house whose remnants were discovered by J. S. Letford several miles south of Lake Minnetonka in 1855?

George Featherstonhaugh, an English geologist, defended Carver and used his book to follow in his footsteps in 1835. "Carver is slightingly spoken of, and I think great injustice done to him," Featherstonhaugh wrote in his book *A Canoe Voyage up the Minnay Sotor.* He "followed him to the extent of his journey, with his book in my hand, I always found his descriptions deserving of very great confidence." Even so, Featherstonhaugh writes of Minnehaha Falls and shows Minnehaha Creek on his map with no source. The big water of Minnetonka was perhaps still hidden to the Europeans.

The "Discovery" of the Lake

French Leave from the Fort

In spite of being by far the largest body of water near what would become Minneapolis, Lake Minnetonka was settled by Europeans relatively late. Some claim that the Dakota tried to keep the sacred lake secret from the Europeans. Father Hennepin traveled through Minnesota in the late 1600s, and the Dakota showed him St. Anthony Falls, but he never ventured west to find the source of Minnehaha Creek, as far as we know. He was, however, taken captive by the Dakota, or at least strongly encouraged to accompany them further north to Mille Lacs.

The best-known story of the "discovery" of Lake Minnetonka dates to 1822. (Of course, the lake was already well known to the Dakota, so "discovery" is a misnomer.) The story begins with Fort St. Anthony (now Fort Snelling), the first substantial European outpost in the area. Soldiers from Fort Snelling often ventured out from the safety (and captivity) of the walls, usually over to Pig's Eye (later St. Paul) to live it up at the squalid watering hole built by St. Paul's first European resident, Pierre "Pig's Eye" Parrant. Mark Twain famously wrote about this seedy settlement, "How solemn and beautiful is the thought that the earliest pioneer of civilization is never the steamboat, never the railroad, never the Sabbath school, never the missionary—but always—whisky. This great vanguard arrived upon the ground which St. Paul now occupies in June, 1837. Yes, at that date Pierre Parrant built his first cabin, uncorked his jug and began to sell whisky to the Indians."

In May 1822, 150 years after Hennepin ventured into the area, four young men set out the opposite direction, deep into "Indian territory." The two leaders of the group were Joseph Renshaw Brown, a seventeen-year-old drummer from the regiment band at the fort, and eighteen-year-old William Joseph "Joe" Snelling, son of Fort Snelling's commander, Colonel Josiah Snelling. The younger Snelling had opted out of West Point in favor of exploring the wilderness and visiting Dakota villages. Two enlisted men, Samuel Watkins and Mr. Stewart, went along, probably to look after the mischievous son of their commander. According to *Minnetonka Story*, the young men "took 'French leave' of the fort"—that is, they left without a pass. Another source, *Once upon a Lake*, describes the four men as having "bodies . . . patched with scurvy, and their gums pale and spongy with it."

Everyone at Fort Snelling had speculated that the source of Brown's River (later called Minnehaha Creek) was either Lake Harriet or Lake Calhoun, just north of Lake Harriet, but this small party went further. Whether this group actually made it to the lake is unclear in early records. They discovered an "inland sea abounding in islands and peninsulas," where they picked wild strawberries and watched the deer frolic. As the story goes, back at the fort, the colonel and other kin looked high and low for the rascals and finally noticed a missing canoe. A search party found the two boys and their minders lounging on the lake shore eating fresh fried fish. When they returned, Papa Snelling went into a rage and wanted no mention made of this cursed lake. Even so, the record books gave credit to these adventurous Tom Sawyers for "discovering" Minnetonka.

Whether Joe Brown and the young Snelling actually arrived at Lake Minnetonka is perhaps less significant than their further contributions because of their reaching out to the Dakota. Even though Brown was labeled "a runaway drummer boy always seeking adventure," he mastered the Dakota language and married a Native American woman, Wakinyasheea (Down of a Bird). He often lived with the Dakota and translated for the encroaching U.S. government. He was torn and shocked when the Dakota War of 1862 broke out in Minnesota. After the conflict calmed down, he was forced to prove his loyalty to the United States, and "he rolled the drum at the Mankato hanging of thirty-nine Sioux Indians," according to *The Early Background of Minnetonka Beach*.

Joe Snelling learned the Dakota language and customs and attempted to write about them without embellishment in *Tales of the Northwest*. He married a young woman who was half Dakota and half French, and his disapproving family tried to hush up all mention of her and his explorations, including his trip to Minnetonka. After just a year of marriage, she passed away. One source says she "died of starvation and cold in her hut outside the garrison walls."

Snelling was one of the first to attempt to document the ways of the Dakota both in fiction and nonfiction. In his stories, he pushed for realism rather than

McLeod County, just west of Lake Minnetonka, is named for fur trader and legislator Martin McLeod, seen here about 1860, who set out to form an idyllic "Indian Kingdom" with the aid of General James Dickson's Indian Liberating Army. Courtesy of the Minnesota Historical Society.

for the glorifying "noble savage" stereotype prevalent in popular novels of the time, but his stormy life got in the way of his crusade. He engaged an enemy in a duel at Fort Snelling and lost a finger from his left hand. He moved back east to write, but he was seriously wounded by an assassin who objected to his writings. In spite of being sued for libel, going on a drunk, and then spending four months in the Boston House of Correction, Snelling helped many understand the way of the Dakota.

An "Indian Kingdom"

McLeod's Liberating Army

While later skirmishes between the settlers and Native Americans are well documented, many of the earliest explorers relied on the Indians' help to escape starvation. Hezekiah Hotchkiss, a trapper, was one of the first Europeans to reach Lake Minnetonka, and he lived there with the Dakota. On October 12, 1852, he wrote back to his family in Boston about his time as a trapper on Lake Minnetonka: "After all these years of trapping with the Indians, I'm pretty nigh a Sioux myself, dress like 'em, act like 'em, eat like 'em, canoe and hunt and fish like 'em; their way is best. I'm the only pale face around this lake." Hotchkiss never bothered to learn their language, so he complained, "I'm never uneasy with them, but I do get deathly sick of their hellish jibberish."

The history of Minnetonka presented in *Once upon a Lake* glorifies the Native Americans of the area: "The

Dakota was a splendid creature. Hodge's *Handbook of American Indians* terms him 'the highest type, physically, mentally and probably morally, of the western tribes.' He was erect, tall, usually superbly built, often handsome by any standards." While these generalizations may be flattering, in contrast to many of the negative stereotypes, they are still "noble savage" stereotypes.

In the 1830s, a Scottish Canadian, Martin McLeod, saw the injustice dealt to the Indians by the U.S. government and dreamed of forming an "Indian Kingdom" on land still controlled by the Native Americans but nevertheless within what the United States deemed its borders. He may have had good intentions, but he was bedazzled by General James Dickson, an Englishman, who was "possibly insane," according to one source, and who had recently returned from Texas, where he fought back the Mexican "intrusion" into what was then still Mexico's own territory. An opportunist and charlatan, Dickson supposedly buried a secret treasure of silver ingots somewhere in the Southwest that he hoped to return to someday.

Having seen in Texas and the West how quickly borders could change, Dickson began recruiting among displaced Indian tribes back east to form an "Indian Liberating Army." This militia set out to unite all Indian nations in a kingdom to be set up in California. Dickson even designed flashy uniforms, which had nothing to do with American Indian clothes, and opted for flashy epaulets. Of course, Dickson was to be the ruler of this Indian kingdom, not a Native American. In honor of past Native American leaders, he even picked out his royal name: Montezuma II.

Dickson's rank as general and his self-serving dream of forming an Indian Kingdom meshed with McLeod's more noble quest. The ragtag Indian Liberating Army went north from the United States looking for some assistance. They wandered into the Selkirk Settlement near Winnipeg, but the white settlers, not surprisingly, would not help, since the Canadian government could have viewed that as treason. The frigid northern winter struck, and Dickson lost his toes to frostbite; his vision of sitting atop a throne as Montezuma II fell to pieces. The campaign for the independent kingdom ended with hunger, arrests, a shipwreck, and a tragic trek to a Hudson's Bay Company outpost. Dickson's requests for credit were all denied—perhaps he wished he had not buried his silver in the Southwest. Most of his Indian Liberating Army either deserted or died.

McLeod went back to the Minnesota River, probably passing near Minnetonka, to escape the even colder Canadian winters. He had given up on his hopes for an Indian Kingdom, and in his diary he oddly wrote "disparaging entries about squaws and white men who associated with them," according to *Once upon a Lake.* He married a beautiful "mixed-blood" woman, Mary Elizabeth Ortley, at Fort Snelling but never mentioned her in his diary, even though she had six of his children.

Early claim houses around Lake Minnetonka relied on felled trees. This photograph shows one of the first frame houses of the area, built by Silas Seaman in Minnewashta, on the southeast side of Lake Minnetonka. Photograph by A. F. Raymond. Courtesy of the Minnesota Historical Society.

Early Trespasses

Europeans Encounter the Dakota

The trappers and traders who ventured throughout Minnesota profited greatly from trading with the Indians, and only later did the idea that the land was valuable become widespread. Land speculators backed by the U.S. government pushed the Indians off this valuable territory.

Before the Treaty of Traverse des Sioux and the Treaty of Mendota were finalized, some settlers sought to move ahead of the impending expansion and trespassed into Dakota territory to make claims. The land did not officially "open up" to settlers until late 1854, and legitimate claims could not be secured until 1855. Although the concept of individual land ownership may not have been familiar to Native Americans, they did not just accept the new settlers on their sacred lake. In fact, the Indian agent at Fort Snelling vehemently protested these trespasses on their land. The government gave him little notice and in fact would probably have helped the settlers if they had had problems.

Franklin Steele, one of the founders of St. Anthony and Minneapolis, ventured out from Fort Snelling into the Indian territory at the lake in the summer of 1846. Steele and McLeod went by horseback to what is now called Gray's Bay, on the lake's eastern end, then went to the north side of Wayzata Bay where Big Six (father of Little Six; both were named Shakopee) and his tribe often pitched their teepees, even as late as 1862. The tribe was probably away on a buffalo hunt, so Steele and McLeod kept exploring the lake. They realized they could not circumnavigate the lake, so they returned to the fort.

Steele had come to the fort via steamboat and worked as the sutler, or storekeeper, so he was privy to local gossip. He heard that the U.S. government was in the process of working a deal with the Dakota to cede the land around St. Anthony Falls. The story goes that Steele crossed the dangerous ice of the Mississippi at night with a sack of potatoes and some lumber and nails. He planted his potatoes, through the snow, and tacked together a little claim shack at the prime spot of St. Anthony Falls.

When morning came, the major from the fort was astonished to see Steele's legitimate claim on this land. Steele thus controlled half the waterpower of the falls and eventually built the first bridge across the Mississippi River. In 1857, Steele also convinced the U.S. government that Fort Snelling was no longer useful, and he bought the fort and eight thousand acres for $90,000 with a down payment of just $30,000. When the Civil War broke out, he graciously let the government use the fort and surrounding land. After the war, the government asked for payment of the remaining $60,000 for the fort. In retaliation, Steele slapped on a rental fee of $160,000 for the use of Fort Snelling. After congressional investigations into Steele, he managed to hold on to almost all the land for his initial $30,000.

With this precedent, many settlers recognized

The most prominent point of land jutting into the lake earned the name "Spirit Knob" from early explorers. In 1867, Benjamin Franklin Upton photographed this sailing party on its shore. Library of Congress Prints and Photographs Division.

that if they acted early they might make a small fortune. One of the first to trespass into Dakota territory and set up shop was Patriarch Robert Trumble. In 1849, with a wagon train pulled by oxen, he followed well-worn Indian paths all the way to the lake, but he was uncomfortable with this dark wooded area. As though working his way to Paradise, his group passed "the lip of a quagmire so hellish miry that they named it Purgatory," according to *Once upon a Lake*, which is where one of Minnehaha's tributaries, Purgatory Creek, got its name.

The claims made on the land, of course, were

SPIRIT KNOB, LAKE MINNETONKA.

The vistas available to tourists from Spirit Knob continued to feature prominently in the lake's mythology well into the steamboat era. This engraving by Willis R. Willard appeared in early periodicals like Tourist and Sportsman *and* Northwestern Tourist. *Courtesy of the Minnesota Historical Society.*

unenforceable until years later. Many land agents sought to sell immigrants untenable titles to questionable parcels of land in areas that had not been properly surveyed.

In spite of the treaties requiring the Dakota to leave their ancestral land, white settlers reported that they often returned during the summer. On May 26, 1858, residents of what would become Eden Prairie, southeast of what is now Minneapolis, complained of noise from Shakopee that they surmised was a battle between rival Ojibwe and Dakota. "The townspeople hurried to the riverbank for ringside seats, undeterred by occasional bullets whizzing by," according to *Tales from Tonka*. "When the ammunition of the Sioux began to run out, the citizens of Shakopee furnished more so that the show could be continued."

Obviously the white settlers were pleased that these two bands fought each other rather than them. One witness described the slaughter as a show, "as perfectly as one could sit in the boxes of a theater and watch a play." A work from 1931, *101 Best Stories of Minnesota*, callously referred to the event as amusement: "The only flaw in the Battle of Shakopee was that the citizens of the town didn't have time to send out invitations for the entertainment."

Where Is the Sacred Stone of Spirit Knob?

A Native American Altar

One of the prevailing myths that has been retold as popular (and unconfirmed) history converges at one spot: Point Wakon, or the "Place of Spirits," according to the *Northwestern Tourist*, a newspaper from the 1880s that was itching to sell articles on supposed Indian myths. This legend is based on eyewitness accounts and on speculation that the Dakota supposedly believed that all the power of Lake Minnetonka's peninsulas and bays converged here. The location, just north of Maplewood on the southern edge of Wayzata Bay at the end of Breezy Point, became known as Spirit Knob to the white settlers because the land protruded sixty feet above the water level.

Many early visitors saw the sacred Dakota site with their own eyes. In *Summer Rambles in the West*, Elizabeth Ellet described her trip to Lake Minnetonka in the early 1850s before the Europeans acquired the territory. She understood that she was "treading ground the white man's claim had never reached as yet." She described her group stumbling on campsites where Dakota had recently stayed, with campfires and poles still standing for teepees and lodges.

Ellet's group visited a site that was probably Spirit Knob (before it had that name) and speculated that it was an important Dakota site. When her group met a Dakota chief, they asked him about a mysterious stone, painted red with yellow spots and elevated by two sticks, on the pinnacle of Spirit Knob. She reported that the chief replied that the stone was visited by warriors who returned from battle. It is unclear how she understood this since she did not speak Dakota.

Captain Arthur Mills and Lucien Parker confirmed her report when they wrote in the *St. Anthony Express* of October 1, 1852, about their visit to Spirit Knob:

> We found on the shore a stone, shaped like an egg, standing on the small end, painted red and all the rocks around were sprinkled with a paint resembling blood. On the top of the stone was placed some Indian tobacco, ready for smoking; and about a rod from the stone was a grave. The bark with which it had been covered was rotten, so that hardly any traces of the grave were left except the mound. . . . It is probably the grave of a Chief, who was killed with the others across the lake, but the warriors out of respect buried him here, and everyone who passes this way paints the stone, and leaves some tobacco, in memory of the departed chief.

Even after the Minnesota territorial government officially allowed white settlers into the area in 1854, Dakota warriors returned to this site. In 1859, George

Francis Davis Millet's painting Treaty of Traverse des Sioux, *from 1905, hangs permanently in the governor's reception room at the Minnesota State Capitol and offers a majestic and grandiose spin on what proved to be a giant land grab by the U.S. government. Courtesy of the Minnesota Historical Society.*

Day recalled a group of Dakota who came back with the scalp of an Ojibwe following a battle. The tribe cleared snow in a circle about thirty feet across.

What happened to this hallowed stone of the Dakota? The 1884 *Guide and Directory of Lake Minnetonka* gives a clue. One of the early groups to the site considered the huge stone "so great a curiosity that the party concluded to send it to Washington as a relic. . . . Mr. Harrington, who still lives near Wayzata, dug it out and hauled it away with his oxen, and tells us it was shipped to St. Paul, where it was conveyed by water to Pittsburgh and thence to Washington."

Several other sources claimed a "Dr. S. of St. Louis" stole the stone in 1852, or perhaps the thief was "a dentist from Ohio." Once Dr. S., or whoever it was, removed the stone, the outcropping that was Spirit Knob began to crumble. When the Breezy Point Club bought the land, members tried to restore it, but the peninsula was too far gone. Instead, they leveled it "to within a few feet of the water," according to *Tales from Tonka*, and now luxury homes stand near the point.

Today, the whereabouts of the stone are unknown. Perhaps it resides in a private collection whose owners probably do not know its spiritual importance to the original inhabitants of Lake Minnetonka.

Treaties of Traverse des Sioux and Mendota

Three and a Half Cents per Acre

Minnesota's first territorial governor, Alexander Ramsey, was eager to open lands to the west of the Mississippi to increase the territory's wealth. Meeting one mile north of St. Peter at a Dakota rendezvous site named Oiyuwege, the European settlers and the Dakota signed the Treaties of Traverse des Sioux and Mendota on July 23 and August 5, 1851. The U.S. government would acquire from the Sisseton and Wahpeton Dakota all the land between the Minnesota and Mississippi Rivers, about 23.75 million acres, for $1.665 million dollars.

Although the treaties ultimately benefited the settlers greatly, many questioned paying so much money when the territorial government could scarcely afford it. Some politicians justified trading food to the Native Americans in exchange for the more than thirty-seven thousand square miles of prime land as a form of charity when the Native Americans needed immediate food rather than the cash. The *Pioneer Press*'s first editor, James M. Goodhue, wrote, "To the Indians themselves, the treaty is now indispensable to their very existence. Especially the ensuing winter, without the treaty, these poor wretches must die off by hundreds. The high water has ruined their corn, and they will entirely lose their summer buffalo hunt, by having spent the season coming to, remaining at, and returning from the treaty."

The Dakota chiefs gathered and spoke to their people about the treaties. "We know that the whites are like a great cloud that rises in the East and will cover all our lands," they said, according to *The Early Background of Minnetonka Beach.* Little Crow (Taoyateduta) spoke with "suavity of manner in which he was gifted beyond any other Indian I ever met," according to Dr. J. W. Daniels in *Indian Outbreak.* Daniels was careful not to heap too much praise on Little Crow and pointed out that he had four wives, all sisters because they could get along better than wives who did not know each other.

Little Crow faced the "scowling braves" who did not want the treaties, but he signed first, saying, "Warriors, it has been said by some of you that the first who signs the treaty you will kill. Now, I am willing to be the first. . . . It matters little to me when my time comes, nor do I care much how it comes, although I would rather die fighting our enemies. I believe this treaty will be best for the Dakotas, and I will sign it, even if a dog kills me before I lay down the goose quill."

The brother of Chief Shakopee, Hochokaduta, disagreed. He argued, "The chiefs don't seem to do anything and we must be heard." He agreed with Little Crow that the borderline in the east was too far north, and he wanted Indian land to include Minnehaha Creek and Lake Minnetonka. Ramsey and the U.S. commissioner of Indian affairs, Luke Lea, held firm.

Further, because of manipulation by the politicians and (perhaps intentionally) poor translation, the Dakota signed what they were led to believe was a triplicate of the treaty that gave them just three cents per acre. In fact, these were "trader's papers," which gave the Indians' profits first to anyone who claimed the Indians owed them money. The result was that the white settlers at the signing immediately profited. For example, Henry Sibley, who would become governor in 1858, was paid $66,459—a fortune at the time. The net result was that the Dakota would receive one cent per acre. This money was put into a trust from which the Dakota would receive annual payments.

Settlers were impatient for Congress to ratify the treaties. The Senate did so in 1852, and soon afterward the Dakota agreed to the treaties' amendments, although the treaties would not be legally adopted for a couple more years.

Hezekiah Brake would not wait for the bureaucracy and had already moved to the lake illegally. He wrote in his memoir *On Two Continents* that in 1852, twenty Dakota visited his family's camp and came right into his house. Others in his group of settlers hid until the Dakota were gone, but he and his wife claimed not to be afraid, even though the men wore black, yellow, red, and white paint. This was the group that came from "Shockapi" (Shakopee). Brake begged the U.S. authorities for help: "I had earnestly entreated Captain Steele of the Fort to have the Indians removed from the neighborhood," despite their legal right to still be there.

Governor Alexander Ramsey (seen here in 1888 at a picnic in Orono with surviving Civil War officers of the First Minnesota Regiment) gave Lake Minnetonka its name after declaring the name "Peninsula Lake" too mundane. Photograph by Palmer and Anderson. Courtesy of Macalester College Archives, DeWitt Wallace Library.

The next summer, Chief Shakopee, along with fifty to sixty members of his tribe, came to visit. He came to sell his canoes and paddles, since Fort Snelling had now forced their removal from the land. Brake wrote that he understood enough of what Shakopee said in the Dakota language to know that he "was telling them that they were leaving forever their favorite hunting-grounds, where they had so long enjoyed freedom and happiness." Brake had a change of heart, even though he had beseeched the authorities to evict the Native Americans.

Not until February 24, 1853, did President Millard Fillmore publicly announce the treaties, but they could not yet take effect. That year civil engineer John Carman was ordered to come to Minnetonka from Ohio to survey the land before new settlers could officially lay claim.

Settlers could not officially come until August 4, 1854, when the U.S. government opened the newly acquired territory, or "Suland," as the newspapers called the area. The earliest colonizers were squatters, and "it was not until 1855 that they were able to enter their lands at the United States land-office and receive good solid titles," according to *The Early Background of Minnetonka Beach*. Even so, by 1852 many settlers had already swarmed illegally across the Mississippi River, into the territory, and around beautiful Lake Minnetonka to stake their claim.

What's in a Name?
Big Water: Minnetonka

The lake is the tenth largest in Minnesota, with a shoreline of ninety-one miles and a depth of up to ninety-one feet, yet what was it called? The first Europeans settlers called it Peninsula Lake because of the many bays and fingers of land jutting out into the deep water. Steele exclaimed, "Here is the most beautiful and perfect climate and country I have ever seen, wanting only a touch of labor to make it a veritable paradise.... Back in Eastern cities, and in Europe, men, women and children are living in filth, idleness and all the squalor of abject poverty. Why don't they come?" Still, he did not name the lake.

The early trapper Hezekiah Hotchkiss wrote back to friends in Boston, "You'd better come out here and see My Lake for yourselves. You can't imagine how she glows in the sunshine and glitters in the moonlight." Fortunately for future generations, he refrained from naming the lake after himself.

"Peninsula Lake" stuck until 1853 when Territorial Governor Ramsey visited the lake after signing the Treaties of Traverse des Sioux and Mendota. He declared to his troupe, "You know, boys, this discovery is a perfect inland sea." Ramsey rejected the ho-hum "Peninsula Lake," and by naming it *minne*, "water," and *tonka*, "big," he gave a nod to the Dakota, who had considered the lake a sacred spot for centuries. ("The original Dakota was closer to 'Mdeatonka' or 'Bdeatonka,'" according to *The Early Background of Minnetonka Beach*.) What's more, Ramsey knew that he was helping polish the identity of the lake to glorify the Indian past that he had just helped erase.

William Keating, who wrote about Jonathan Carver's early trip, claims that the original Indian name for the lake was Manha Tanka Otamenda (Lake of Many Large Birds), but French sources claim it derives from Marrah Tanka (Swan Lake), the name of a large lake just northeast of Mankato. In any case, early documents show various spellings—sometimes it's "Mi-ni-tan-ka"—but the sounds are always similar.

Preserving the lake's Dakota name kept a certain mystique and sometimes made white immigrants to the area edgy. Before the treaties even took effect, many white immigrants moved to the lake. The book *Minnetonka Story* tells of settlers who were nervous in Indian territory being assured by land speculators that Native Americans believed the lake was sacred: "This lake is sacred to the Great Manitou who loves peace. Thousands of moons ago he gave Minnetonka to the Sioux on the promise never to defile its shores by bloodshed." This reassurance often guaranteed the sale.

Hotchkiss had not gotten the message about the naming of the lake, and he reported that he heard rifle shots and axes chopping in the distance when "I was canoeing along by the outlet of My Lake." He knew times were changing as he listened to "somebody on the shore [who] was laughing fit to split. (Indians don't laugh.) Now what does all this mean? Just one thing—the whites are coming." The publicity of Franklin Steele and others about the beauty of this lake near St. Anthony and Minneapolis began attracting thousands of new settlers. ❧

The early white settlers to the area often had to fend off claim jumpers who sought to cash in on the newly opened land. Here Joseph Chowen and his family pose outside their house at what would later be known as Chowen's Corner at Minnetonka and Northome Boulevards in Deephaven. Courtesy of the Excelsior–Lake Minnetonka Historical Society.

2

The Settlers Settle

Early Skullduggery

Feuds, Charlatans, and Claim Jumping

Some of the early settlers around the lake fancied themselves as Robinson Crusoes in the wilds of Indian territory before it was officially U.S. land. The trapper Hezekiah Hotchkiss wrote in 1852 about a trip with an Indian friend: "[We] were canoeing along the southeast shore when we caught sight of a man stepping off land and stopping to drive stakes now and then." His time in the wild away from white society was coming to an end.

James M. Goodhue, editor of the *Minnesota Pioneer* (later the *Pioneer Press*), wrote to readers that same year, "The treaties *will be ratified.* There is no room for ifs or buts about it." Jonas Howe, an artist from Petersham, Massachusetts, took these words to heart and informed his wife Margaret that he would like to farm along Lake Minnetonka. More important, the family doctor had told Howe that he had tuberculosis and needed the "fine, dry climate of Minnesota Territory," according to a journal about Plymouth Township kept by his daugh-

Early visitors to Lake Minnetonka relied on hunting and trapping to survive in the wilderness. Here Henry McKarmick is cleaned up and poses for the camera with his hunting dog. Courtesy of the Excelsior–Lake Minnetonka Historical Society.

ter Laura Negus Howe. His wife reluctantly agreed to uproot the family and move to the Wild West, where her husband might well die of TB, leaving her all alone. They settled north of Wayzata in what would become Plymouth.

While most of the settlers spoke English, the town of Plymouth was home to many Germans who could not understand anything but their own language. When a local government was set up, "there was a French Canadian who could neither read nor write any language, but he was one of the three supervisors—an office of the first importance," according to *Once upon a Lake.* Settlers communicated through sign language, drawings, and the simplest words. Even so, divisions formed along ethnic lines.

As soon as Goodhue and others put out the word that this beautiful new land filled with lakes would be open for settlement, settlers invaded, arriving before the surveyors did. By 1855, "the enterprising and audacious squatters . . . had no troublesome scruples . . . no restraints but the ethics of the frontier," according to *The Early Background of Minnetonka Beach.*

Pioneers lugged in lumber and tacked up little claim shacks in hopes of keeping the property. James Shaver saw the pristine shore around the lake and claimed 700 acres, far beyond the legal limit of 160. He was only able to keep the allowed amount, but he stayed nevertheless. During the first five years of Minnesota's statehood, "claim jumping, skullduggery in fulfilling requirements and hard feelings between neighbors cropped up here and there," according to *Happenings around Deephaven.*

Many land prospectors, such as Charles Morris, Charles Hargin, and James McMahon, put vast claims on acreage near Deephaven, on the east side of the lake, in what would later be Cottagewood. By 1856, William Ferguson already had a claim on much of the land and was living on it: "I was so angry with their deceitful conduct in declaring on my claim," he wrote. Morris, Hargin, and McMahon allegedly spread false rumors that Ferguson tried to claim four hundred acres, even though he actually only claimed forty-nine. Then Hargin jumped the claim by asserting that Ferguson did not even live there.

Ferguson noted that when these three rascals laid claim to the land, they had not built a claim shack, felled any trees, or "even stayed long enough to eat a meal." Ferguson admitted defeat to these "scoundrels" on January 16, 1856, and said he would give up his house. Meanwhile, Hargin had built a "pen-like claim shack" that stood from three to five feet high, not even high enough to stand up in. When Ferguson peered inside, he saw a pile of flannel undergarments inside a trunk and one old turnip—obviously, not enough to survive a Minnesota winter.

The feud continued after Ferguson died, as his widow, Lydia Ferguson Holtz, wrote in the 1860s in her diary, one of the earliest written sources of Lake

This watercolor by Edwin Whitefield, circa 1856, shows two early cabins on the lake. Cabins like these often served to mark a claim to property, whether anyone actually lived in them or not. Courtesy of the Minnesota Historical Society.

Minnetonka history. She told of feeling "worried and badgered . . . by dishonest men" every way she turned. Lydia inspected her land one day in 1870 and found nothing but a series of stumps in one area. Sixteen ironwoods and four giant oak trees had been chopped down and the lumber hauled away. Other foragers roamed through her acreage in search of ginseng, without any thought of ownership.

Then, in 1877, the price for hoop poles for barrels skyrocketed to seven dollars per thousand, so scavengers ignored property lines and went through the woods to gather branches. "Worse yet, strangers could

This rustic land-claim cabin is similar to those erected by settlers around the lake. Hoping to hold on to the land once the Dakota treaties were signed and ratified, feuds raged between early pioneers, and accusations of claim jumping were common. Courtesy of the Minnesota Historical Society.

work unseen in the deep woods. . . . Touring her land in search of hoop-pole thieves, Lydia . . . learned that six men, who had been staying in a neighbor's cabin, had probably made off with thousands of chair poles and hoop poles," according to *Happenings around Deephaven.*

Lydia chronicled these dangerous burglaries and expressed her bitter feelings about her dastardly neighbors and kin in her diary. When her daughter Alice married the no-good wastrel Chester Bingham, he promptly broke into Lydia's house and "purloined" all her diaries from the 1860s. He burned them, effectively destroying a treasure trove of early Minnetonka history.

Suspicion of trickery ruled the minds of the settlers, who did not want to be duped. Just as the Dakota had been manipulated into signing treaties that brought them far less than their land was worth to the settlers, swindlers now tried to sell titles to lands that had not yet been legally surveyed. A dispute over property lines led to a vicious feud in Wayzata between neighboring hotels owned by Abel Day and William Dudley. Abel's wife, Eliza Day, was notoriously confrontational and ran the hotel with a "sharp tongue, sour bread and haphazard housekeeping," according to *Tales from Tonka.* Abel kept building a fence on land he thought was his, but Dudley had the "legal" claim to it. Dudley reclaimed what was rightly his by pulling up Day's fence and replacing it with his own. Day, in turn, pulled that one out. The screaming battle caught the guests, looking for a bit of rest and relaxation, in the middle of threats and brandishing of firearms. One day, "Mrs. Day, armed with a pistol, directed her husband's resistance from the top of a haystack," wrote Warren Wakefield in his memoir of the time. Finally the owner of a third hotel, Ben Keesling, took away Mrs. Day's firearm while she "kicked and screamed" in protest.

Local governments were not organized enough to settle claims or help the settlers; in addition, banks often gave dubious loans or shaky advice. Settlers often did not trust these banks with their funds, so they squirreled away their savings, burying them in the yard or secreting them in other hiding places. In Wayzata's early years, Herbert Jevons stuffed gold coins into a sack hidden inside his bed. Another settler with the last name of Warner sewed gold pieces worth twenty dollars each into the lining of his coat, so he would never be separated from his money and could even get the jacket wet without losing his fortune.

Not only did the banks and claim jumpers try to part the settlers from their money, but a "sensational" charlatan came to the area, a man who paralleled the story of the duke and dauphin from *Huckleberry Finn.* A certain Lord Gordon graced the lake with his presence in the 1880s claiming that he was a personal friend of Queen Victoria and wanted to find land for investment to help hundreds of poor Scottish families start a new life. He was courted by the management of the Northern Pacific Railroad, which wanted to sell him much of the land the Minnesota territorial government had

After the University of Minnesota rejected a plan to move its campus to Lake Minnetonka, early settler Charles Galpin tried to lure Carleton College to the area. Meanwhile, locals constructed their own school buildings, such as the beautiful two-story Excelsior Elementary School pictured here around 1890. It burned to the ground in 1898. Courtesy of the Excelsior–Lake Minnetonka Historical Society.

given the railroad. With no way to check his royal connections, the railroad executives took him at his word, wined and dined him, and gave him the best accommodations. "He fleeced them for thousands," according to *Once upon a Lake.* "When cornered, he killed himself."

Minnetonka University?

Schools on the Lake

Early settlers had big plans for Lake Minnetonka. William F. Russell, a captain in Hiram Berdan's Civil War sharpshooter regiment, proposed creating the territorial capital of Minnesota in "Tazaska" on the northwest shores of Crystal Bay, which looks out on what would later be the Lafayette Club. According to *Once upon a Lake,* he wrote to his friend Colonel John H. Stevens in 1857 asking for help: "I want your help in the matter of locating the Capital by a vote of the people on the Big Peninsula in Lake Minnetonka. The scheme is pretty well under way. I can get over four thousand acres of land from the settlers on the lake in the way of donations to aid in the project."

When that plan failed, Russell attended a meeting of the regents of the University of Minnesota with university president William Watts Folwell. There, "with his usual clear-eyed view of reality . . . [he] profoundly disturbed the peace of [the] meeting with the suggestion that the university be moved" to "the south shore of Lake Minnetonka . . . where all the departments could be together in the midst of a forest, by the side of a lake, with a stream to supply water power," according to James Gray's *University of Minnesota.* The approximate location of the University of Minnesota could have been in Excelsior.

The dream of a college on Lake Minnetonka was not lost, however. Reverend Charles Galpin, one of Excelsior's earliest settlers, tried desperately in the 1870s to convince another college to move to Excelsior. Galpin had already adopted the "the old English custom of setting aside a piece of land to be reserved for public use," according to *Tales from Tonka,* and he had reserved 15.5 acres to become the much-loved "Commons." Now he would even give up large tracts of his own land to lure a new college to the area. "Then one day word come that the new college was to be built in Northfield on the banks o' the Cannon River, 'stead of Excelsior on the shores of Minnetonka," according to *Minnetonka Story*. "Yes sir! Excelsior'd lost out on gettin' Carleton College."

Perhaps these prestigious institutions took a look at early schools around the lake and opted to go elsewhere. For example, Excelsiorite George Day recalled one of the earliest schools in the area, an old log schoolhouse from the 1850s, two miles west of town. He told author Thelma Jones, "The cracks between the logs were imperfectly closed with mud, and the cold blasts of winter used to whistle in and make it somewhat uncomfortable." A more respectable two-story schoolhouse was built in Excelsior in 1857, to which a stockade was added during the Dakota War of 1862.

Many of the prickly issues of the day, however, were not discussed in detail—or at all. During the Civil War, a teacher at Parker's Lake near Plymouth, Miss Sophie Bushnell, "never uttered a word to her pupils about the great historical struggle," since the town was mostly Democrat and against the war. In her journal about Plymouth Township, Laura Negus Howe recalled the first lessons being taught, in 1858 in a log hut that was fifteen feet wide and long. A few little desks faced the teacher's table at the front. The school had no blackboard, maps, or any other such accessories for teaching. Miss Shaw started the lessons at the very beginning with readings from Genesis—so much for separation of church and state.

In nearby Wayzata, the atmosphere was very different, according to Charlie Gibbs. He is quoted in *Once upon a Lake* as remembering the "big shaky wooden building. Us kids used to make it shake on purpose. It was a wild place. Teachers were hired to beat education into us. Then they got lady teachers. They weren't much good at beating kids up."

Mound's first school, in the then new District 85, was a log schoolhouse set up in March 1860 at the request of Frank Halstead, the Hermit of the Lake. "The first teacher in the new school . . . received $8 a month for the three months of school, with $4 more per month allowed if he paid for his own food," according to *Tales from Tonka*.

Deephaven youngsters used a yellow frame building that doubled as the Deephaven post office and meat market until the one-room schoolhouse went up in 1892. In 1916, in a similar situation, students ended up in two large tents while a new school was being built. The only playground equipment for the active rascals was the "turning poles" used to tie up horses.

Up until 1930, if students did not walk to Deephaven School, they were driven by local Bert Knight, who "simply laid a board across the jump seats of his big old Cadillac limousine and packed them in with his own youngsters," according to *Happenings around Deephaven*. Nearby Groveland School had a much fancier operation and boasted that students hitched a ride in a modified Ford truck. Although these school districts may be some of the best in the state today, no doubt the University of Minnesota and Carleton did not see the potential in this backwoods lake community.

The Quick and the Dead

Insanity, Ghosts, and Ax Murders

Giving birth in the rustic conditions of the early settlements on Lake Minnetonka could be deadly. And children often died young of illnesses with such bizarre diagnoses as "inward tumor, foul blood, worm convulsions," according to *Once upon a Lake*. The settlers' prayers were answered when a doctor moved to Excelsior in 1854. Dr. Ebenezer S. Snell taught at the Excelsior Institute and specialized in phrenology, the study of people's mental capacities as displayed by the shape of the skull. Through this pseudoscience, Snell could supposedly deduce thirty-two separate personality traits and mental faculties (including "sexamity," "suavity," and "sublimity") simply by reading the contours of one's noggin. Snell and other phrenologists measured heads and cataloged the bumps to determine intelligence, unwanted impulses, and even criminal behavior.

As a doctor, Snell insisted on being paid and had no interest in charity work. A settler near Chanhassen, southeast of the lake, Theodore Bost, wrote in 1861 that he ran desperately to Dr. Snell to get help for the childbirth of the twins of a neighbor, Mrs. Sarver. "I urged him to hurry, even insulted him, telling him that if not as a doctor, then at least as a Christian he ought to come when called; but he said that a Christian should not work when he isn't paid." Bost could not convince the doctor, or "miserly bandit" as he called him, and Mrs. Sarver lost one of the twins at birth.

Bost was even more appalled when the situation happened again a half year later and Snell would not come:

> . . . the same refusal and the same result, but that time there were two babies dead by his fault. Well, this animal (that's what he looks like too) passes for being one of the most ardent Christians in this vicinity; he holds a high place in the church, and when I told Mr. [the Reverend] Sheldon that his conduct was not Christian, he told me that Mr. Snell has a prejudice against the Chanhassen people. . . . Apparently, the doctor is a very good Christian merely because he speaks during meetings.

Not only did many kids risk drowning, but some suffered from the frigid water in the spring and autumn. Sue Sidle was sixteen years old in 1883 and the belle of the lake. After one festivity at the Hotel Lafayette, she decided to swim in the cold water and later

Prominent phrenologist Dr. Ebenezer S. Snell moved to Excelsior in 1854—and immediately threw the Hippocratic oath out the window. Seen here in a portrait from 1856, he had no desire to be a pro bono country doctor but preferred to hobnob with the elite and discuss skull size and shape as a sign of "sexamity," "suavity," and "sublimity." Courtesy of the American Antiquarian Society.

died, reportedly from her weakened state. The heartbroken family could not cope with the tragedy. Sue's niece, Katherine Barber Boynton, would sleep out in a tent and claimed to have seen a ghost, "a lady in white—a tall, willowy lady in a trailing white dress," who held a mysterious letter in her hand and asked young Katherine where she could post the letter. A terrified Katherine claimed she recognized the ghost as Sue, who then disappeared into thin air.

The early settlers got used to death. Daniel Parker, namesake of Parker's Lake, arrived in 1855 with his family after a grueling voyage. Soon after they set up camp, his mother died and was buried in the woods, near what is now the intersection of Seventh Street and Highway 55 in Minneapolis. The debatable honor of being the first to be buried in the Groveland Cemetery goes to a Mr. Waters in 1855. His widow remarried two years later, in the spring of 1857, in the first marriage in Minnetonka Township, which took place at William Chowen's home. The dead sometimes gave the quick a surprise. The funeral of Mrs. David Locke on July 19, 1872, took an unexpected turn when the local women were preparing her shroud: they discovered "the body had swollen till it burst the coffin lid open" from all the gas that had accumulated inside the decomposing body.

Living on the edge of civilized society took a toll on these pioneers, whose behavior often bordered on insanity. The fear of not surviving often led settlers to suspect everyone else of conspiracy to commit terrible acts. One example is the widow Lydia Ferguson, mentioned above, whose daughter Alice married the rascal Chester Bingham. He quarreled with Lydia, physically beat her son Willie, and abused his own wife. He somehow gained custody of his children and committed Alice to an insane asylum to get her out of the way. Lydia could do nothing about her daughter's situation. Instead, she married another man, William Holtz, who soon afterward died of consumption, presumably tuberculosis.

On the other side of the lake, one of the founders of Wayzata, Oscar Garrison, sold his holdings in the town to Lucius Walker, an "Ojibway agent." Walker in turn sold off the sawmill and other assets but stayed in the town, even as the area floundered financially. In 1862, "Walker, insane from fear his Ojibway were joining the Indian uprising, put a bullet through his head, thus leaving Wayzata's legal status in a tangle that went on for years," according to *Once upon a Lake*.

One of the early names for Big Island was Morse Island, after William Bradford Morse and his brother John, who owned the island in the 1850s. These two brothers were uncles of Lizzie Borden, and they just

By the 1890s, phrenology had been largely dismissed by the scientific community as a pseudoscience, but in its heyday it was a subject of intense study by leading scientists. This cover of an issue of the Phrenological Journal *from 1876 features a typical phrenological illustration. Archives and Special Collections, Amherst College.*

happened to be visiting their niece in Massachusetts when Lizzie's parents were savagely murdered. The Morse brothers had to testify at Lizzie's murder trial about the terribly gory scene, but the jury considered their alibi legit and set them free. The case held the country's attention for months, and the court acquitted Lizzie, much to the shock of the reading public. The case was never solved, leaving some to question the alibi of the Morse brothers, who returned to the relative calm of Lake Minnetonka.

Slaves in Wayzata

Abolitionists in Plymouth

Attitudes toward slavery varied widely among immigrants to Lake Minnetonka. Before the Civil War, the Chilton brothers from Virginia brought slaves to Wayzata to work in the ginseng drying plants set up on the edge of town. Many disapproved, but few protested. Fort Snelling also employed slaves, since some of the officers would venture down to St. Louis to the slave markets. They were euphemistically called "servants" in Minnesota because of the distaste many had for the treatment of slaves in the South. Technically, slavery was outlawed in Minnesota Territory by the Northwest Ordinance of 1787, but it was tolerated at the fort.

Although owning slaves was illegal and selling slaves was prohibited in Minnesota before the Civil War, Alexis Bailly "purchased at least one slave directly from an officer at Fort Snelling," according to Mary Wingerd's book *North Country*. Since these slaves accompanied the officers and the well-to-do, they often had much more luxurious lives than settlers or enlisted men at the fort. Still, they were slaves.

Dred Scott famously was a southern slave brought to Fort Snelling who sued for his freedom after his owner, Dr. John Emerson, died. Scott argued that because he had lived in the free states of Minnesota and Illinois, where slavery was illegal, he and his wife Harriet should still be free. The U.S. Supreme Court ruled against him, 7–2, with the decision that no one of African ancestry could become a U.S. citizen. Of course this enraged the abolitionists and intensified the feelings leading up to the Civil War.

One of the first settlers to venture to Lake Minnetonka was Eli Pettijohn, an ardent abolitionist who helped organize the Republican Party in Minnesota along with Alexander Ramsey. Apple guru Peter Gideon also declared himself a fervent enemy of human bondage and went "lecturing against slavery in strong slavery localities. He almost got himself lynched," according to *Once upon a Lake*. Many New Englanders who came to Minnetonka were dedicated abolitionists, such as Margaret and Jonas Howe. This area was proudly Democratic early on, which meant that the majority opposed freeing the slaves, or at least did not want to get involved in the South's business. Laura

Howe remembers her father being called a "Black Republican" and a "red-hot Abolitionist." The abolitionists often passed around copies of *The White Slave* and *Uncle Tom's Cabin* to convince their neighbors of the evils of slavery. Laura remembered her father lending *The White Slave* to a friend who "boasted of having torn it up to light his pipe with."

Jonas Howe was proud that the Union wanted to abolish slavery, so he was appointed deputy provost marshal in Plymouth and given the difficult task of serving draft notices to young men called up for duty. Some of the local Democrats viewed Howe as a sort of grim reaper and warmonger because of his support for Lincoln. *Once upon a Lake* tells of Howe finding drafted men hiding in cellars or haystacks to avoid conscription, leaving the man's wife or mother to receive the notice. "To her mind it was equivalent to a sentence of death. . . . One violent woman threatened to scald him, another threatened to shoot him," according to Thelma Jones. For some settlers, freeing the slaves meant losing a son to war.

Civil War!

The Halstead Hermits Lead the Fight

On April 12, 1861, shots rang out at Fort Sumter in South Carolina; the Confederate forces had started the American Civil War. More than 600,000 soldiers and civilians died in the bloodiest war our nation has ever fought. Although far on the frontier at the time, Minnetonka was not immune to its effects.

Minnesota offered the first regiment of soldiers to Lincoln to fight in the Civil War. Governor Ramsey put out the call for volunteers, and A. B. Robinson, postmaster of Minnetonka Mills and the namesake of Robinson's Bay, was one of the first to enlist. He served in Company A of the Third Minnesota Volunteers. He was wounded in June 1862 but reenlisted that October and for three years served as a musician for the troops—a loud target for Confederate cannons. Sharpshooters Elbridge Barnes, Wilbur Coleman, and David Archibald from Lake Minnetonka volunteered at sixteen years of age. They exaggerated their ages and joined Minnesota's First Regiment, optimistic that the war would end quickly. They originally enlisted for ninety days, but soon after that the Union secretary of war changed all enlisted soldiers' time to three years. It was too late to reconsider their decision, and all three were gravely wounded in the war.

The Lake Minnetonka area also boasts the first civilian to be commissioned during the war. The Halstead brothers, George and Frank, settled on the shores of Lake Minnetonka in the 1850s; Halstead's Bay is named for them. The day after hostilities erupted, George enlisted in the Union Navy. Frank was traveling to New Jersey at the time, and he soon signed on the dotted line as well.

ado.
are
s the
e –
t here.
C — o —
rom sailors
s –

U. S. Frigate Minnesota

Commodore Stringham

She Roanoake is the same rig as the M– but somewhat larger –

18 Port holes in her white line

– thus –

they may all be of value sooner or later –

The two of them served on the USS *Minnesota*, the flagship of the North Atlantic Blockading Squadron, which fought the southern navy in Virginia and North Carolina. The ship engaged in several naval battles—one against ironclad Confederate ships. The recoil of *Minnesota*'s side cannons ran her aground near Newport News, Virginia. Tugboats and a steamer lugged the *Minnesota* from the mud. It later survived a Confederate torpedo attack, one of the first ever used in naval warfare. During the Civil War, the U.S. Navy also commissioned the construction of the USS *Minnetonka*. The three-masted steam frigate was completed in 1867, two years after the end of the war, and never saw any military action. Since the hull was made of seasoned wood, the boat rotted, and it was dismantled in 1875.

On April 3, 1865, the news that General Robert E. Lee had surrendered and that the Union had won the war spread to Minneapolis. Residents of Excelsior, including Reverend Charles Galpin, traveled to Minneapolis to see the flags hanging from all the buildings and the marching bands parading in the streets. Church bells clanged ecstatically. Galpin's group returned to the lake the next day bringing newspapers, waving flags, and spreading the news.

Following the war, many vets moved to Lake Minnetonka to escape the memories of the carnage. Minneapolis entrepreneurs started an artificial limb industry, and the city was soon established as the "prosthetic capital of the world," serving the Civil War veterans who came home without arms and legs. Soon the arrival of the dangerous mills at St. Anthony Falls also kept the artificial appendage business thriving.

When the lake was connected to the city by a railroad in 1867, many wealthy southerners fled the ravages of the land after the war to summer on Lake Minnetonka. Memories of the war lingered and sometimes sizzled, such as when President Ulysses S. Grant visited the Hotel Lafayette and met an old enemy, the Confederate general Braxton Bragg. Grant had routed Bragg's southern troops at the Battles for Chattanooga, and the southern secessionist lived in luxury for a spell at the lake.

Union officers, such as Frank Halstead, who achieved the rank of captain in the navy, also moved back to Minnetonka. Halstead settled on the westmost bay of the lake near Minnetrista; he built a small house and named it his Hermitage. The captain, sporting long hair and a goatee, hardly deserved the name "hermit," since he often met with visitors and became a well-known character on the lake. Drawing on his naval experience, the Hermit of Lake Minnetonka helped dredge out the Narrows and made the lake more accessible to large boats. The sole steamer on the lake, the *May Queen*, provided poor service, so Frank mortgaged

George and Frank Halstead served on the U.S. Frigate Minnesota, *depicted here in a sketch by Alfred R. Waud, circa 1860–65. Morgan Collection of Civil War Drawings, Library of Congress Prints and Photographs Division (LC-DIG-ppmsca-21103).*

Civil War veterans, including Major George Halstead (twenty-first from the left), assemble on Water Street in downtown Excelsior for a parade in their honor. All the buildings in this photograph were destroyed by a fire in 1895. Courtesy of the Excelsior—Lake Minnetonka Historical Society.

(Opposite) George Halstead was a major in the Volunteer Army of the United States and moved into his brother Frank's house, the Hermitage, where he regaled visitors with battle stories of the Civil War. He died in the house when it went up in flames in 1901. Courtesy of the Minnesota Historical Society.

his house to build his own competing steamer, the *Mary*.

Building the boat led him to financial and, ultimately, emotional ruin: he rowed to the middle of Lake Minnetonka, tied a bag of rocks around his neck, and threw himself overboard. Newspaper headlines screamed on July 8, 1876, about the tragedy, which most surmised was suicide. Rumors spread about why he died: some speculated that he was in love with a Mrs. Dunbar, a widow in Excelsior; other reports noted that five members of his family had already taken their own lives, and suggested that the captain was probably haunted by the Civil War. His body eventually surfaced near Crane Island, and he was buried at the Hermitage. This morbid scene took place the day before the grand celebration of the Fourth of July 1876, the centennial of the United States. "The death of Captain Halstead cast a gloom over all the gatherers, and it was the quietest Fourth we have had for many years," said a newspaper at the time. "There were no contestants and no audience for the steamboat and rowing races. . . . The string band did not tune up their instruments and departed for other fields of labor."

His brother George, a major in the Volunteer Army of the United States, moved to the Hermitage and took over the estate and the *Mary*. The Hermitage had become a popular tourist stop, where visitors could spend twenty-five cents to see Civil War relics and hear battle tales. According to *Once upon a Lake*, "morbid thousands trooped ashore and wrote their names and bits of verse on the sidings of the house." Halstead would often greet the visitors, and he placed glass and a frame over the graffiti poems on his house if he liked them. In 1901, a fire quickly burned the Hermitage to the ground, with Major George Halstead inside. The site was still visited by curious onlookers, who did not find much left except the charred metal bedsprings and some bones. One young visitor, John Moore, took home a rib bone to his disgusted mother, who buried it immediately.

The Battle for Lake Minnetonka

The Dakota War of 1862

By the early 1850s, when Governor Ramsey signed the Treaties of Traverse des Sioux and Mendota officially allowing European settlers into the Lake Minnetonka area, the U.S. government had long debated the merits of a "homestead" act that would allow citizen farmers to own their own land. This Jeffersonian idea was opposed by southern Democrats, who preferred plantations with slaves. When the country erupted in civil

Reverend Galpin used the steamboat Governor Ramsey *to transport women and children safely across the lake during the U.S.–Dakota War. When the boat's boiler conked out, passengers were left floating helplessly on the water before eventually reaching the shore. Photograph by Whitney's Gallery, circa 1870. Courtesy of the Minnesota Historical Society.*

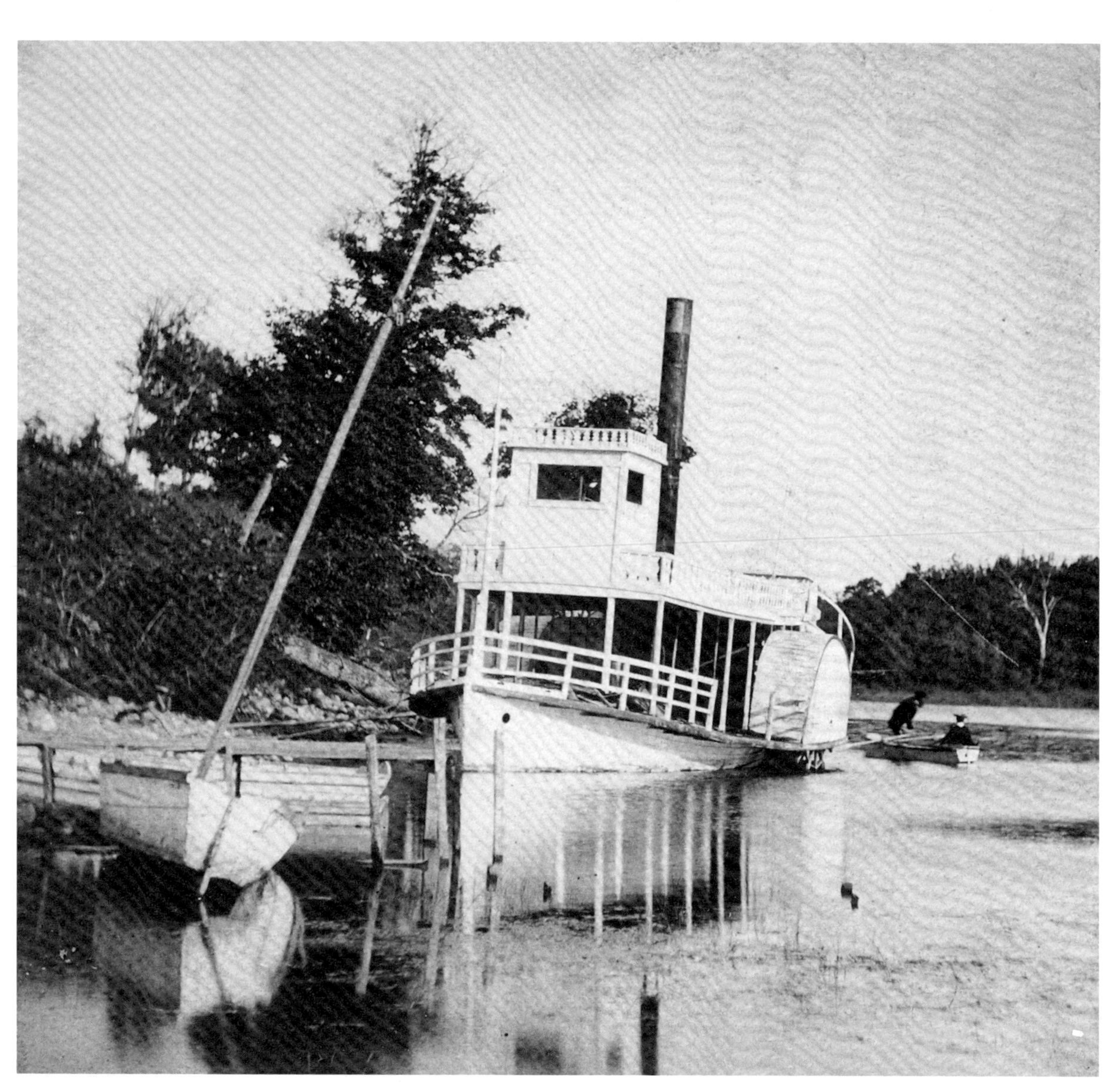

war in 1861 and the southerners were out of Washington, D.C., Lincoln seized the opportunity to sign the 1862 Homestead Act. This further enticed pioneers to move to Lake Minnetonka and claim land; to make it their own, they merely had to improve it and live on it for five years.

A drought struck, and the federally run Lower Sioux Agency refused to give the Dakota the payments owed them under the treaty. News spread quickly about an "uprising" and about Dakota "murdering, mutilating, pillaging and burning," but these early reports could not be confirmed, so exaggerations followed, such as that "all the tribes clear to the mountains" were moving. An estimated thirty thousand panicked settlers moved out immediately. Many immigrants, such as Dan Parker of Plymouth, simply let his animals loose, figuring he might be able to retrieve them if he could come back soon.

Farmers and their families came to the towns, and a stockade was built around the schoolhouse in Excelsior in hopes of making a stand against the Dakota. Rather than risking a potentially dangerous trip into Fort Snelling or St. Anthony, women and children were sent to Gooseberry Island (later called Gale or Brightwood Island). Their boat's engine died en route, and the boat eventually drifted to shore in Tonka Bay while the helpless passengers fretted about their fate. Reverend Galpin had his steamboat ready at the docks in Excelsior to bring the residents to Big Island, if need be. Other settler groups included veterans from the Civil War and stayed in their cabins with guns loaded.

Wayzata hotel owner William Dudley made steel traps to catch any intruders. He fabricated a "goose gun" for protection; he used to brag jokingly that it could "shoot a mile, kill fourteen geese at a time." Dudley refused to run when the Dakota War broke out, even as everyone else fled. Instead, in his fireplace, he forged several long harpoons with which he could impale invaders. He and his wife, armed with the harpoons, waited for an attack.

Settlers gathered together, assuming there was safety in numbers, and they grabbed whatever arms they had. In Excelsior, one of the men accidently fired his rifle while trying to clean it. A collective scream of terror rang out as "the sound of the gun was understood to herald the arrival of the savages." Then a bell in Excelsior rang furiously after someone claimed to have seen a Dakota warrior hiding in the woods ready to pounce. The "warrior" turned out to be an old woman in a straw hat gathering blackberries.

The conflict spread around the Minnesota River and left the Lake Minnetonka area essentially untouched. Chief Shakopee (Little Six), who had once lived on the lake, fled to Canada with his friend Medicine Bottle. Two Americans, one from Lake Minnetonka, took to heart Governor Ramsey's proclamation that "the Sioux Indians of Minnesota must be exterminated." They tracked Shakopee over the border,

Cut Nose was a regular visitor to Lake Minnetonka before the U.S.–Dakota War. After the conflict, he was hanged with thirty-seven other Dakota warriors in Mankato, Minnesota. Photograph by Joel Emmons Whitney. Courtesy of the Minnesota Historical Society.

a blatant infringement on then British territory. They kidnapped Shakopee, fed him whiskey, and drugged him with laudanum and chloroform to bring him back to the United States along with Medicine Bottle. He was tried in a kangaroo court, and even though there was no evidence of his guilt, he was hanged at Fort Snelling alongside Medicine Bottle in 1865. His body was taken to Jefferson Medical College in Philadelphia and dissected by a Professor Pancoast.

The "Indian Massacre of '62," or the "Sioux Uprising," became the main topic of conversation for years among white settlers. "In the store, farmers would expatiate on tomahawked womenfolk and babies nailed to burning cabin doors," according to *Once upon a Lake*—in spite of the fact that the war never made it to Minnetonka.

By 1882, though, the topic had already become a subject of fascination rather than terror. That year James J. Hill launched his massive *Belle of Minnetonka* steamboat on the lake; he hired Dakota children and dancers to provide the entertainment for tourists. W. D. Washburn's rival steamboat, the *City of St. Louis*, would not be outdone and "hired Indians in war paint and feathers as an attraction" aboard the boat, according to *Happenings around Deephaven*. From 1916 to 1926, several hundred Excelsior residents would dress up in pioneer and Dakota clothes and reenact the early days of the town for entertainment.

Church Services in a Stockade

Religious (Land) Claims

Trinity Episcopal Church in Excelsior began when it allegedly jumped a claim on Mr. McKensie's log cabin and land. Even before the land was officially opened up to settlement, Reverend Jacob Chamberlain put a claim on McKensie's log cabin on the shores of St. Alban's Bay. To make this tiny cottage do as a church, "a fine imitation of stained glass on a curtain of linen [was] stretched over the chancel window," according to the church's centennial literature. Parishioners William and Lydia Ferguson generously donated five dollars in 1855 to put in a large stained-glass window above the makeshift altar in the log cabin.

According to *Happenings around Deephaven*, Chamberlain used his "devious ways" to make "dubious claims" on the land for personal gain. After Ferguson donated the expensive window, he learned how the church had acquired the land and lamented in his journal about this corrupt pastor. Ferguson claimed that Chamberlain gave "40 town lots to the church to pay for his sins in robbing McKensie of his town and houses." Ferguson, for his part, wanted to get in on this newly opened land as well, but the minister would not divulge when the land would go on the market. Ferguson complained that Chamberlain "couldn't tell the truth—[about] so simple a fact as that." He was convinced that Chamberlain was being paid by land developers. He went on, "I find that the Rev. Mr. Chamberlain whom we respected as a devoted minister of the gospel, whom we also dearly loved as a friend, is an abettor of all the perjury and villainy, if not the contriver of their wicked designs."

Right after Christmas 1855, when the land went up for sale, Chamberlain failed to show up at Trinity Chapel to preach and give communion one Sunday. Ferguson steamed, "I fear after the false swearing of the last two weeks the sacrament would have . . . choked him some." The next November (1857) Ferguson fell through the ice when walking home from Excelsior. His nemesis, Reverend Chamberlain, presided over his burial service. If that was not insult enough, Ferguson's body was exhumed years later when the new owners of Ferguson Point wanted to build on the spot.

Trinity Chapel had been established during lean times on Lake Minnetonka. For Thanksgiving supper in 1853, the new settlers had resorted to eating raccoon (for the lucky; squirrel pie for the others). Thankful Episcopal pioneers held church services in their homes before "acquiring" McKensie's log cabin.

The Dakota Indian tribes and Ramsey had signed the Treaty of Traverse des Sioux in 1851, ceding all of Lake Minnetonka to the new Minnesota Territory, but the European pioneers complained that the Native Americans had hunted out all the deer. Chief Shakopee (Little Six), explained to his bitter tribe that they had to leave their hunting grounds and push on further

Early settlers fought over the land claimed by Reverend Chamberlain of Trinity Episcopal Church, but a chapel was built on it between 1852 and 1854 regardless. When the U.S.–Dakota War erupted in 1862, nervous settlers preferred to attend services behind the safety of a stockade in case of an attack, which never came. A fortified fence like this was built around the Excelsior schoolhouse, and not around the church. Courtesy of the Excelsior–Lake Minnetonka Historical Society.

west. Many new settlers who moved to the lake before the land officially opened in 1854 were disturbed by the continued presence of the Native Americans.

The small community of Episcopalians who built the log cabin chapel wanted to found a proper chapel in Excelsior to keep the errant settlers from going astray. A string of bad luck plagued the congregation. The sawmill in St. Alban's burned to the ground, and the Civil War broke out in 1861. The devout persevered, and Englishman Arthur Vickers raised funds by asking for donations in England to spread the word into Indian territory.

The congregation raised Trinity Chapel (by an unknown architect) in 1862, the same year the Dakota War (Minnesota's own Civil War) erupted, triggered by famine and nonpayment to the Native Americans. After the siege of New Ulm, about seventy miles southwest of Lake Minnetonka, nervous settlers around the lake stayed on guard. The congregation at Trinity Chapel gathered closely, and church "services were held inside a stockade to insure protection against hostile Indians," according to *The WPA Guide to Minnesota.* The guide was probably referring to the fortified fence built around the schoolhouse, because records show the church was never stockaded.

Probably the oldest building in town, the Trinity Chapel in Excelsior almost met the wrecking ball when the Minnetonka Electric Railroad deemed that, standing where it did downtown, it hindered progress. Fortunately, the congregation saved the church by moving it down the block. Courtesy of Hennepin County Library Special Collections.

The chapel survived the conflict, and it was officially consecrated by Bishop Henry Benjamin Whipple in 1864. In 1907, the building was moved to Excelsior's Third Street; it was expanded to include a guild hall in 1928 and an addition in 1949. According to local historian Bob Williams, "Trinity Chapel is the oldest Episcopal church in the state and possibly the oldest building in Excelsior."

Jesse James Visits Minnetonka

A Social Call before the Northfield Heist

The "last battle of the Civil War" happened in Minnesota eleven years after the South surrendered. During the war, William Quantrill raised a band of guerrilla fighters, including a couple of young Missourians, Frank and Jesse James, to attack Union sympathizers in Kansas. The guerrillas slaughtered 150 people in a raid on Lawrence, Kansas, that burned the town to the ground on August 21, 1863.

Once the war was over, Frank and Jesse James would not let it die. In August 1876, the Jameses and their cousins (the Younger brothers) came to "Yankee" Minnesota, which had been the first in the Union to send troops when Lincoln called for volunteers in 1861. They cased banks from Faribault to Mankato looking for the right one to avenge the war.

Lake Minnetonka was growing fast, and wealth

Before meeting his violent end in Missouri, shot by one of his own, Jesse James and his band of thugs visited the area around Lake Minnetonka in 1876. His body was photographed before his burial. Library of Congress Prints and Photographs Division [LC-USZ62–26562].

was more plentiful than policemen. Martha Baier recalled that when she was twenty, she ran into eight to ten attractive men with dashing southern accents who were watering their horses in the lake near her family's cabin outside Jordan. The polite gentlemen in expensive riding clothes asked her where they might buy some food. She told them of a nearby general store and curiously asked where they came from, since their accents gave her the idea of a distant state with glorious southern plantations. They cryptically replied that they were from Belle Plaine and going south; they asked if they could rest by her creek and unsaddle the horses for a bit. Martha's father let the men relax down by the creek since, apparently, the gang had paid "a social call" on her father, who had some southern affiliations. The handsome men intrigued Martha, and they invited her to eat with them. She sat to chat with the pleasant men and ate sausages and bread. Little did anyone know that they were destined for a notorious raid and heist.

Fortunately for Minnetonka, "We came to the conclusion that [the banks] had enough to do to take care of the farmers . . . ; therefore, we went to Northfield," recalled Cole Younger after the raid. On August 25, the gang stayed in the Maurer Hotel in Wayzata under false names and then the Nicollet Hotel in downtown Minneapolis before splitting up to descend on Northfield. Half of them took a train to Red Wing and the others went to St. Peter, where they bought horses and ammunition.

The James brothers heard that $200,000 lay waiting for them at the First National Bank in Northfield. What better way to rally the gang than remind them that the bank was owned by a former Union general and notorious carpetbagger who profited from the South's loss? The dapper bandits dressed in leather spats, tall boots, and long coats; carrying their rifles in scabbards, they galloped into town in 1876.

A member of the gang, Clell Miller, was keeping watch on the street as the others went into the bank. On seeing this unusual entourage, the owner of the hardware store asked him, "What's going on here, young man?"

Clell famously replied, "Shut your damned mouth and git!"

Two bandits were gunned down by the people of Northfield from the roofs. Clell Miller was scalped and his skeleton put on display in the Northfield Museum in homage to the foiled bank robbery. The rest of the gang fled town, followed by a posse of one thousand men. Charlie Pitts and the three Younger brothers were showered with bullets near the town of Madelia. Pitts's bloody corpse was sent to St. Paul to be displayed in the Capitol before a doctor boiled it down to study the skeleton. The Younger brothers were captured at the old Flanders Hotel in Madelia, where locals gathered eagerly to hear stories of bank heists. The robbers' outlaw tales enthralled the audience so much that the locals gave them flowers before they were sentenced to life in prison at Stillwater State Penitentiary.

Though Northfield claims its valiant residents defeated the bandits, Frank and Jesse James escaped to form another gang of Missouri thieves to stage train heists. A fellow gang member, Robert Ford, shot Jesse to collect a giant ransom.

News of the robberies and shoot-outs traveled to Lake Minnetonka. Martha Baier Spandel, then married, still carried warm memories of sharing sausages and bread with the southern gentlemen, who just happened to be bank robbers and murderers.

"Mosquitoes with Trunks like Elephants"

Wolves, Bedbugs, and Insect Plagues

Don't put the baby too close to the cabin wall because a wolf might eat him through the holes! James Shaver, who settled on the lake in 1853, had twin sons and lived in a log cabin with no chinking between the rough logs. The front door was just an old blanket nailed up to keep out the wind. One night he almost lost one of his sons, while the rest of the family slept, when a hungry wolf came to the outside wall and tried to claw his son through the gaps between the logs.

Nellie B. Wright told author Blanche Wilson about her father risking dangerous wild animals during the frigid winter when he came back late at night to Minnetonka Mills: "A pack of wolves, howling fit to kill, would start following him. If anything went wrong with his lantern, he'd drag chains behind to scare 'em off."

George Bertram and Hezekiah Brake had a similar tale to tell from their days establishing Excelsior. In June 1852, Brake wrote in his journal, "Night overtook us, our boat leaked, and, despite our efforts at bailing out the water, we felt it about our knees, while the howling of wolves on the shores added to our terror and fear of landing. Our jolly boatman tried to cheer our fainting spirits by telling us there were no bears in the woods, and that the sounds we heard were made by bullfrogs."

Wolves roamed the area into the twentieth century. The *Hennepin County Review* reported in 1908 that "Casper Geisen of Minnetonka Township recently shot a wolf on his neighbor's farm. . . . It was probably the last wolf bounty paid in the Minnetonka area," according to *Tales from Tonka*. Settlers may have been terrified of wolves, but the incessant buzzing and biting of insects may have made the settlers want a quicker death. The English mother of pioneer Hezekiah Brake wrote to her son who was going to Minnesota "where nothing but trappers and Indians live" that "it will cost you your savings, and then [you will] be murdered in the wilds of Minnesota, or drowned on Lake Minnetonka, or have your precious blood sucked out of you by mosquitoes, for a woman told me they have trunks like elephants." Brake ignored his mother, but later wrote that she was right about the mosquitoes. One night, he wrote that he "climbed a tree and hid in the branches, but my companion could not climb, and his moans and cries would have made a passerby believe he was being murdered." Once they had a place to stay inside, settlers often made a smudge, or smoky fire, to get rid of the bugs. What was worse, inhaling thick smoke all night or being bitten by bugs?

Charles Moore, a painter from the East Coast, came to Priest Bay on the far west side of the lake in the winter with his wife and children. He did not admit his own fear, but he wrote that his wife was terrified: "The temperature never got above twenty-five below, the wolves frightened the wife, and the bed-bugs in the cabin walls horrified her."

If bedbugs and mosquitoes did not drive the settlers away, the plague of grasshoppers in the 1870s might have. Clouds of them rose up "a thousand feet into the sky" and ate anything green; trees would bend under the weight of the whistling insects. A hundred grasshoppers would attack a single stack of wheat, eat everything, and move onto the next. Clothes hung out to dry were eaten right off the lines, leaving only the buttons on the ground. Even some cattle were killed from blood poisoning.

People dug ditches around their fields and lit huge fires to try to keep the insects at bay. Farmers made "hopperdozers": sheets of metal sopped down with tar, which they dragged across their fields. Once the metal was covered with bugs, they would toss a

The grasshopper plagues of the 1870s led to ingenious inventions that killed thousands of bugs, but their vast numbers still ate any plant, and even clothes hanging outside on the line. William Smith portrayed the hopeless battle of the "Grangers versus Grasshoppers" in 1880. Courtesy of the Minnesota Historical Society.

match onto it, let it burn down, and "harvest" some more.

According to *Once upon a Lake*, "Some of the men tried to frighten them by running down the fields, flailing their arms, and they lit on the men, a metallic horror, and chewed their clothing. Some of the women ran out with bed-quilts to cover gardens . . . and the locusts ate the bed quilts and then the green stuff and flowers." Many viewed this as a plague of biblical proportions and cursed the triple-tailed Donati's Comet as a dark omen that had passed in the skies warning of wars, such as the Dakota battles, and insect scourges.

During the winter of 1876–77, settlers beseeched the Minnesota government to do something, since the state entomologist declared that two-thirds of the state was covered with grasshopper eggs ready to hatch in the spring of 1877. Governor John S. Pillsbury, who later built the grandest mansion on the lake on Brackett's Point, was stumped. In desperation he called for a statewide day of prayer on April 26, 1877, on which all businesses had to be closed for "a day of fasting, humiliation and prayer in view of the threatened continuation of the grasshopper scourge," as he wrote in his gubernatorial proclamation.

Priests and pastors praised the governor because some viewed the grasshoppers as God's punishment for the sins of the settlers. Critics scoffed and mocked "Pillsbury's Best," a parody of the famous flour slogan, saying that the day was "a marked discredit to the intelligence of Minnesotans," adding, "There is not one well-authorized instance of such prayer having been answered, not one." Newspaper reporters from around the country ventured into Minnesota to witness this day of statewide prayer. Then a miracle happened. Sleet appeared out of nowhere and rained down ice on the eggs, freezing many of the grasshoppers just as they were hatching.

The settlers rejoiced, but not for long. As soon as the grasshoppers died back, the chinch bugs came. "You could smell them a mile [away]!" complained one Minnetonkan. The bugs would devour straw, so many of the tired pioneers lost their mattresses and did not sleep so well that year.

Medical Miracles at the Lake

Antiseptic Mud and Devil's Dung

Doctors recommended the vigorous climate of Lake Minnetonka as a sort of natural spa where the sick and infirm could come for a cure. Before Minnesota was even a state, newspapers trumpeted, "We have never known of a case of fever or ague in Minnesota Territory." Goodhue of the *Minnesota Pioneer* wrote, "The whole world cannot produce a climate more salubrious than that of Minnesota. We have as good land as there is in the world." Early settlers drank the crystal clear water of the lake before any wells were dug. Charlie Gibbs, who lived near Wayzata, said, "Nobody ever got typhoid or anything from drinking from the lake," according to *Once upon a Lake*. The invigorating waters and environment were the ultimate antidote to dirty eastern cities. "The lake boasted that nine out of ten left wholly restored."

A clammy Englishman disagreed and according to *Minnetonka Story* wrote in 1879 about the lake: "Hot? These Americans do not realize that Minnesota lies in the tropics, but I swear it does. Under heat, we Britishers suffer and grow surly; the Americans simply sweat, and the more they sweat, the more cheerful they get. Infernally queer, I say. Late afternoon, we started home,

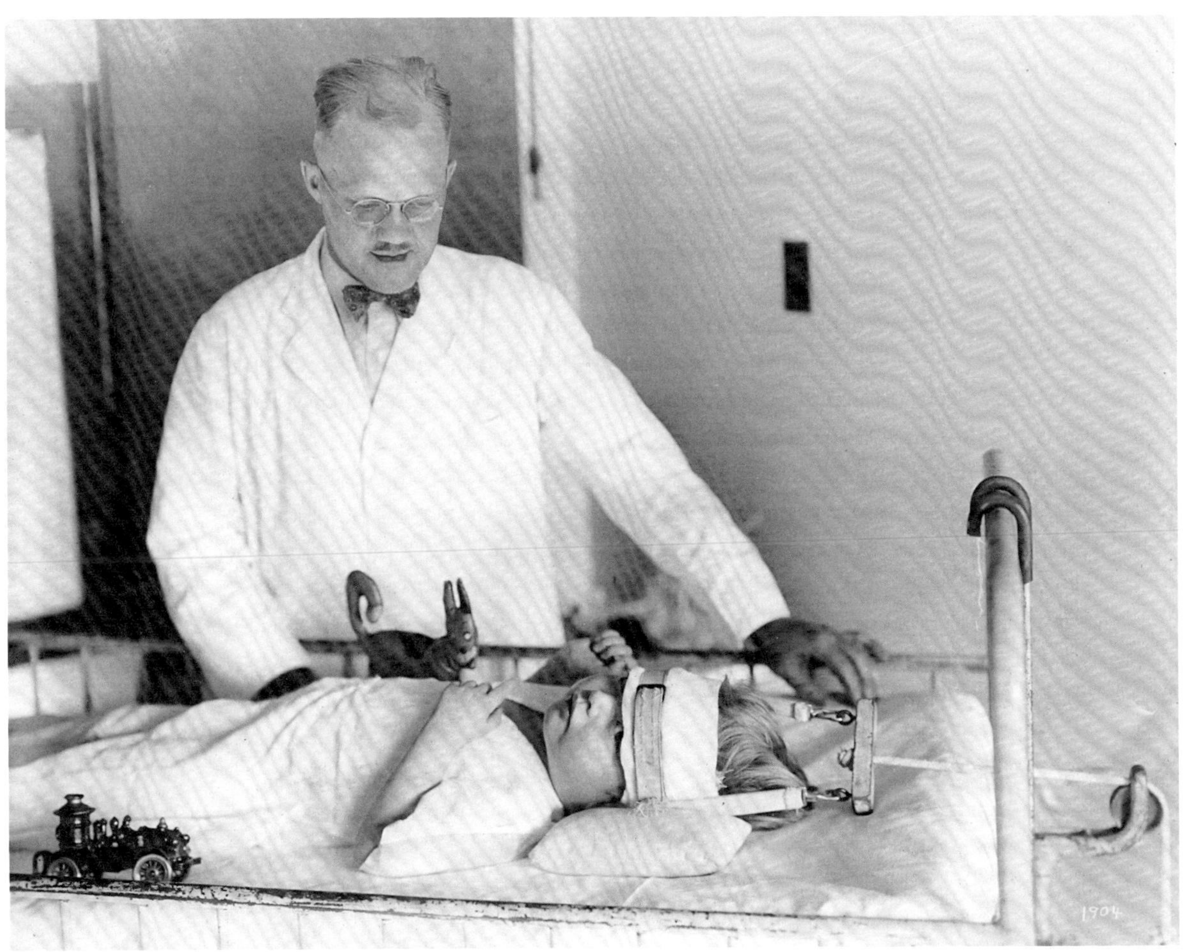

Minnetonka's gigantic Glen Lake Sanatorium opened in 1916 and treated hundreds of tuberculosis patients. Desperate doctors were known to use unorthodox methods of treatment, like the one pictured here. Photograph by Freeman Gross Engravings. Courtesy of the Hennepin History Museum.

wilted and wet from the heat but with our hands full of wild flowers for the ladies and with our faces full of smiles, for had we not been walking in paradise?" The report from this squeamish Brit contradicts nearly all the other raves about the lake's curative climate.

If the lake air did not heal a patient, other remedies might be tried. Howard Amundson from Minnetonka recalled what his grandmother would do "to repel all airborne sickness including the flu," according to *Remedies and Rituals: Folk Medicine in Norway and the New Land.* "Grandma would take out a small, soft leather bag . . . [and] open it up and take out a strange lump of waxy material . . . [that] looked like brown bee's wax. We were never allowed to touch it, but were able to sniff its strong smell." The old woman would put the strange lump on the wood stove to produce "a small puff of smoke and the room would fill with the strong and unpleasant odor." This was asafetida, commonly called "devil's dung."

Before John Harvey Kellogg or C. W. Post even dreamed of digestive cereals and refreshing enemas at the Battle Creek Sanitarium to cure the nation's sexual promiscuity, Lake Minnetonka had its own cereal man. Probably the first legal settler in the area, Eli Pettijohn was a strong abolitionist and teetotaler ("never drank enough to fill a cup") who ardently believed in the health of breakfast cereals. He warned that "predigested and partially digested foods tend to lower the tone of digestive system just as the brain or muscles are weakened by disuse." He marketed his own Pettijohn's Breakfast Food in 1854. It used his secret recipe for rolled wheat cereal that was originally manufactured at Minnetonka Mills. The advertisements advised that "Parents Should Know that children cannot grow on medicated and unnatural factory-processed foods." Instead, his hot cereal kept the digestive tract working hard and healthy because "wheat is the natural food of man!" Quaker Oats took notice and bought his recipe, distributing Pettijohn's across the country with a picture of a strong, healthy bear on the box.

Another local settler benefited from wholesome whole wheat. Samuel C. Gale built the Maplewood Inn in 1869 and stayed there with his family during the summer months. He became the advertising director for General Mills and saved the struggling Wheaties cereal from the chopping block when he invented the modern radio advertising jingle. The little ditty sung in 1926 by the Wheaties Quartet slyly skirted restrictions on advertising on the radio because it was just a song, with lines suspiciously similar to Pettijohn's advertising of years earlier:

> Have you tried Wheaties?
> They're whole wheat with all of the bran.
> Won't you try Wheaties?
> For wheat is the best food of man.

Another pioneer to the area brought along his unusual ideas for remedies for what ails you. Dr.

Edward R. Perkins, a proud member of the Odd Fellows, "shipped in various kinds of earth from five different states to be ground and mixed with pure glycerine. He paid ten cents an hour to boys who filled little tins with the gook, soldered on the lids and applied the labels. He called his analgesic, antiseptic balm 'Excelsine,' but the boys called it mud, made at the Mud Factory," according to *Tales from Tonka*. Some speculate that his salve had an antibiotic effect, possibly from chlortetracycline (Aureomycin), but this chemical was not even identified until much later, in 1945.

Perkins heard about the terrible fires in 1894 in Hinckley, in the northeastern part of the state, and he took a large supply of his "mud" up to help the victims. He reported back that his antiseptic salve helped alleviate the suffering of countless burn victims from the fiery inferno that torched several towns. He returned to Excelsior to raise money for disaster relief—and perhaps to reimburse his expenses for making Excelsine.

Eli Pettijohn, possibly the first legal settler on the lake, warned against eating predigested foods rather than wholesome whole grains. His secret recipe for rolled wheat cereal from Minnetonka Mills is advertised here in an early trade card. Collections of the Boston Public Library.

Visitors to the Excelsior docks in 1887 could choose their steamboat for a trip around the bucolic lake. Today, the docks at the end of Water Street boast towering trees and a much more tourist-friendly atmosphere. Courtesy of the Excelsior—Lake Minnetonka Historical Society.

3
Harvesting the Lake

Mill City
Minnetonka?

Traveling toward Lake Minnetonka from Minneapolis along Minnetonka Boulevard brings visitors past the historic Burwell House, built in 1883 by milling money earned from one of the earliest settlements of the area. The small but majestic Italianate house shows that the first permanent white settlers in the area had visions of turning the area into a European-style haven.

To most Minnesotans, Minnetonka may evoke leisurely cruises over the crystal waves, but in the nineteenth century the name was synonymous with the finest flour in the Midwest. Initially a sawmill took advantage of the gushing Minnehaha Creek at Minnetonka Mills, which was originally called Minnetonka City. The millers from St. Anthony, known as the Stevens–Tuttle crew, erected a small dam that was completed on January 1, 1853, where the McGinty concrete bridge is today. The dam afforded pressure to feed the mill a constant water flow and to help float logs from the lake. The sawmill was completed by April, so the first logs floated down the creek by fall. Many of the freshly hewn boards were "poled upstream on large bateaux to pioneers building their homes around the lake," according to *Happenings around Deephaven*. The mill cut giant old-growth timbers for the first bridge across the Mississippi connecting Minneapolis and St. Anthony, bringing the two towns together as one.

The mill burned to the ground the next year, but a larger one took its place, along with a furniture factory making a reported two thousand chairs and beds a week, according to the *Minnesota Republican* in February 1857. Visitors venturing out from the city and up Minnehaha Creek always passed by Minnetonka Mills, and two new hotels serviced these tourists: the Newark Hotel and the Minnetonka Hotel. That same year, the manager of the mill drowned in the lake. Flames took down the mill once again in the summer of 1860. This time the furniture factory burned to the ground as well, leaving Minnetonka Mills practically a ghost town for nearly a decade.

No mills profited from the laughing waters of Minnehaha at Minnetonka City for nine years, at which time Thomas Perkins built a large, three-and-a-half-

The area around Lake Minnetonka is not typically associated with farming, but this photograph shows that fertile soil produced abundant grain. Steam-powered threshers separated the stalks from the wheat, which was then shipped across the lake to Minnetonka Mills to be ground into flour. Courtesy of the Excelsior–Lake Minnetonka Historical Society.

story flour mill to grind the bumper crops from nearby farms. The flour was packed in barrels, so a coopery was set up next door to pack the three hundred to four hundred barrels of flour a day. Charles Burwell moved to Minnesota in 1874 as the new manager of the mill. From a blue-blooded family that traced its American roots back to the Revolutionary War, Burwell became Minnetonka's most prominent citizen and took advantage of his situation to pay farmers just a dollar for a bushel of wheat, selling the ground flour for three dollars per hundred pounds. By October 20, 1874, the Minnetonka Milling Company was the first mill in the state to

The first mill in Minnesota to ship flour to Europe, Minnetonka Mills relied on the water flow from Lake Minnetonka into Minnehaha Creek. The Minneapolis and St. Louis Railway provided transport from the depot at the right of the mill in this photograph. Courtesy of the Minnesota Historical Society.

export flour to Europe, and "business at Minnetonka City exceeded that of Minneapolis," according to *Tales from Tonka.*

Still, the local farmers were pleased to be able to have a prominent nearby mill that could grind their grain while they camped out for two days in Minnetonka Mills. Perkins would generously let them set up tents on his property and make campfires for cookouts. Steamboats such as the *Governor Ramsey* even sailed across the lake to deliver wheat to the mill, and ox carts creaked from fifty miles away to bring the harvest. According to *Minnetonka Story*:

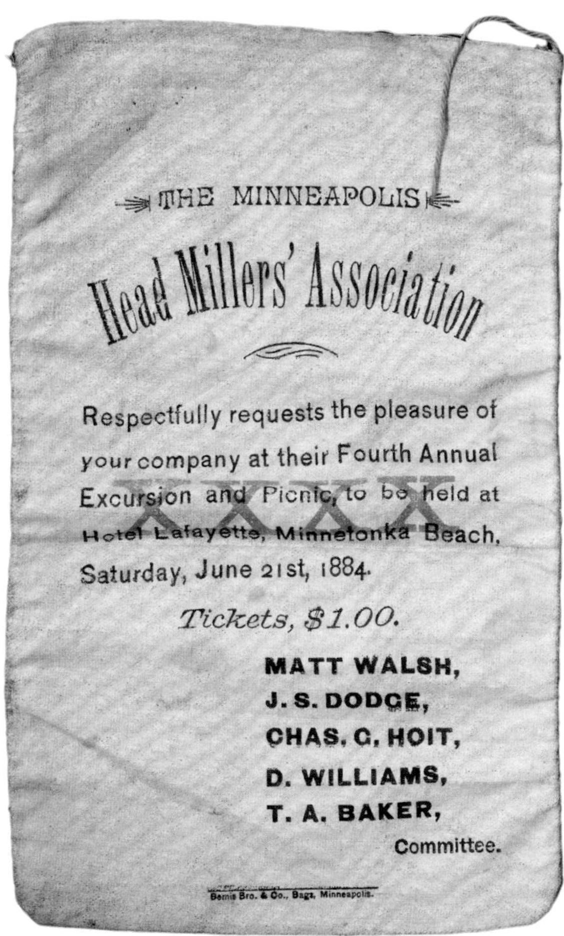

A picnicking mecca, the shores of Lake Minnetonka attracted both tourists and titans of industry. This clever invitation to the 1884 Minneapolis Head Millers' Association excursion and picnic at the Hotel Lafayette, Minnetonka Beach, is printed on a small flour sack. Courtesy of the Minnesota Historical Society.

> To visit the mill was enough to make a fellow's heart beat double-quick. . . . The smell of that newly crushed wheat was the evasive fragrance of mignonette heavy with dew. White powdery dust from the flour clung to walls and rafters and roof, turning cobwebs into fairy lace. The mill hands turned white from head to foot.

Not all customers were so pleased, however. One day eight angry German farmers yelled that the mill's special Snow Ball flour was second-rate sawdust. Mary Burwell quickly whipped up some of her special homemade bread with the supposedly tainted flour, and the Germans hailed the loaves as manna from heaven.

With this newfound fortune in flour, Charles Burwell built near the mill a majestic Victorian/Italianate house that has been placed on the National Register of Historic Places. With Minnetonka becoming more of a pleasure playground, lake dwellers complained that the water level of the lake was lowered because of the mill; residents proposed a dam at Gray's Bay to maintain the level. Over the years, Minnehaha Creek from Gray's Bay to the mill had been widened by twenty feet and deepened by eighteen inches. When the dam was built at Gray's Bay, canoes could no longer go directly from the lake to the creek. The dam raised the lake's waterline, but even as late as September 1951, residents complained that the dam flooded their land.

Minnetonka Mills could not compete with the

giant Pillsbury Company and other mills at St. Anthony and Minneapolis that took advantage of the power of the mighty Mississippi, and it was shut down by 1895.

Ginseng Fever in Wayzata

The Weed That Saved Minnesota

The name "ginseng" comes from a Chinese term meaning "man root," in reference to the plant's potent man-shaped roots, which were thought to be a powerful aphrodisiac, or at least a stimulant. According to the *St. Paul Daily Pioneer and Democrat* from 1859, the Chinese esteemed the plant and dried, mashed, and smoked it. They viewed these gnarly herbs as an opiate and an intoxicant.

This snake oil tonic and early Viagra was American ginseng (*Panax quinquefolius*), which grows wild across the Big Woods of Wisconsin and Minnesota. Native Americans used ginseng as medicine, and early European settlers thought that it might make them immune to mosquito bites. These early pioneers dubbed the plant "sang," and "sangers" went foraging for the wild roots under the shade of deciduous trees in the lush forests of Minnesota. This little weed with yellowish-green flowers under hardwood maple trees was undiscovered gold.

After the economic panic of 1857, farmers in Minnesota needed new income fast. Edward and Joseph Chilton moved from Virginia to Wayzata to open a ginseng station to buy and dry the plants from foragers sanging in the woods. Harvesting of ginseng throughout New England had left the area depleted of the vigorous roots.

Thousands of pounds had been shipped to China for top dollar, and now merchants were desperate for more. China had long since been mostly depleted of its plants. When the Chilton brothers ventured north from Virginia, they advertised in Minneapolis that they would pay eight cents a pound for washed ginseng. They had another branch of their business across the lake in Excelsior, where ginseng entrepreneur J. H. Clark bought up plants and shipped boatloads of roots over the lake to them. From there, the plants traveled first to the East Coast and then on to the Orient.

The Chiltons kept their business relatively quiet at first to avoid a ginseng rush, but when this edible gold reaped ten thousand dollars in 1858, the news was out. A distributor in Virginia tried to run a competing ginseng distributor in Pennsylvania out of business by paying even more for the plant, but the supply from Minnesota seemed endless.

Hundreds of unemployed workers now scoured the forests for plants, unconcerned about land claims. The Chiltons set up a giant drying plant in Wayzata and paid out thousands of dollars "in gold" for all the ginseng gathered. Each year, the price for ginseng rose as foragers found less and less. "These diggings will

Before the Civil War, two brothers from Virginia set up shop in Wayzata to buy ginseng plants from foragers. In this photograph from 1910, a group of Minnesota growers try to cultivate a crop of "man root." Photograph by Briol Studio. Courtesy of the Minnesota Historical Society.

bring the *gold* more certainly than those at Pike's Peak," according to the *Minnesota Statesman* newspaper of St. Peter on May 6, 1859. Diggers could make five dollars a day, a hefty sum at the time, and the Chiltons were rumored to have as much as $50,000 to pay out, so the woods were filled with ginseng hunters. In one week of 1859, twenty-five tons of dried ginseng root was shipped to St. Paul.

Immigrants moved from Wisconsin just to dig ginseng, and many pioneers set out on long excursions through the Big Woods in search of this buried treasure. Practically every general merchandise store in the Big Woods dealt in ginseng on some level. Once the dirt was washed off, the roots were typically laid out to dry on wooden platforms, but the Chiltons in Wayzata used a special ginseng kiln for quicker results.

This gold rush of roots inspired the "Ginseng Polka," written by a Mankato musician, and another Minnesotan wrote a parody of Henry Wadsworth Longfellow's poem "Excelsior," naming it "Dig Ginseng":

> There through the livelong summer day,
> 'Tis dug, and washed, and piled away;
> But, whether clarified or dry,
> Celestials will forever cry,
> Dig Ginseng!

During the entire ginseng wave, the Chinese market paid an estimated $200,000 to desperate immigrants in the area. One ginseng merchant, Godfrey Scheilin, paid settlers $50,000 for ginseng in 1861, but four years later he lost double that in his trade with China.

The ginseng boom had gone bust by late 1860. Millions of roots had been dug up in the shade of Minnesota's Big Woods, and the market on the East Coast was saturated. At Lake Minnetonka, though, the Chilton brothers went too far: they imported slaves to work in the drying plant in Wayzata. Although Minnesota was not a slave state, the boom took place before the Civil War, when most northerners scowled on the savage practice but had little way to fight it. Whether the ginseng foragers combing the woods were abolitionist Republicans or noninterference Democrats, they took their ginseng to other buyers in protest. The Chiltons ended up moving their ginseng-drying operation elsewhere.

Demand for ginseng stayed alive, though, and the Minnesota state legislature passed the Ginseng Law of 1865, which protected plants still in the wild and only allowed very limited harvesting after August 1 of any given year. To avoid long treks into the wild to dig clandestine plants, residents of Mound cultivated their own ginseng in their shady gardens as early as 1909. Today, ginseng poachers still try their luck to find some ancient roots filled with energy to stimulate the spirit.

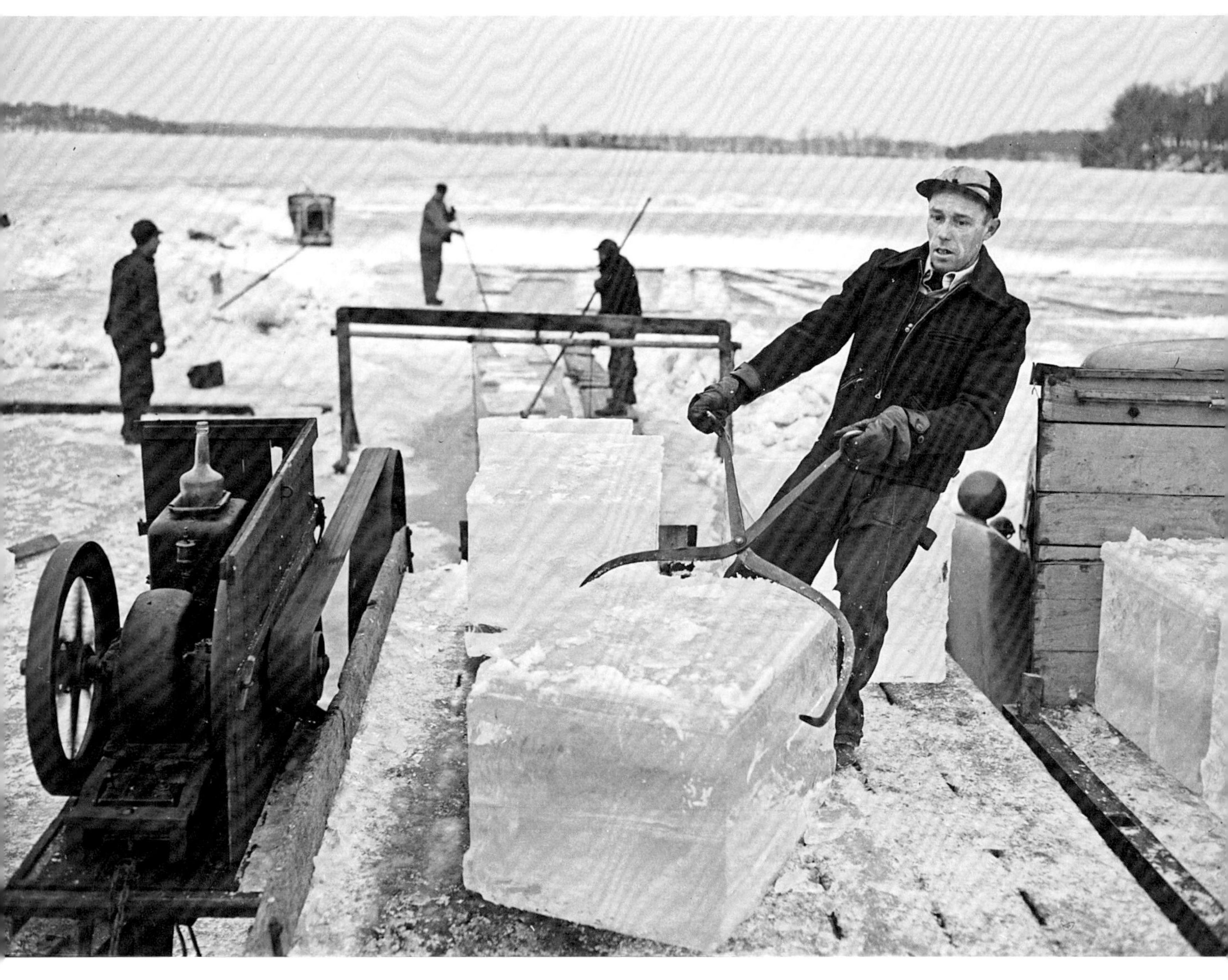

Diamonds in the Ice
Ice Harvesting on Lake Minnetonka

Lake Minnetonka was Minneapolis's playground during the summer, and the lush land produced crops such as ginseng, fruit, and berries by the bushel. As the winds howled in the bitter off-season, many hunkered down to wait out the winter or set up fishing shacks to lug in lunkers from the deep. Enterprising settlers unwilling to sit on their idle hands took out the long handsaws, bundled up in their parkas, and set out across the frozen lake on snowshoes. Digging and drilling deep into the ice, these brave souls endured the "crystal harvest," cutting thousands of pounds of frozen Lake Minnetonka water for about six to eight weeks in January and February. Horses hauled the load to shore on sleds; there, large barns, the summer icehouses, stored the year's yield in a snug bed of sawdust. Sweaty urchins would sneak into these barns during the dog days of summer, as they were the only air-conditioned buildings around.

In the memoir *My Island*, author Isabel Thibault recalls growing up on Crane Island in Lake Minnetonka, including summer trips to the icehouse:

Though automated machinery made the task easier, ice harvesting was still backbreaking work. Here Alfred Hilgers of Spring Park maneuvers a giant block into position for the Cedar Lake Ice Company. Photograph by Minneapolis Star Journal Tribune. *Courtesy of the Minnesota Historical Society.*

> Getting the ice was the most challenging duty. The icehouse was at the foot of the little hill at the north end of the island. We wheeled a barrow down to the tall dark building. At the beginning of the season the house was packed full. We climbed a ladder to the door at the top, carrying the tongs, swung it open and stepped into the cool darkness. An axe and broom were kept up there.
>
> It was always Kate, the eldest of our trio, who did the chopping. The chunks as first cut and packed were too large for the old icebox up at the house, to say nothing of our handling of them. Kate chopped, strengthening her vocabulary as she did so, then dragged the block to the open door and shoved it to the ground. From there we dragged each piece to the lake beside the icehouse, washed it off and loaded it on the wheelbarrow.

An industry magazine, *Cold Storage and Ice Trade Journal*, from 1909 reported, "About 500,000 tons of ice have been stored in the various homes about St. Paul, and the product is very good. The average thickness was 18 inches. Most of the supply for next summer's use in St. Paul was taken from Bass and White Bear lakes and Lake Minnetonka in Minneapolis. It was then loaded on cars and shipped to St. Paul by the trainload." Icemen stored most of these blocks to fill iceboxes year round, but boosters of St. Paul stacked twenty-seven thousand extra chunks to make an ice castle for the Winter Carnival to prove wrong the New York newsman who bashed St. Paul in 1885 as "another Siberia, unfit for human habitation."

The *Star Tribune* reported in 1890 about the "one and only crop in Minnesota which is never a failure." The reporter hailed this natural resource that southern states bought to keep their lemonade cool and their food wholesome. "The ice that is now being taken out of the lakes is as clear as crystal and so pure that no typhoid germs lie concealed within. It would make a St. Paul man sick to look at it and reflect that his city decided not to have an ice palace this winter."

Lake Minnetonka historian Bob Williams remembers residents putting signs in their windows to tell the iceman what size blocks they needed to tide them over: twenty-five, fifty, seventy-five, or a hundred pounds. He said, "Then the ice companies were threatened by those new-fangled electric refrigerators." In fact, advertisements for the Coolerator, which could freeze ice cubes, appeared in January 1939 in Excelsior. Even with the arrival of a freezer, the icemen still came, as Carl Gustafson harvested ice at Cottagewood and a Mr. Peterson harvested it from Robinson's Bay to supply the many iceboxes in the area.

During the late nineteenth century, Lake Minnetonka was one of the premier lakes for ice cutting. Giant blocks were stored in barns insulated with hay and hauled to iceboxes across the state. Courtesy of the Minnesota Historical Society.

Monsters of the Deep
Bury the Extra Fish in the Yard

The Dakota had long known that Lake Minnetonka, with its huge stock of fish, provided easy dinners. One of the first recorded fishing trips to the lake dates back to September 11, 1852, when Colonel John P. Owens wrote in the *Weekly Minnesotian* about several prominent men from St. Anthony who went on a trip to visit the claim shanty of Simon Stevens along the shore. They needed some lunch. A couple of the party "cast in their lines, and quicker than it will take us to relate the fact, they flung to shore more bass than twelve hungry men could devour in one meal. They continued fishing fifteen or twenty minutes, and the product was about forty pounds—all bass of the largest size," Colonel Owens reported. The first recorded ice-fishing house on the lake belonged to Simon Stevens as well. He built a small fire inside his dark shack and cut a good-sized hole in the ice. The fish came to investigate, and he speared them as fast as a neighbor could sell them.

Before the joke postcards of giant walleyes chomping at lures, photographs such as this one from about 1885 show real scenes of Lake Minnetonka—without another boat in sight. Photograph by Charles A. Zimmerman. Courtesy of the Minnesota Historical Society.

While Minnetonka is known today as a good walleye lake, walleye were not introduced to the lake until May 27, 1926. The Minnesota State Game and Fish Commission at the Mound hatchery introduced approximately 5 million baby pike, and the lake has been stocked with more than 41 million fish since 1875. Before stocking, the lake probably held mostly northern pike, bass, and panfish. Early reports claimed that trout were unsuited for the lake because even though it is very deep and cold, the depths lack oxygen. Therefore, both trout and salmon stocking failed. Now the most common fish are northern pike, bluegill, walleye, largemouth black bass, black crappies, white crappies, pumpkinseeds, and perch.

Occasionally visitors witness bizarre fish or think they see monsters in the deep. The late 1800s were an

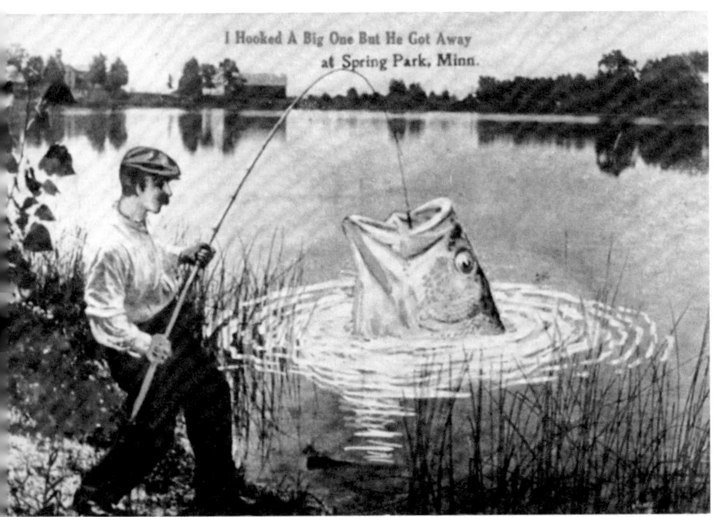

I Hooked A Big One But He Got Away
at Spring Park, Minn.

This postcard, dated 1912, advertises the best fishing in the state in Spring Park. Was anyone actually fooled by these classic images of anglers hooking giant freshwater fish? Courtesy of Westonka Historical Society, Mound.

era of unknown-creature sightings in the northern wilderness, so news spread quickly about the giant lake snake of Minnetonka. "Dozens of people reported having seen, evenings, a grayish-green sea-serpent at least fifty feet long, and with a horrid head. Some of them saw two hideous forearms with claws on them," according to *Once upon a Lake*. Some kids claimed that this monster chased them and that they had barely escaped. Some historians speculate that these were just oversized carp, but carp were not even introduced to the Midwest until the 1880s, and even then not in every watershed. What was this bizarre beast? Or was this another prank?

In spite of tales of vicious prehistoric reptiles beneath their boats, fishermen came in droves to catch dinner or hoping to be the one to land a "freshwater whale." Nellie B. Wright told author Blanche Wilson that her family's livelihood relied on the fishermen: "Whenever the men guests wanted to go fishing, Pa would row them around all day for $2—fine wages at the time! Like as not they'd bring home so many fish, Ma and Pa would be up all night cleaning 'em. Next day we'd have fish every meal."

The early fishermen had no limit on how many fish they could haul in. The trains stopped in Wayzata, and the fishermen might go back to the city with as many as fifty fish or more. "The length of the string was the limit. . . . The supply seemed inexhaustible," fisherman reported at the time. Male vacationers at the hotels would go out fishing, and it was a wife's "prerogative to admire the catch before [her husband] proudly ordered it to the kitchen to be cooked for them," according to *Once upon a Lake*. "So many fish were caught that the hotels did not always try to keep them separated. They were stored in sacks in the ice-houses and when there was no more room, the staff dug holes and quietly buried the fish."

Just another early morning fishing trip on Lake Minnetonka in 1909. Anglers brought catches like this to nearby hotels for the cooks to prepare. Courtesy of Westonka Historical Society, Mound.

No Bad Apples

The Wealthy, Haralson, and Honey Crisp

Native Americans and early settlers around Lake Minnetonka knew of the abundant berries, chokecherries, plums, and grapes that grew wild in the rich soil along the lake. Still, many considered the subzero winters of the frozen northland of Minnesota to be far too extreme to raise apples, which many settlers assumed belonged back in the Old Country with the strudels and ciders of Europe. After all, Johnny Appleseed had not dared venture this far north.

LAKE MINNETONKA
APPLES
Home of the Wealthy Apple
Plums
Grapes
Currants
Cherries
Raspberries
Strawberries
Blackberries
Gooseberries
Crabapples
Grown and Packed by
Excelsior Fruit Growers' Association
Excelsior, Minn.
Copyright. Excelsior Fruit Growers' Association

Reverend Gideon Pond planted some of the first apple trees in Minnesota when he received a letter full of seeds from friends back in his native New England. Some years later, around the 1840s or '50s, hungry settlers found small sour apples on the trees. The disappointed pioneers resolved to grow wheat rather than apples, and Pond returned to his initial mission: converting the Native Americans to Christianity.

Peter Gideon, on the other hand, was an intrepid agriculturalist who envisioned himself as a northern Johnny Appleseed when he settled on 160 acres on the bay that was soon named for him. His friend Robert McGrath tried to discourage this greenhorn from joining the apple biz after Pond's debacle, but Gideon could not be swayed. McGrath wrote in his diary about this "apple-crazy man, crazy even to imagine apple trees can stand a frigid climate as this." In fact, Gideon had a reputation as an "early advocate of abolition, prohibition and woman suffrage. He was almost vegetarian and never indulged in liquor, tobacco, tea or coffee. Clean-shaven himself, he detested beards," according to *Tales from Tonka*.

Gideon relied on an apple-obsessed colleague in Bangor, Maine, to send him seeds from that northerly state, which had similarly chilly winters. Gideon's original experiments left him with a single crab apple seedling that had withstood the cold. He knew that this hardy little sprout would serve to graft scions of preferred, plump apples. By 1862, this tough Russian crab had produced a decent orchard of full-fledged apple trees, but the hot, dry summer wiped out every one. He needed a tree that could withstand not only the cold winters but the tropical summers.

Minnesota's own Johnny Appleseed, Peter Gideon made Lake Minnetonka "Home of the Wealthy Apple" with his agricultural success, as advertised in this promotional poster. Courtesy of the Minnesota Historical Society.

Many of the other settlers around the lake wondered about Gideon's quixotic vision of a promised land full of fruit. Some scorned the high-minded experimenter as "a red-hot abolitionist, a fighting temperance man, and, as to religion, he was first a Universalist, and next a Spiritualist," according to *Once upon a Lake*.

Rather than give up on his dream of cornucopias of fruit for everyone, Gideon chose not to replace his tattered clothes and instead scrimped and saved for more apple seeds. "Springtime found Mr. Gideon precariously clad in a suit tailored from two vests and an old pair of trousers, but exuberantly happy as he planted a new orchard," according to *Minnetonka Story*. With high hopes, he named his pride the Wealthy apple, after his wife, Wealthy Hull Gideon. After ten years of trial and error, Gideon introduced the Wealthy in 1864. It was a fruit tough enough to last through the chilly Minnesota winters and was considered by some to be "the best apple discovered since Adam and Eve left the Garden of Eden," according to *Tales from Tonka*.

In less than twenty years, Gideon's Wealthy harvest filled the local fruit stands, and horticulturalists deemed Gideon's fruit the best in the Midwest. As Minnesota's premier horticulturalist in 1878, he was the "father of fruit breeding in the Midwest." When others around the lake planted his trees, however, they ran into many of the same difficulties as he had with the weather. In October 1873, a fierce wind whipped through Deephaven and uprooted William Chowen's prized seven-year-old apple trees.

Eager apple growers heard about this new "Minnetonka apple" with the ambitious name. A member of the audience at the Minnesota State Horticultural Society asked in the early 1900s, "We have received several orders for the Minnetonka apple. How can we fill them?" Mr. Philips of the society responded, "If the Minnetonka apple is not a child of the imagination, why in the name of God don't you make them shop up the apple so outsiders can see them?"

Never mind these skeptics. Not only did the Wealthy live up to its name for dozens of orchards, but it was also one of the parent plants for the famous Haralson apple produced by another undaunted horticulturalist: Charles Haralson from Sweden, who grew his fruit at the Minnesota Horticulture Research Center, aka the Arboretum. Haralson served for fifteen years as superintendent of the University of Minnesota Fruit Breeding Farm before moving to Hummingbird Road and Minnetonka Boulevard. He developed the Latham raspberry, six kinds of plums, the Deephaven strawberry, and the Red Lake currant. Mostly he was known for the eponymous Haralson apple, which was generally preferred over the Wealthy. Thanks to these experimental gardens, dozens of new varieties of fruit fill our cornucopias, including the practically perfect Honey Crisp Apple.

With fruit trees overflowing, Excelsior chose September for its annual Apple Day Festival. In 1930, festival promoters selected only the best of the bunch to exhibit as perfect specimens of that year's harvest. Courtesy of Hennepin County Library Special Collections.

Woodchuck Stew and Baked Raccoon
Living off the Land

The earliest white settlers around Lake Minnetonka had to learn how to live off the land—and fast. They usually could not afford to buy all their provisions from general stores and transport them to their distant cabins, and waiting for crops to sprout and grow to harvest could mean starvation.

The trappers and settlers who chose to listen to the Dakota learned the edible plants of the area, so the settlers did not live exclusively on the staples of dried corn and pork. In addition to the wild cherries, plums, and cranberries, the Dakota of the area ate swamp potatoes; *psinchenchah*, a white bulb; *oomenechah*, a sort of bean; *teepsinna*, a root similar to a turnip; and

Hunting was both popular and necessary around the lake. Here a dapper group of hunters displays a mound of trophies in front of a railroad car. Courtesy of Hennepin County Library Special Collections.

(Opposite) Towering sugar maples provided perfect spring sap to boil down for syrup for flapjacks. This photograph, circa 1925, features a father and his two sons drilling for liquid sugar near Lake Minnetonka. Courtesy of the Minnesota Historical Society.

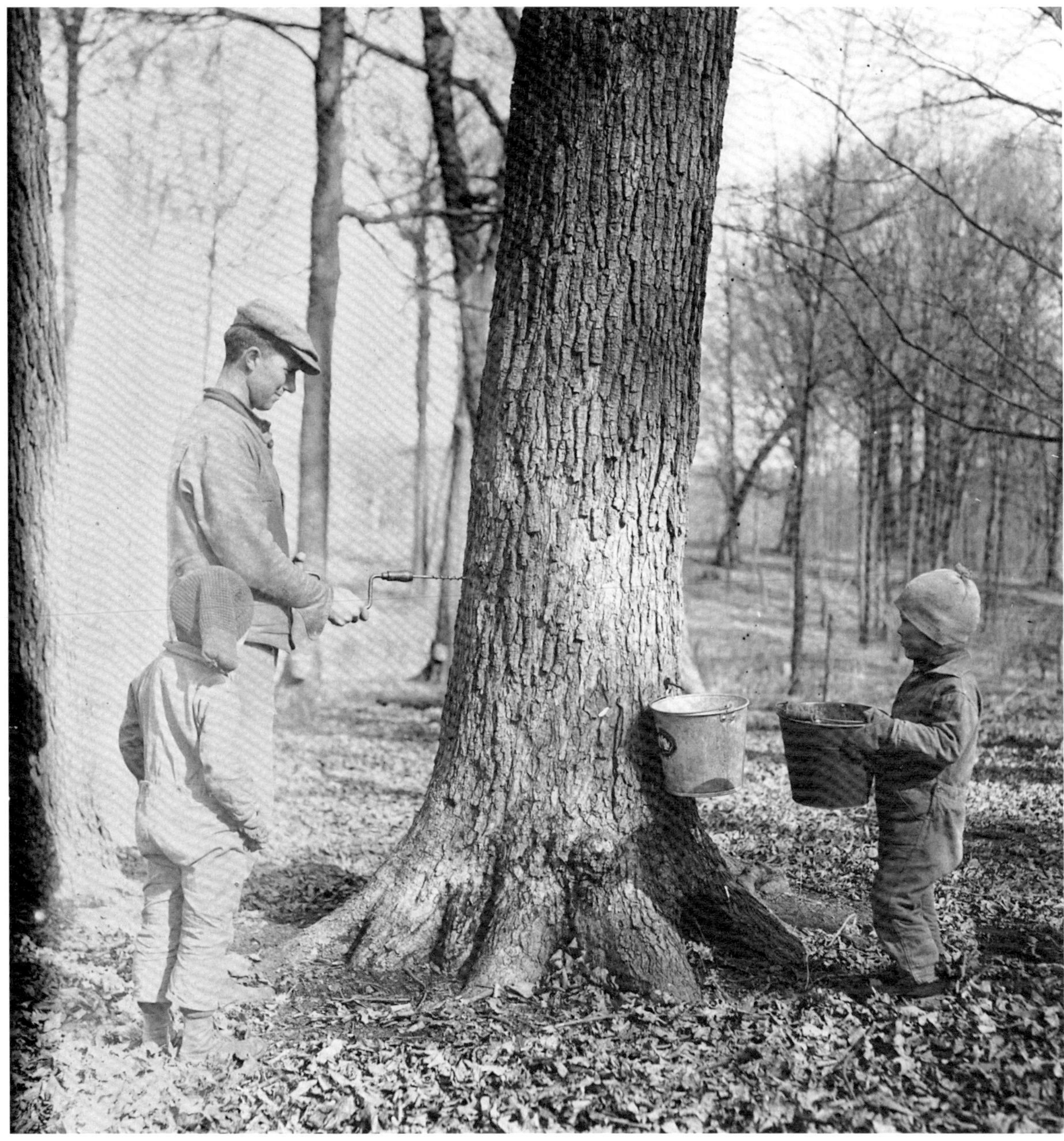

tawahpah, a lotus root. Besides the plentiful fish, the water's of the area were an abundant source of wild rice. Gleason Lake, just north of Lake Minnetonka, and Gray's Bay were once covered with wild rice plants. In fact, Gray's Bay in 1852 was "scarcely worthy the name of 'lake' as the greater portion of its surface is covered with a thick growth of wild rice," according to Colonel John P. Owns in 1852, writing in the *Weekly Minnesotian*.

One of the sweetest lessons the Native Americans taught the pioneers was how to boil down maple sap to make syrup. In 1853, Hezekiah Brake set up troughs under five hundred maple trees to collect the sap along Lake Minnetonka. He did not have big enough containers, so he used the canoes that he had bought from Chief Shakopee. The next year, Brake sold a barrel of syrup to a merchant in St. Anthony for two hundred dollars, or a dollar and a quarter a gallon—a fortune at the time.

The "sugaring parties" when the sap was boiled down were festive occasions in the spring where black soot covered everyone. Rather than lugging around hundreds of buckets, some settlers split small trees in two and hollowed them out with an adze to make troughs to move the syrup to a giant, hollowed-out log (or canoe in Brake's case). For ideal sap, the temperature needed to drop below freezing every night and climb into the forties during the day. Large pots boiled the watery sap; it took forty gallons of sap to produce just one gallon of high-quality maple syrup.

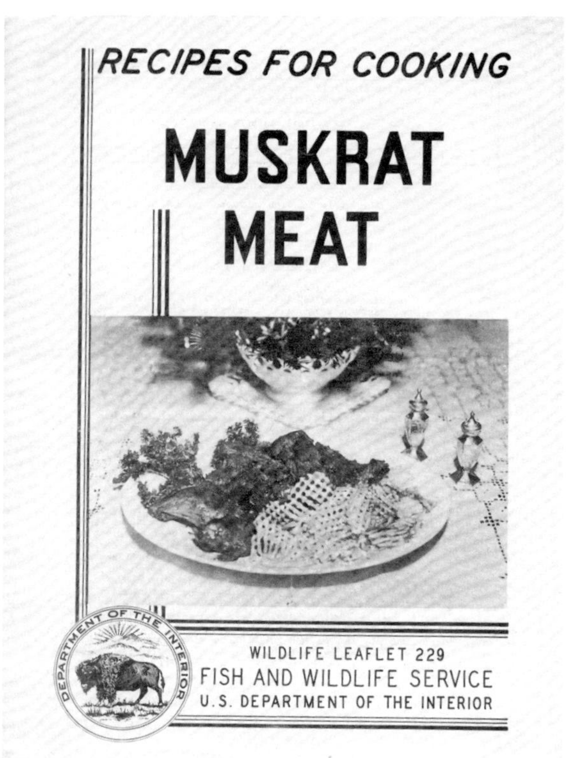

Interest in unusual game continued well into the twentieth century. This cover of a publication from the U.S. Fish and Wildlife Service from 1943 gives scrumptious recipes for muskrat, an animal common in the Minnetonka region.

With snow still on the ground, settlers would make a sort of ice cream by "carameling syrup," dripping syrup into the snow and then beating the sweet mixture until it turned white. Laura Negus Howe wrote in the 1850s that the maple syrup they made at the lake was used as sweetener in everything except coffee and

Shooting animals from the windows of train cars was considered sporting but was not looked on favorably by residents, who feared flying bullets from speeding locomotives. Courtesy of the Hennepin History Museum.

tea, for which they used "boughten" sugar. Her favorite concoction involved putting doughnut batter "into a large hot iron spider" and then cracking eggs into boiling syrup, beating the mixture, and pouring it over the doughnuts to make "Yankee pie." Some settlers skipped these fancy recipes and just used the syrup as mixer to make a brandy hot toddy.

When hunting, the settlers bagged a deer whenever they could, but they often had to rely on smaller creatures for meat. Wild turkeys provided an exceptional feast, but Blanche Wilson wrote in *Minnetonka Story* that meager quantities of expensive salt left the meat less flavorful than it could have been. At one turkey feast, each eater was allowed "only three pinches apiece, salt was that scarce!" Squirrel stew helped keep away the hunger pangs, since the playful creatures were plentiful. William Dudley's hotel in Wayzata bragged about its woodchuck stew and "baked 'coon." Eli Pettijohn recalled an especially unusual dinner at the house of Henry Sibley in Mendota. He ate a "'boss' of buffalo"—that is, the hump on the back of a young male bison—and what he thought was dried beef but turned out to be "boned dried beaver's tail." Sibley bragged about the beavers, "Over 5,000 of them, as well as the skins, have been brought in here during the year."

In spite of the potential for feasts of unusual delicacies at Lake Minnetonka, one peninsula stands in contrast to this strange cornucopia: Starvation Point. The name derives from a white trapper whom the Dakota called Hairy-Faced Man. He had lived among the Indians for decades (perhaps one of the earliest Europeans in the area) and had disappeared and was later found lying dead on the point.

George A. Brackett bought the peninsula. He renamed it after himself, partially because "Starvation Point" no longer fit since Brackett had brought back three large cauldrons for beans from his time as a cook in the Civil War with General Henry Sibley and Franklin Steele. Brackett, Sibley, and Steele had been sent back from fighting the Confederate Army to combat the Dakota in Minnesota in 1862. To ensure full stomachs after a long day of fighting, Brackett would bury his cauldrons of beans in a smoldering pit, and the Dakota never noticed dinner cooking underground. When Brackett and his squadron returned at night, they would have enough beans to feed three hundred men, as well as a nice warm spot for sleeping. Brackett brought his bean-hole cauldrons to Starvation Point and renamed the remaining area Orono. The Minnetonka Yacht Club made him its first commodore, and he had famous bean-hole feeds for three hundred sailors and crews. No more starvation here.

Animals Amok!

Farm Animals in Our Midst

The early European immigrants who ventured to Lake Minnetonka relied heavily on their animals, and decades later the local village councils struggled to free themselves from all these beasts in their midst. Delilah Maxwell wrote in *Old Rail Fence Corners* about traveling by oxcart from St. Anthony to Wayzata in 1856 along the hilly "Indian trail": "As we started down a terrible steep hill, Jerry [the ox] switched his tail around a young sapling. It was wet with dew and it lapped tight, and we were going downhill so fast something had to give way. It was the tail! There was only a stump left . . . and the ox like to bled to death. Mrs. French kept worrying for fear the wolves would get Jerry's tail, and when we had gone about a mile, she made Mr. French go back and get it." The ox did survive the loss of his tail, and the settlers would have struggled without their beast of burden. The average farmer in the area could only clear about an acre a year, and that only with the help of oxen.

Hezekiah Brake wrote about transporting a Mr. Payson to his claim forty miles from the lake. The mud on the trail came up to the knees of a horse, and it took them a week to make the trip. Brake later rented his horses to Christian Biblizen of Buffalo Lake, who needed to till his land. Brake hesitated, but he knew he should help his neighbors. On the way out to the farm, Biblizen accidentally went through a "floating swamp," and the mare sank all the way down and was never seen again.

In spite of the settlers' best efforts, their animals lived in constant danger not only of mishaps but of wolves and of human encroachment on their land. The trains, or "Iron Monsters," often killed cows before fences enclosed the pastures. Well into the years when Wayzata was established, the railroads still allowed deer to be shot from the windows of the passenger cars once they were out of St. Anthony. Surely some poor bovine would make an easy target, and the culprit would be long gone.

In the 1870s, "livestock also ran at large, their whereabouts unknown until the finder posted notices in public places or spread word via the grapevine," according to *Happenings around Deephaven*. Lydia Ferguson wrote in her Deephaven diary that in 1871, "some mysterious cows . . . came out of the woods, trampled her garden and had to be penned up and fed until posted notices finally brought the owner."

For this reason, when citizens incorporated the villages around the lake, one of their first acts was to control the animals. An ordinance passed by the Wayzata Village Council when it formed in 1883 made it illegal for goats, horses, cows, or mules to have the run of the town. The owners would be charged fifty cents for each stray animal and twenty-five cents for each loose chicken. Soon the duties of the police included rounding up the animals. The Deephaven council sent the village marshal out to warn Oskar Carlson "to keep his garbage dumping place in Gale's pasture covered up so that there would be no odor from it and no chance for the cows to eat any of the refuse," according to *Happenings around Deephaven*.

Many of the earliest edicts of these new village councils were enacted to solve problems between neighbors. As early as the 1880s, Lydia Ferguson's dog

Early farms around the lake rarely had fences to keep animals penned up, so some livestock practically became pets. Courtesy of the Minnesota Historical Society.

was poisoned, probably by a disgruntled neighbor, perhaps even the owner of the renegade cow mentioned earlier. By the turn of the century, all dogs in Deephaven were ordered muzzled when a rabies scare spread through the area after Walter Douglas's dog died of the disease.

Soon keeping farm animals required official approval. Pigs were especially contentious around Deephaven, even though Carson's Bay was originally called Pig Inlet, and nearby Spray Island was called Hog Island. In 1921, the Deephaven Village Council passed a decree, by a wide margin, stating that residents could still keep one pig but needed to apply for a license if more were kept at home. Sixteen years later, records show that the council conceded a license to local H. J. Burke to have nine cows and three horses, but absolutely no pigs. Wayzata was a little more lenient, announcing a big lakeside festival with "a yacht race for a stake of $50; rowing races and a $5 prize for the one who could catch the greased pig." Animals now doubled as entertainment.

Winning the Heads, Hearts, Hands, and Health

One Hundred Years of 4-H in Excelsior

In the late 1800s, agricultural discoveries at some of the large land-grant universities, such as the University of Minnesota, were often ignored by immigrant farmers, who brought with them from Europe agricultural techniques that had been passed down for generations. Frustrated researchers fed up with backward-thinking peasants turned to young people, who were much more open to experimenting with new techniques. Thus youth agricultural programs took root.

Although Ohio is often given as the birthplace of 4-H, a Minnesota group in Douglas County began a youth farming program the very same year the Ohioan club was formed, in 1902. A group of about thirty boys in Excelsior formed a tomato-growing club in 1911 that eventually merged with the rest of the 4-H groups. Typically, 4-H clubs had different divisions for boys and girls, but the forward-thinking Hennepin County group integrated them from the beginning. The Excelsior club did not use the classic four-leaf 4-H symbol when it first formed. A preliminary three-leaf-clover design was adopted in Ohio in 1907, with the three Hs standing for "head," "heart," and "hands." Everyone knows that a four-leaf clover is much better luck, so the symbol's designer recommended "hustle" to fill the void. By 1911, "health" replaced it for the final four.

Once the U.S. Congress officially recognized farm clubs in 1914, the groups—including the one in Hennepin County—united under the 4-H banner when it passed to the Cooperative Extension System. Just as 4-H offered opportunities early on to both young men and young women, the extension system was administered through land-grant universities, which had to be open to all races. (Most southern states have two land-grant universities since they did not want blacks and whites at the same school. The University of Minnesota, however, never had that policy.) The 4-H organization broke away from the one-room schoolhouse and was an early proponent of experiential learning, which enables young people to learn by putting their ideas into practice. This educational philosophy has since been widely lauded as being much more effective than lectures and rote learning.

During World War II, as part of its "Food for Free-

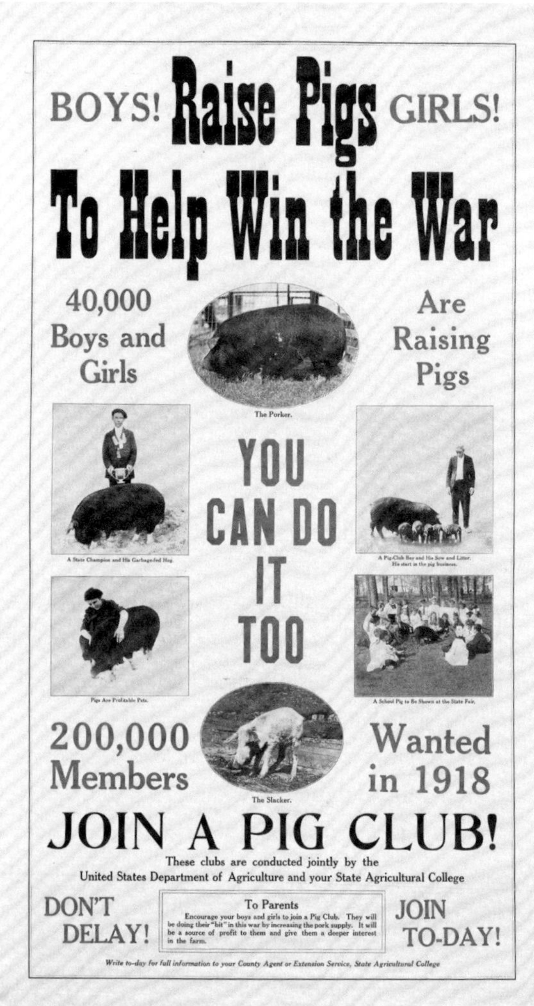

To aid the war effort, the U.S. government promoted activities like victory gardens and animal husbandry to groups such as 4-H. This World War I–era poster encouraged kids to get involved and do their part. Courtesy of the Minnesota Historical Society.

dom" campaign, 4-H clubs were instrumental in establishing Victory Gardens to augment food production on the home front. Some 4-H groups collected scrap metal to help the United States build ballistics, and many clubs invested in war bonds. Today, 4-H boasts more than 6 million members nationwide, with alumni such as Walter Mondale, Jimmy Carter, and Al Gore.

In 2011, the 4-H club that began in Excelsior celebrated its hundred-year anniversary at the Hennepin County Fair in Corcoran, Minnesota. Before retiring in 2002, Bill Svendsgaard worked for twenty-six years as the extension educator for the Hennepin County 4-H. Following its anniversary, Svendsgaard began compiling a book about the history of 4-H in the county. He told the *Star Tribune*, "I grew up in northern Minnesota on a farm and was a 4-H club member there for thirteen years. So it's in my blood."

While this worldwide nonprofit started with a "Corn Growing Club" and by planting tomato seeds, it has branched out beyond farming and animal husbandry to include science and technology, engineering, nutrition, and civics. A trip to the 4-H Building at the Minnesota State Fair shows each county's handiwork. Hennepin County's 4-H entries range from modular origami to a duct-tape dress. Although formed along the shores of Lake Minnetonka, the Hennepin County 4-H looks back to its roots and is based in the extension program at the University of Minnesota so young people can learn about the latest techniques and apply them in the field.

This 4-H float in the 1939 Raspberry Day Parade in downtown Hopkins proudly shows a cow with its udders ready for milking. Photograph by Minneapolis Tribune. *Courtesy of Hennepin County Library Special Collections.*

Since 1895 the Cottagewood Store of Deephaven has served elegant southerners, cabin-dwelling vacationers, and the residents of this picturesque neighborhood. Today the store looks remarkably similar to the way it did here in 1920. Photograph courtesy of Jon and Mary Monson.

The Cottagewood Store

An 1895 Relic

Lake Minnetonka was a vacation destination where city slickers could cozy up in quaint cottages nestled under oaks along the many bays of the pristine blue waters. A little general store with gingerbread trim opened its doors in 1895 in the Cottagewood neighborhood near Deephaven to sell dry goods and basic foodstuffs to summer visitors.

As a kid, I viewed the Cottagewood Store as the halfway point on my bike ride to Excelsior, the spot to refuel with an ice cream cone or root beer and marvel over the nearby caged-in paddle-tennis courts. The local kids wandered in from the beach or wrung hands sore from rope burns gotten on the sailboats of the nearby Minnetonka Yacht Club. In spite of the encroaching mansions (often built on the foundations of quaint lake cabins), the Cottagewood Store was a refuge from the big-box stores of suburbia and showed that people do need human contact along with parking lots and checkout lines.

In 1995 the owners of the Cottagewood Store recognized that they could not compete with the prices of their giant competitors in the strip malls along Highway 7. The doors were closed, and the building was put up for sale. A community meeting was called to determine the fate of this historic monument at the core of Cottagewood before it was bulldozed or turned into a residence. More than one hundred neighbors gathered and acknowledged that this historic general store was more than a simple convenience store. Families pitched in $180,000 to buy the building and preserve it for future generations. Today, the general store is a gathering place for morning coffee and community events. Kids stop in for ice cream from April to October, and diners munch on Reuben sandwiches. Nearly a thousand festivalgoers celebrate at the store and at the Cottagewood Children's Park on the Fourth of July, then hop in their boats or on their bikes to see the fireworks in Excelsior. Although flour mills are gone and ginseng harvesting is just a memory, the Cottagewood Store preserves the past with historical photos on the walls, letting visitors be grateful that pigs are not roaming the streets and woodchuck stew is not on the menu. ☙

Southerners were delighted to savor cool northern breezes off the water from wrap-around porches. The Lake Park Hotel, pictured here around 1890, offered five floors of views to the steamboats below. Courtesy of the Excelsior–Lake Minnetonka Historical Society.

4

Hotels and High Rollers

The Grand Hotels of Lake Minnetonka

The President Supposedly Hit with a Pie Plate

After the Civil War, southerners invaded Lake Minnetonka. Well-to-do ex-Confederates took the trains to the lake to lounge on the extended porches of the Hotel St. Louis (named so the Missourians would feel right at home), the Lake Park Hotel, and the Hotel Lafayette.

Lake Park Hotel, later called the Tonka Bay Hotel, was built in 1879 and had giant balconies and tall ceilings so guests could breathe in the breeze. The building was five stories high, all with verandas that wrapped around the hotel and were wide enough "for promenading." According to *Minnetonka Story*, "On those verandas they would have seen Minnetonka's guests at their best—laughing, talking, singing, taking no thought for the morrow, even entertaining Dan Cupid on the sly. The day came when those verandas swayed with the gayest of the gay crowds."

As part of the health craze of the era of John Harvey Kellogg's sanitariums, the Lake Park Hotel allowed its thousand guests to escape the filth of the city. It was included on the Chautauqua assembly lecture circuit and presented concerts, adult education classes, and temperance society meetings. No modern convenience was spared, and visitors could even buzz electric call bells for maid service.

The Hotel Lafayette was James J. Hill's capstone of the Victorian era. His newly acquired St. Paul, Minneapolis, and Manitoba Railway ran right to the doorstep of his three-hundred-room hotel at Minnetonka Beach. In 1883 the Lafayette hosted an elegant ten-course banquet for a thousand guests to celebrate the completion of the Northern Pacific Railroad. The event "made the triumph of a Roman Emperor pale in magnificence," according to publicity at the time, and it was attended by the most prominent politicians of the nation and the state, brought by special trains from New York, according to James Ogland's *Picturing Lake Minnetonka*.

One of the German dignitaries, Herr N. Mohr, wrote about the fabulous event in a diary called *Streifzug durch den Nordwesten Amerika* (Ramble through Northwestern America): "Lake Minnetonka and the Hotel Lafayette will from this day on be renowned, for

The Hotel Lafayette was nicknamed "Saratoga of the West" for the lakeside decadence it provided wealthy visitors. Courtesy of the Minnesota Historical Society.

Newspapers described the new hotels on the lake as "veranda crazy." The wide covered porches wrapped around the buildings, giving every room a view; they doubled as a promenade path in the evening. Here a group of dapper youngsters lollygag on the Lafayette's porticos, circa 1890. Courtesy of the Minnesota Historical Society.

it is assembling about itself a company which attracts the gaze of the whole United States. . . . And the tables, *ach Himmel!* Never shall I see such long tables again during my life's span! My hand goes lame at the faintest endeavor to describe such a banquet."

President Chester Arthur, former president Ulysses S. Grant, architect Cass Gilbert, environmentalist John Muir, Governor Alexander Ramsey, eight other governors, nine generals, royalty from England, and German nobility joined nearly a thousand guests to honor Hill's railroad triumphs, but the elegant evening was interrupted by a brawl among the kitchen staff, who had been drinking on the sly and began throwing plates. Rumor had it that the police stormed the kitchen to stop the kerfuffle, but not before Grant was whacked with a pie plate and others suffered minor injuries from tea cups and champagne glasses. This is probably hyperbole, but the local temperance societies—and owners of rival hotels—called for the Lafayette to be shuttered, or else the "magnificent hostelry [could degenerate] into a beer garden," according to A. S. Dimond, a journalist writing for the *Minneapolis Tribune* at the time.

One of the busboys who worked after the melee was appalled by the treatment of the wait staff at these grand hotels. The busboy, W. E. B. Du Bois, was summoned to a table by one of the corpulent capitalists. "Thus Caesar ordered his legionaries or Cleopatra her slaves. Dogs recognize this gesture. . . . Then and there I disowned menial service for me and my people." After such treatment, Du Bois went on to become one of the founders of the National Association for the Advancement of Colored People.

The Lafayette burned to the ground in 1897, and the Lake Park/Tonka Bay Hotel was closed in 1911. Today, no hotels stand on the shore of Lake Minnetonka.

The Hotel St. Louis Pleasure Resort

"Very, Very Gay"

When Deephaven was a wild woodland with nothing more than a twisty wagon trail winding under the maple trees, Charles Gibson visited and envisioned a grand hotel on the spot. Gibson claimed to be an English knight (many called him "Sir Charles") and was a well-known attorney from St. Louis who owned other hotels in Missouri. He knew this pristine northern lake could attract southerners eager to escape the scorching heat of their summer. He put cash down to purchase the peninsula of Breezy Point on the lake for his "North home," or "Northome."

Gibson developed the first real resort on the lake, the Hotel St. Louis, and also named the bay it over-

A favorite among southern tourists, the opulent Hotel St. Louis on Carson's Bay was one reason Minnetonka was deemed "among the leading pleasure resorts of the American continent" in 1881. Courtesy of the Minnesota Historical Society.

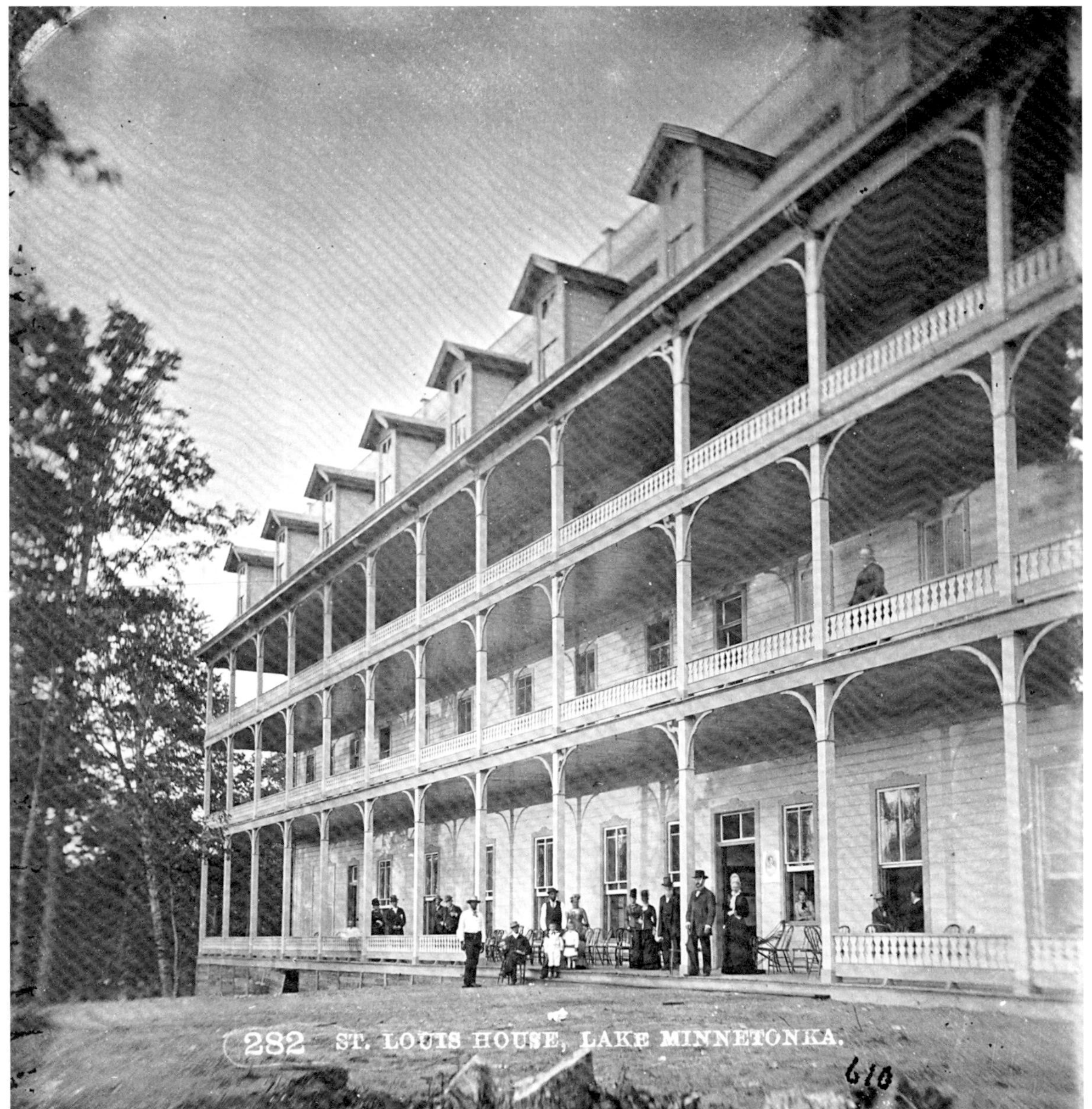
282 ST. LOUIS HOUSE, LAKE MINNETONKA.
610

looked St. Louis Bay. Construction began in 1879 for a July 1880 opening of the giant gray building with green trim. No expense was spared for Gibson's "Health and Pleasure Resort," which boasted not only indoor plumbing and electricity but a bathing room on each floor. Marble-topped dressers, elegant drapes, and large brass beds filled the plush rooms, which all had a large veranda overlooking either Carson's Bay or St. Louis Bay. A five-mile-long system of electric bells helped the staff attend to every need of the upper-crust guests. Evening entertainment included dances to live music, plays, musical revues, and poetry readings. If that was not enough, guests could lounge in one of the four parlors or the smoking room or shoot pool in the billiard pavilion.

No wonder the newspapers proclaimed the Hotel St. Louis "the first first-class hotel to be built on Lake Minnetonka . . . one of the most complete summer resorts in the Northwest," according to *The Magic Northland*. This 1881 guide to the area also proclaimed that the hotel had officially "placed Minnetonka among the leading pleasure resorts of the American continent." Gibson's hotel was a hit, but he was mostly an absentee owner who had to attend to his businesses in St. Louis.

Southerners came up in droves to fill the two hundred rooms, which could accommodate four hundred guests at a time. A series of white cottages were built behind the hotel for "the help," the African Americans who took care of the rich southern children. The southern tourists came for the rowing and the sailing, but mostly for the Northwestern Lawn Tennis Tournament held on the grass courts of the hotel. In July 1891, a $250 prize was offered to the winner. (Contestants were all men since women were not allowed to compete until 1913.) The famed Victor Etting traveled from Chicago to win the singles championship, and according to *Happenings around Deephaven*, "He overcame all opponents. Yet he was immaculate in white flannels, starched collar, bow tie and narrow brim straw hat." Or as *Once upon a Lake* described life at the St. Louis, "Existence there was said to be elegant, lazy and very, very gay."

Gibson knew that getting the guests to the front door was half the battle, so he had a horse-drawn carriage waiting at the Deephaven depot for any visitors who needed a lift. Most southerners took the Minneapolis and St. Louis Railway, which stopped in Minneapolis, but soon a spur of the Chicago, Milwaukee, and St. Paul Railway (often called the Milwaukee Road) took them right to the back door of the hotel.

Soon, however, Gibson had competition from none other than James J. Hill and his enormous Hotel Lafayette across the lake. Four years after its construction, Gibson spent another four thousand dollars to update his hotel to keep up with his high-class neighbors. Gibson's hotel did outlast Hill's, which burned to the ground in 1897, but the wooden structure eventually met the same fate. Walter and Mahala Douglas built a French-revival mini-chateau on the site of the burned-down Hotel St. Louis. Completed in 1911, that house still survives. Walter Douglas was able to enjoy his house only for a short time, as he had a ticket on the *Titanic*'s maiden voyage.

James J. Hill's Legacy on the Lake
Stations, Snuff, and Hotels

Some called James J. Hill the "Empire Builder"; detractors snubbed him as the "Robber Baron." He was inextricably linked to Lake Minnetonka and helped establish its pristine waters as a playground for the well-to-do.

The Homestead Act of 1862 had opened up the land to homesteaders, but some settlers were already squatting on land that the federal and state governments had given to the railroads. Minnesota alone gave an estimated $51 million worth of land and grants to the railroads—mostly to railroad barons such as Hill. In August 1867, the St. Paul and Pacific Railroad finished its line to Minnetonka Mills and Wayzata. With the new railways, commuting to the cities from the beautiful lake became possible. "In those days so many businessmen took the train to and from their homes at Lake Minnetonka that trains ran every hour, with two trains a half-hour apart scheduled at supper time," according to *Tales from Tonka*. With glorious speed, people around Wayzata could arrive in downtown Minneapolis from Lake Minnetonka in the same time it takes today by automobile.

Hill began his career in earnest by snatching up the floundering St. Paul and Pacific Railroad, formerly the Minnesota and Pacific Railroad, after Black Friday on September 19, 1873. He saved the company from bankruptcy and renamed it the St. Paul, Minneapolis, and Manitoba Railway. As part of the huge purchase, Hill acquired the first locomotive maintenance center in the state, which had been set up on Jackson Street in St. Paul in 1862. His shrewd business savvy led him to invest when markets were abysmally low in St. Paul as a result of an 1872 outbreak of equine encephalomyelitis, or "sleeping sickness" in horses.

As Hill expanded his railroad, he wielded his power mercilessly by threatening to bypass Minnesota towns unless they gave him their best real estate for free. Risking being left in obscurity, the town of Wayzata battled the powerful businessman but finally surrendered to Hill's tactics and "donated" prime downtown Lake Minnetonka property to him. To be unconnected to the burgeoning railroad system was economic suicide for a town. "Give me Swedes, snuff, and whiskey, and I'll build a railroad through hell!," Hill proclaimed, since strong Scandinavian immigrants were his favorite beasts of burden—that is, until they organized into unions. Before Hill laid railroad tracks throughout Minnesota, the best way of reaching the northwest part of the state was aboard a giant oxcart.

James J. Hill hosted elegant parties for senators, ambassadors, and even the president of the United States at his luxurious Hotel Lafayette. After the building burned in 1897, the parties continued at the Lafayette Clubhouse, where the railroad baron celebrated his seventieth birthday. Courtesy of the Minnesota Historical Society.

The trains did not come without a price, however. Sparks from the rails would fly from the metal wheels and set dry hay fields on fire. In the mid-1870s, an engineer fell asleep at the wheel, causing a train wreck between Long Lake and Wayzata of eleven freight cars, which caused even more damage because the engine kept plowing into more buildings. The temperature—a frigid thirty-two degrees below zero—did not help the cleanup crews, and landowners were livid with Hill.

Hill celebrated the completion of his railway at his fabulous Hotel Lafayette at Minnetonka Beach. The hotel cost him $815,000 in 1882 dollars. Imagine the monstrous five-story hotel, which was 745 feet long and 95 feet wide, with little immigrant cabins nearby. The style was remotely Queen Anne, but Thelma Jones wrote in *Once upon a Lake* that it was more "a mongrelizing of Elizabethan, Jacobean, and other styles quite unidentifiable." "How had that prize location been overlooked so long?" some asked, but Hill had scoped it out long before. The Hotel Lafayette went up between Crystal Bay and Holmes Bay (now known as Lafayette Bay), on a hill so that all rooms, front and back, would have a view of the water. Rather than keep the beautiful old-growth trees, Hill gave the order he gave to the workers who prepared the land for the railroads: "Clear!" Lumberjacks chopped down every tree, and clean little lollipop trees were planted on the grassy grounds.

Hill used his railway empire to transport passengers right to the door of his fabulous hotel in Minnetonka Beach. Here a steam locomotive puffs its way along the shore in 1885. Courtesy of the Minnesota Historical Society.

The grand opening on Independence Day 1882 saw the launch of the *Belle of Minnetonka*, the largest steamboat on the lake, twice the size of the next biggest boat, and it had the entire Fort Snelling band aboard for entertainment. Guests included many generals, governors, senators, and European ambassadors, who were carried by Hill's own train right to the door of the fabulous hotel. The Northwest Traveling Men's Reunion Association was there at the gala, but most notable was an appearance by ex-president Grant. "It was a monstrous stretch of luxury, easily the finest resort in the Northwest," according to *Once upon a Lake.*

By 1897, Hill was losing money on the fabulous hotel and planned to tear it down the next year to avoid further losses. Right after the water was turned off for the winter to prevent pipes from bursting, a blaze ripped through the building, and the extensive five-story building with its wide wooden porches burned to the ground. In spite of the terrible inferno, the Lafayette Clubhouse took the place of the hotel and hosted many prominent guests, such as Vice President Adlai Stevenson, in its summer cottages in 1900. President William Taft, all 354 pounds of him, dined there to honor a Japanese diplomatic mission coming through in 1910. In *My Ditty Bag*, Captain Charles W. Brown wrote this about the unusual meeting of Asians in far-off Minnetonka: "It is difficult to remember and correctly place Orientals, but President Taft gave what seemed to me to be a very unusual exhibition of a fine memory. . . . Pointing out of the open window looking toward the Lake he would ask, 'Does not this remind you of that place near Tokyo?'"

But losing the Lafayette was small potatoes for Hill, who focused on his ever-expanding railroad, which he had renamed first the St. Paul, Minneapolis, and Manitoba Railway and eventually the Great Northern Railroad. Hill's shrewd business deals formed the largest railway system in the world at the time, and its center was in St. Paul.

Southern Carpetbaggers

Mint Juleps on the Verandas

Following the Civil War, many of the upper-crust plantation owners from the South looked for a place to vacation away from their war-ravaged land. A direct train line could bring these gentlemen, their ladies, and their "colored" servants right to the door. Often they brought their own carriages and riding horses along with them.

The Hotel Lafayette provided all "the social amenities and gaieties of the mint-julep-drinking planters and traders, their regal ladies and fair southern belles who came up the river by steam packet of the 'Diamond Joe Line' from St. Louis to St. Paul," according to *The Early Background of Minnetonka Beach.* The two ballrooms of the hotel could each hold an orchestra.

Author Blanche Wilson wrote, "If the Lafayette was a thing of splendor, the St. Louis proved to be something that stood for American aristocracy—not eastern, but southern." She interviewed Judge Weatherby from

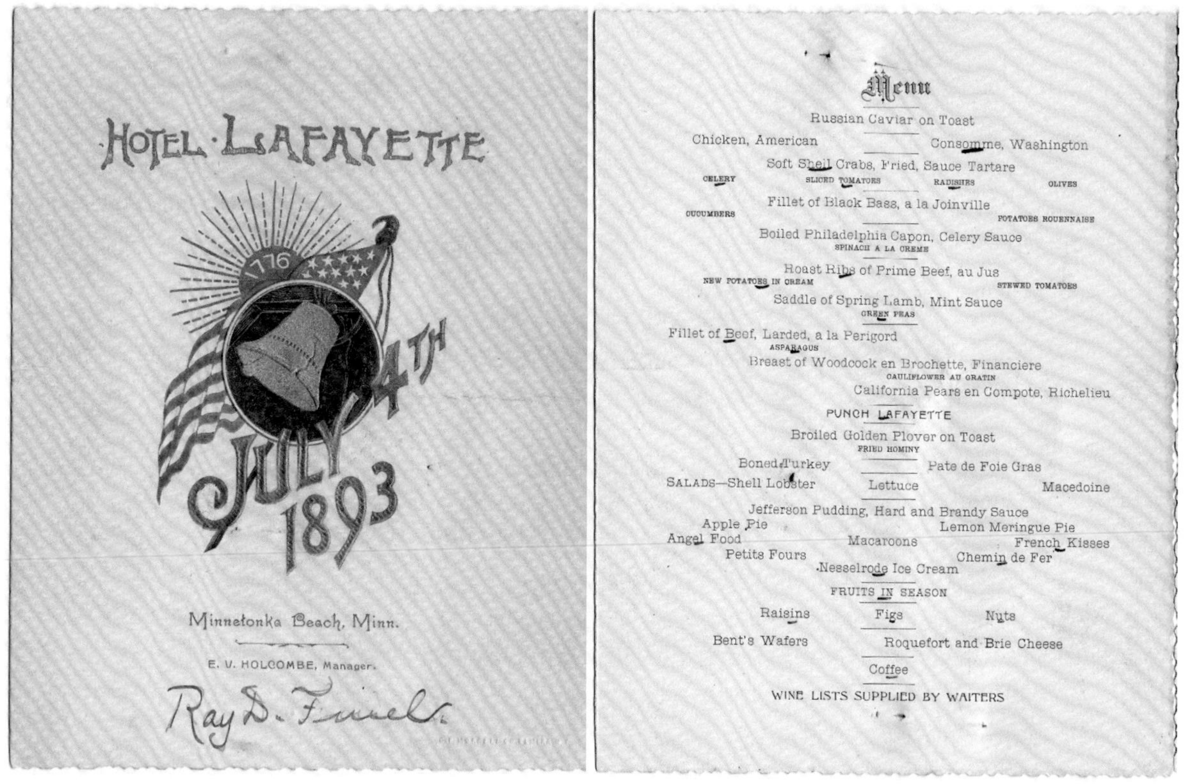

HOTEL LAFAYETTE

1776

JULY 4TH 1893

Minnetonka Beach, Minn.

E. V. HOLCOMBE, Manager.

Ray D. Fruel

Menu

Russian Caviar on Toast

Chicken, American — Consomme, Washington

Soft Shell Crabs, Fried, Sauce Tartare

CELERY — SLICED TOMATOES — RADISHES — OLIVES

Fillet of Black Bass, a la Joinville

CUCUMBERS — POTATOES ROUENNAISE

Boiled Philadelphia Capon, Celery Sauce

SPINACH A LA CREME

Roast Ribs of Prime Beef, au Jus

NEW POTATOES IN CREAM — STEWED TOMATOES

Saddle of Spring Lamb, Mint Sauce

GREEN PEAS

Fillet of Beef, Larded, a la Perigord

ASPARAGUS

Breast of Woodcock en Brochette, Financiere

CAULIFLOWER AU GRATIN

California Pears en Compote, Richelieu

PUNCH LAFAYETTE

Broiled Golden Plover on Toast

FRIED HOMINY

Boned Turkey — Pate de Foie Gras

SALADS—Shell Lobster — Lettuce — Macedoine

Jefferson Pudding, Hard and Brandy Sauce

Apple Pie — Lemon Meringue Pie

Angel Food — Macaroons — French Kisses

Petits Fours — Chemin de Fer

Nesselrode Ice Cream

FRUITS IN SEASON

Raisins — Figs — Nuts

Bent's Wafers — Roquefort and Brie Cheese

Coffee

WINE LISTS SUPPLIED BY WAITERS

Southerners vacationing on Lake Minnetonka expected fancy desserts such as macaroons and lemon meringue pie. Other delicacies for the aristocracy on this Fourth of July menu from 1893 included Russian caviar, breast of woodcock, golden plover, and saddle of spring lamb in mint sauce. Courtesy of Hennepin County Library Special Collections.

Mississippi who would summer at the glorious Hotel St. Louis on Carson's Bay: "Mother liked dressing for dinner every night too. I can see her yet all togged up fit to vamp even father. Those Minnetonka nights made me feel downright religious."

This high-class living was in sharp contrast to the lifestyle of the pioneers who scrimped and saved, eating woodchuck stew to survive. Many settlers would watch the wealthy southerners and listen to the orchestras from a distance. Ada Hoefer Bowers's family would

Fish fries and chicken dinners were among the down-home dishes available to diners at the Excelsior Bay Hotel. One would be hard-pressed to find this southern cuisine around the lake today. Courtesy of the Excelsior–Lake Minnetonka Historical Society.

let her go from their farm to take a peek at the fabulous wealth. "I liked them so much, the summer people, and they liked me," she recalled. "One of them wanted to take me back as a lady's maid," she declared, according to *Once upon a Lake*.

Suddenly there was a distinct class system at the lake. Early settler Laura Howe recalled, "We were no poorer than our neighbors and no richer." Another settler also wrote in a diary, "There were no classes, all were on the same level." Of course this does not take into account the way the Native Americans were treated or the position of some of the very wealthy land speculators and robber barons such as James J. Hill.

Not everyone liked the southerners. The settlers who lived near the Arlington House in Wayzata were not impressed. Charlie Gibbs remembered, "They weren't healthy looking. They wouldn't get in the sun, just sit around in the shade and smoke cigars and drink whiskey," according to *Once upon a Lake*. They never fished nor swam; "what the southerners did like to do was gamble. . . . They were high-class looking, real dudes. . . . I remember one coming back from the Arlington with a cigar-box full of jewelry." Obviously much of the wealth of the South still remained with this group.

The Lake Park Hotel, on the other hand, had a mix of northern and southern clientele with family suites on one floor. A spur of the narrow-gauge railway of the Minneapolis and St. Louis line ran right to the front balcony, and visitors were awed by the sixteen electric lights of the hotel. At the same time, the hotel prohibited liquor on the grounds, and no steamers could dock there on Sunday, in deference to the Sabbath. Lecturers came, such as a missionary to the Native Americans who educated the visitors on the history of the local Dakota, who had since been banished to desert-like land in South Dakota. Full academic courses were offered to guests staying for weeks, including scientists and physicists. Five hundred people could fit in the dining room, which doubled as the lecture hall. One presentation featured a large cartoon that showed "The Traitor, Jefferson Davis." Many southerners stormed out in protest; the Civil War was not forgotten.

Servants Stay Out Back

Minstrel Troupes and Separate Barracks

The victory of the Union over the Confederacy made the Emancipation Proclamation law over the South as well. The "forty acres and a mule" promised to freed slaves did not materialize, and some ex-slaves became servants reliant on rich plantation owners.

Charlie Gibbs remembered the arrival of the southerners, as quoted in *Once upon a Lake*: "Some of them had slaves. Yes, some of them had been . . . They'd ship the colored waiters back in the fall. And the pretty Negro girls that were maids for the southerners." Many of the residents of Lake Minnetonka had not seen African Americans since the Chilton brothers illegally brought slaves to Wayzata to work in their ginseng-drying operation.

The Hotel St. Louis on Carson's Bay catered especially to the "St. Louis people," who brought their horses and African American coachmen up by steamboat. As a young girl, Bertha Whipple, who lived on a farm near Lake Minnetonka, would tarry outside the Hotel St. Louis to listen to the music. She would

As part of the Excelsior Commons Pageant in 1919, a white entertainer dresses up in blackface to perform a minstrel show for the crowd. Courtesy of the Excelsior–Lake Minnetonka Historical Society.

admire the beautiful carriages and clothes that the wealthy brought up on the steamers from St. Louis. At the beginning of the summer "it was always the same. We'd see forty, fifty Negroes walking from Minnetonka Mills, where they'd got off the train," she recalled, according to *Once upon a Lake*. Even though they were venturing into the wilderness of Minnesota, the rich southerners from St. Louis brought along their African American servants, French chefs, and all the amenities of the South.

The view persisted that African Americans were quaint, simple folk who needed to be cared for by the rich southerners. Just as the Dakota sometimes provided "authentic" color to the wealthy on the steamboats, the ex-slaves put on minstrel shows after the Civil War.

W. E. B. Du Bois worked at the Hotel Lafayette in 1888 and was outraged that to get the best tips, waiters had to act like minstrel clowns. "I saw that it paid to amuse and to cringe," he wrote. "One particular black man set me crazy. He was intelligent and deft . . . [but] he was playing the clown—crouching, grinning, assuming a broad dialect when he usually spoke good English—ah! It was a heartbreaking sight." This waiter made more than any of the others through his demeaning acting skills.

The African Americans rarely slept in the actual hotels; they stayed in "separate barracks for colored servants." The management of the Hotel St. Louis "also provided separate quarters on the grounds for Negroes working at the hotel or serving guests from the South," according to *Happenings around Deephaven*. Such segregation was not practiced just at the big hotels: one of the little vacation colonies of cottages on Casco Point had a large carriage house and stable where the "colored coachmen got leftovers and they ate them alone," according to *Once upon a Lake*.

The black women often took care of the children of the rich white southerners. The main character in Borghild Dahl's partially fictional story *A Minnetonka Summer* "always got a thrill out of the sight of the beautiful Hotel Del Otero [where] . . . fashionably dressed grownups and children with Negro nurses strolled on the green velvety lawn." In an interview in the nonfiction book *Once upon a Lake*, Charlie Gibbs recalled the southerners who came to Wayzata with African American wet nurses giving milk to the white children.

While the black servants at Lake Minnetonka proved to be mostly a novelty to the locals, one of the African Americans became the de facto postmaster of Deephaven. Sidney Woodford, "a colored man from Kentucky," is mostly referred to disparagingly in historical records, since he "used to toss letters into an empty beer case and leave them for villagers to come and sort out," according to *Happenings around Deephaven.* He was soon replaced by a white settler, Carl Fogelmark, who added the post office to the Deephaven railroad station.

Many northerners viewed the African Americans as a potential menace, as evidenced in the *Knut Book*, a songbook from the Glen Lake Sanatorium that featured the song "They're Hanging That Poor Devil in the Morning," a parody of Rudyard Kipling's "Danny Deever":

> What is that moan?" the Colored Party said.
> "It is a patient awaiting death," said
> Flies-On-The-Bed.
> "He's guilty of the blackest crime, a most
> horrendous thing,
> They caught him visiting a woman, a
> WOMAN mind you, in West Wing.
> So they're hanging Danny Deever in the
> morning.

When the black servants from the hotels started appearing in the lakeside towns on their free days, some northerners were uncomfortable. In 1881, tragedy struck when four waiters from the Hotel St. Louis rowed over to Wayzata to have a good time on their day off. Charlie Gibbs remembered that they got in their rowboat after some time in Wayzata. "They started home, drunk. Nobody knew exactly what happened, but the bodies came up in nine days, they all came up. I can still see those white shirts come drifting in to shore." The townspeople were not quite sure what to do with the bodies. The coroner covered them up, but some townspeople protested that they should not be buried with the revered pioneers in the Wayzata graveyard. Finally the grave digger, Mr. Perry, "made a grave in our cemetery," according to *Once upon a Lake*. "There were some in town who found fault with that."

With time, the grandiose hotels and the southern culture that went with them disappeared. Cottages took the place of the hotels, and as Blanche Wilson wrote in *Minnetonka Story*, "There were no servants around now, so parents played with their children."

Riffraff from the Railroads
James J. Hill's Feud with Wayzata

To supply Lake Minnetonka with tourists in 1867, the St. Paul and Pacific Railroad ran its lines right along the shore to drop the wealthy clientele in front of the lobbies of the grand hotels. Wayzata had become a major transportation hub for the lake when railroad baron James J. Hill bought the line.

Rich vacationers stayed home following the financial disaster of the Panic of 1873, and in the 1880s summer cottages sprouted up on the lake to replace some of the giant hotels. The new residents complained that Hill's "box-cars . . . [brought in] a very rough element." What's more, Hill had clear-cut all the trees around the railroads, leading some to say, "Actually the only thing you could say for Wayzata was its convenience to the cities."

Wayzata became known as the toughest stop on Hill's railroad line. "And it wasn't just the railroad [that] brought the toughs, they'd come out in hacks, too, all liquored up," according to Thelma Jones. "Drunks or men who became drunk as soon as possible piled off the train at Wayzata in 1877. . . . And drifters used to come through. We would give them so much to move on. Other towns did the same. This was a notorious place for a while." The women organized to stop the madness with a local temperance society. At the time, Wayzata was still part of Minnetonka Township, which allowed alcohol. The women pushed to make Wayzata its own village to halt the intoxicated visitors. But they were not yet able to make a difference.

Wayzata was becoming known as a town of cottagers rather than of rich vacationers like other spots around the lake. Residents of Excelsior disparagingly dubbed Wayzata "Caretakers' Town." These pithy Excelsior teetotalers in their quaint bungalows lamented that not only were Hill's hotels bringing in the riffraff, but they were boozing it up when they arrived. One shabby hotel in Wayzata was run by Eliza Day, "who could not boil water. . . . Transients avoided both if there was lying-down room in a bed elsewhere. She bullied her husband until he was a quailing creature who seldom spoke and then only in mysterious little whispers," according to *Once upon a Lake.*

Minnetonka Beach on Lafayette Bay, a dry town at the time, demanded that all the wine ordered for the opening of Hill's Hotel Lafayette be sent back to Chicago. Hill scorned them as small-town bumpkins with small-minded attitudes toward alcohol. The stage was set for a showdown.

Wayzata became its own town in 1881 and swiftly banned bars from its city limits when it officially incorporated in 1883. Anyone caught "loitering, lurking or possessing a gaming device" was labeled a vagrant and locked up in a watchtower that the council had built. Emboldened, as its first order of business in 1883 the Wayzata Village Council passed a resolution

James J. Hill took the best land for his business and thought nothing of running his railways right along the shore, effectively cutting Wayzata off from its beach and igniting a furious protest from the town council. Courtesy of Hennepin County Library Special Collections.

that Hill's railroad could not "allow said streets to be blocked up with cars, trains, engines, or otherwise, for a longer period than five minutes at any time." Each transgression would cost the railroad fifty dollars. Two days later, the council upped the ante and voted to "move the main track from the center of Lake Street so as to give the Village sixty feet of said street . . . [and] to move the water tank and pump house from its present location . . . and [to put] the railroad . . . on [the] grade of Lake Street." Essentially, the new city council demanded that Hill move his railroad tracks back three hundred feet from the shore of the lake so that residents could enjoy both the beach and a view of the waves.

As the story goes, Hill promptly parked a long line of boxcars filled with garbage in Wayzata and demanded that the council drop the law or he would move the town's station a mile away for the next twenty years. The council also sued Hill to remove his railroad "from the public streets they have occupied in Wayzata." Hill was not pleased but lost his case in court. Wayzata held its ground. Hill kept his promise, ignored the law, and moved the depot one mile east of town into a swampy area on Bushaway Road; he called it Holdridge Station. Hill proclaimed, "Let them walk a mile for the next twenty years!"

Hill did not stop there. Since the law now required Hill to move some of his buildings from the waterfront, he moved Wayzata's water tower and pump house from what he deemed his property and set them smack dab in the middle of the road. Hill had always allowed Wayzatans to water their horses on his shoreline property, but now signs were posted that warned of penalties for trespassing. He also leased the one big hotel in Wayzata, the Arlington, which suspiciously burned in 1887, leaving less competition for his Hotel Lafayette. Hill ran trains filled with silk from the Orient right through downtown Wayzata, in spite of the danger, because the station was now east at Holdridge.

While the rest of Minnesota's population boomed, Wayzata only grew by three people between 1890 and 1900. Hill wanted to crush the town's resistance, so soon only fishermen came to town, and Wayzata floundered. Hill had essentially doomed Wayzata to oblivion. According to Jason McGrew-King in the *Lakeshore Weekly News*, Wayzatans wrote a saying about this robber baron:

> *Twixt Hill and hell there's just one letter;*
> *Were Hill in hell, we'd feel much better!*

In 1905 a windstorm destroyed the depot at Holdridge Station. That same year, the Wayzata council sought to make peace with the powerful businessman and passed a Reconciliation Ordinance. It effectively annulled the old law, which Hill had ignored all along. Hill was thrilled and built the grandest railroad station on his line to thank the town.

Ironically, the coastline in Wayzata has been

By 1905, Wayzata had tired of its war with James J. Hill and reached a truce with him. The railroad baron was so pleased that he built Wayzata the finest depot on the line. Courtesy of the Wayzata Historical Society.

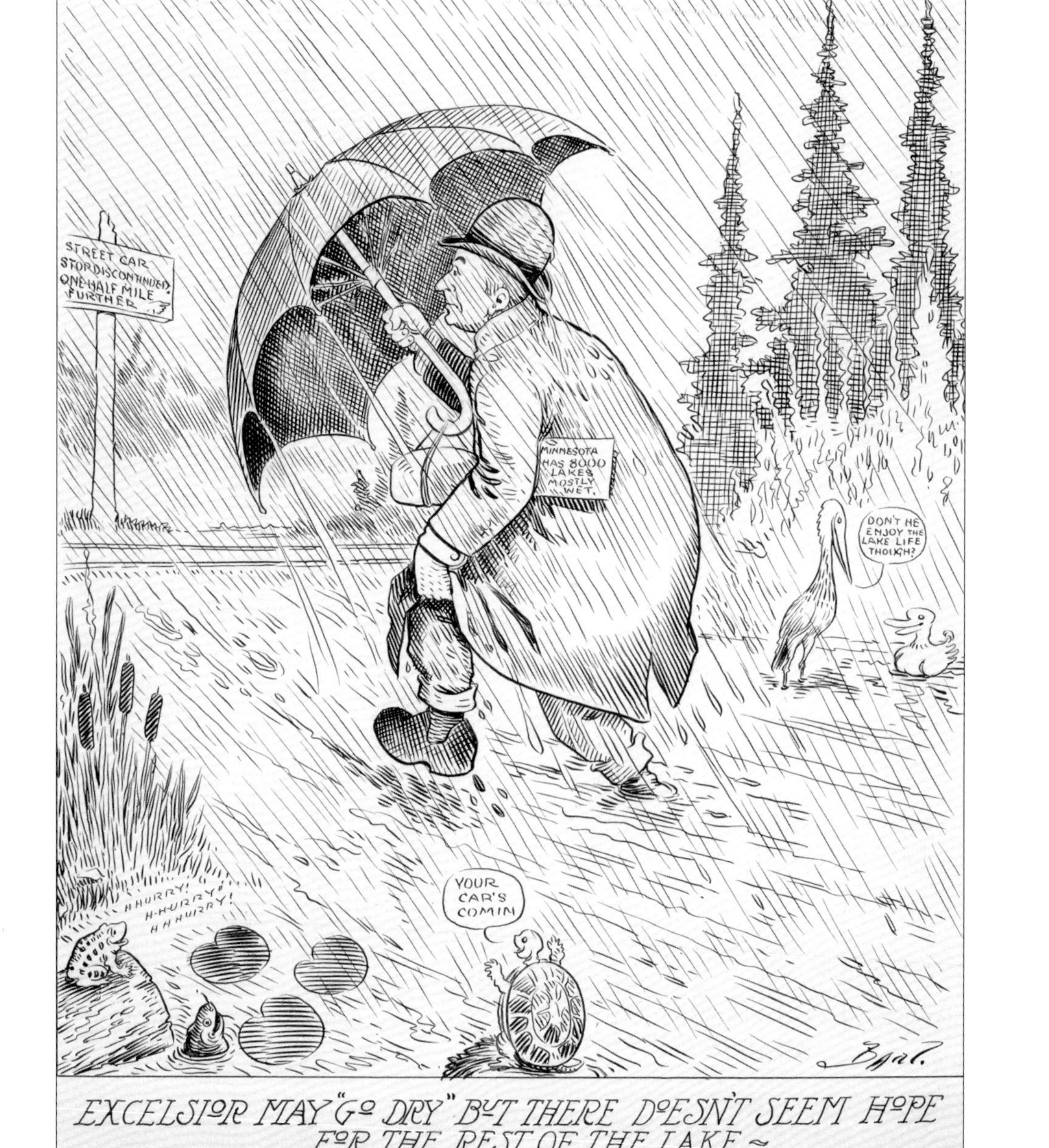

EXCELSIOR MAY "GO DRY" BUT THERE DOESN'T SEEM HOPE FOR THE REST OF THE LAKE.~

preserved and mostly kept open from development because of the railroad tracks and thanks to the robber baron. The station closed in 1971, was placed on the National Register of Historic Places, and is the centerpiece of the annual James J. Hill Days in September that began sixty years after the reconciliation.

A Pastor Reportedly Shoots a Saloon Owner

A War of Words between the Wets and the Drys

Lake Minnetonka has a long and grand tradition of drinking. When Governor Ramsey visited the lake in 1852 to fish, his group forgot to pack salt to season the catch. "It was the governor who suggested that brandy did just as well and who took the flask from the medicine chest. They all agreed that the dram made a piquant sauce," according to *Once upon a Lake.* Ramsey was generally well liked, though Helen Austin, who recalled that as a young girl she would sit on the lap of this "wonderful old man," also remembered that he perhaps tipped back a few and was "given to strong language."

This cartoon by Charles Bartholomew from 1909 was published in the Minneapolis Journal *and spoofs the fight between the Wets and the Drys around Lake Minnetonka. Towns like Excelsior struggled to keep saloons away, but the nearby hotels and steamboats openly defied local laws and flooded the area with liquor. Courtesy of Gustavus Adolphus College Archives.*

Ramsey's territory of Minnesota saw a giant influx of Scandinavian immigrants, many of whom had left northern Europe to escape the rampant drinking fueled by home stills back in the Old World. In 1868, a group of Finnish settlers walked from Minneapolis, past Lake Minnetonka, and on another twenty-five miles to settle Temperance Corners, now Cokato, where they built the state's first sauna. Nordic teetotalers were torn, for early Viking traditions stated that "beer had to be served to make an agreement legally binding," according to *The Norwegian Kitchen.* "The Gulating law also states that nobody should be declared incompetent, so long as he has his senses, can ride a horse and drink beer." Herr Mohr wrote in his diary, *Streifzug durch den Nordwesten Amerika*, "Upon one island, Germans from St. Paul have built themselves a charming place, where, far from the tumult of the world, they can drink a good glass in peace." At least for the moment.

This split between the "Wets" and the "Drys" played out across Minnesota. In Excelsior, the "Wets met in the Fred Hawkins Hotel," according to local historian Bob Williams. "The Drys met in church." The Drys also pushed through legislation in 1870 that made Excelsior ban snuff, cigars, and all other tobacco.

Led by the antiliquor crusader Pastor Charles Sheldon, Excelsior denied Charles Stout a license for a saloon in town. A report by John Parker in the *Minneapolis Tribune* of August 20, 1874, tells of the two men meeting by chance when they were hunting outside of town one weekend. Stout screamed insults at the clergyman, who in turn preached against demon drink. Taking the law into his own hands, the pastor decided Stout was better off in hell. Sheldon shot at Stout's head and took off one of his ears. During this "disgraceful and bloody affair," Stout, gushing blood, stabbed the pastor in the stomach with his hunting knife. As the gory pair rolled around punching and trying to kill each other, a storekeeper heard the fuss and tried to pull them apart. Stout ran after the storekeeper and knifed him from behind. Sheldon "was taken home and his wife was nearly overcome with grief at the sad sight." Friends of Stout had to guard him vigilantly against "many threats of lynching" by angry townspeople.

The next day, the *Tribune* ran a retraction of the entire article after an Excelsior resident claimed that the "Excelsior Hoax" was "all a canard made out of whole cloth." The *Tribune* reported that "we frequently receive communications from our friends in the country" but added that "no such person as John Parker is known in Excelsior." The angry editors promised to prosecute the "scoundrel" John Parker "who could perpetuate such a cruel and malicious falsehood implicating a respected clergyman in a shooting affray." Mostly, the newspaper sought to shift the blame for the hoax to "certain liquor dealers who are anxious to go into business at Excelsior." This fictitious tiff, however, showed that emotions ran high.

Excelsior Village was incorporated on March 17, 1877—only later was St. Patrick's Day met with widespread parades and drinking—and the council voted on whether to allow the sale of alcohol. The Wets and the Drys had their say. The teetotalers won, and the town became a "pronounced temperance community." Across the lake in Wayzata, which incorporated in 1883, twenty-five council members (out of thirty-two) voted to keep the town dry. All the wet votes had connections to the grand hotels around the lake.

The battle heated up when James J. Hill scoffed at what he considered puritanical do-gooders. On September 3, 1883, he held his gala banquet to celebrate the completion of the Northern Pacific Railroad. As already noted, the elegant evening was marred by a skirmish among the supposedly smashed kitchen staff. The journalist Dimond not only panned the event, claiming that the food was mediocre and the wine subpar, but wrote that the drunken brawl between waiters toward the end of the meal was indicative of the debauchery at these supposedly elegant establishments. He railed against Hill for his "open defiance of the Excelsior township no-liquor law."

The debacle embarrassed Hill and rallied the temperance movement to enforce the liquor laws, which allowed beer and wine but nothing served by the glass (in other words, hard liquor). Police booked the Hotel Lafayette's bartender several times for ignoring the rules. However, the elite hotel succeeded in keeping

This postcard of a Shriners' convention at Lake Minnetonka epitomizes the drunken merrymaking along the shores that drove local cottagers crazy and pushed the city councils to pass dry laws even before Prohibition. Courtesy of the Minnesota Historical Society.

the liquor cabinets filled. The profits from spirits kept these hotels and the accompanying steamboats afloat. For example, the *City of St. Louis* steamboat sailed twenty hours a day and earned an average of $1,500 per day on alcohol sales.

The jury was out on whether liquor was indeed detrimental to health. Numerous elixirs and bitters contained alcohol as their main ingredient. A Lake Minnetonka store in the 1890s advertised "Mexican Mustang Liniment," which could also be taken orally, as a "long tested pain killer for housewife, farmer and raiser of any sort of animals. You will need it every day for the children!" Charlie Gibbs, who had not thought much of the southerners' sickly looks, hailed the Irish who came to Wayzata, saying they looked healthy, strong, and muscular: "Biggest men I ever saw; strong and tough. Six foot, two and four. Wore a fourteen boot," according to *Once upon a Lake.* "Terrible fighters when drunk. Everybody had a black eye after pay-day."

Then the streetcars arrived, thanks to Thomas Lowry, who envisioned Lake Minnetonka as a playground for everyone, not just for the crème de la crème. Well-heeled visitors sometimes shunned the riffraff picnicking on Big Island, who often brought bottles of beer. Established residents feared that Excelsior would become a haven for taverns, as had happened to White Bear Lake, north of St. Paul, at the other end of Lowry's trolley line. Walter Douglas complained of the streetcars bringing the hoi polloi to his quiet Deephaven. On June 13, 1910, he lamented to the Deephaven Village Council of a "blind pig" behind his house. Since Douglas was the most prominent man in the village, the town marshal undertook an investigation "to find out if there are any places in the Village where intoxicating liquors are sold," according to *Happenings around Deephaven.*

In fact, one of the earliest acts of the newly incorporated Deephaven Village was to condemn locals Lars Pederson and John Carlson for "disorderly carousals on their premises." Most disturbing to locals was the colorful language used by the imbibers, which raised calls to prohibit profanity. These supposedly rowdy, drunken bashes became the subject of "a committee of one," boat builder Arthur Dyer, who was to "consider the advisability of an ordinance against profane and indecent language within the Village," according to the *Recorder* for the Deephaven Village Council. Once again the lines were drawn, not just between alcohol and its prohibition but also between decent and indecent language.

A History of Arson?
The Excelsior Siren Warns of Fires

Lunch is at noon, supper is at six, and kids must be off the streets at nine. The Excelsior siren says so. Every day since the 1940s, an old fire alarm atop City Hall in Excelsior has blared out these hours. The siren, however, triggers memories of terrible infernos before an adequate firefighting team was established.

Most of the early buildings around the lake succumbed to flames; the big hotels burned, probably resulting in a payoff for the owners who "lost everything." Proving arson was nearly impossible unless witnesses happened to catch the culprit in the act. However, the sheer number of important buildings that went up in flames, only to be replaced by grander structures, leaves skeptics scratching their heads. The first hotel built for summer use, the Maplewood Inn, burned in 1904. The Northwestern Christian College, which began as the Excelsior Academy in 1885, burned to the ground in 1896. The famous Hermitage house burned in 1901, killing the Hermit of the Lake. Both the Moore Boat Works in Wayzata and the Dyer Boat Works in Deephaven burned, in 1902 and 1910, respectively. The Keewaydin Hotel burned in 1924 and took down a cottage next to it. Fire destroyed the Minnetonka Ice Yacht Club in 1904 and the spectacular Minnetonka Yacht Club on Lighthouse Island in 1943. The list goes on . . .

Early fire departments often could not arrive in time to save the structures, often because of the lack of efficient communication. The Excelsior siren is a reminder of this problem. In an earlier world, when not everyone relied on a wristwatch (or a cell phone), people kept track of time by the sun or by the peals ringing from the church steeple. As a holdover from earlier days, the Excelsior siren still sounds the divisions of the day with extended blasts; shorter bursts of noise signal distress or a fire. Before the alarm was in place, a bell rang out the time to call the farmers from the fields, the sailors from their boats, and the vacationers to the table.

The daily siren is now triggered by a clock, but the fire alarm was once set off by "a telephone exchange on Water Street." Retired firefighter John Sweeney explained the process to the *Lakeshore Weekly News* in

The number of buildings around the lake that burned, sometimes under suspicious circumstances, often led to speculations of arson. In August 1933, the Minnetonka Country Club in Shorewood erupted in flames as onlookers watched. Courtesy of the Minnesota Historical Society.

2008: "[The exchange] would receive a telephone call about a fire. Then the operator rang the siren. The first one to the fire station called the operator for the address of the fire." (The siren should not be confused with the much louder tornado siren.) If a decent warning system had been established earlier, many of Lake Minnetonka's famous hotels might have been saved. However, sinister intentions are difficult to foil. For example, James J. Hill leased the Arlington House in Wayzata, only to watch it burn in 1887, which conveniently destroyed a competitor to his Hotel Lafayette.

Hill's Hotel Lafayette was slated to be torn down by the summer of 1898, but in October 1897, a blaze beat the wrecking ball. "There were those who remembered having seen box-cars being loaded with linen and silver from the hotel a couple of weeks before the conflagration," according to *Once upon a Lake*. When a small fire in an outbuilding swept to the grandiose wooden hotel, a telegram was sent to Hill's St. Paul office. But with the power already turned off and the big water tanks drained for the season, the people who first arrived on the scene could not do anything. The hotel was locked, including the telegraph room that could have sent for help, and the watchman had somehow skipped out of his duties for the day to take a jaunt to Minneapolis.

Architect Harry Wild Jones's fabulous Minnetonka Yacht Club on Lighthouse Island, with its third-story lookout, was an icon on the lake until it burned in August 1943. Courtesy of Hennepin County Library Special Collections and the Excelsior–Lake Minnetonka Historical Society.

The blaze began at just after eleven in the morning. A curious fisherman noticed smoke, but he and others could not get the hoses hooked up. The smaller fire extinguishers were not powerful enough. Someone made it to the Spring Park station two miles to the west and asked the train engineer to call for help, but, mysteriously, he said he would not act without orders from above. Not until twelve thirty did a telegram finally reach the Minneapolis fire chief, Frank Stetson, who sent out Engine Company No. 4 on a special Great Northern flatcar. The fire engines drawn by the Great Northern switch engine No. 5 made it in fifty minutes. The flames had burned freely for three hours before the Minneapolis Fire Department arrived to see the charred remains. All that was left was a smoldering mass. The total value of anything salvageable was fifty dollars.

To avoid such calamities, a second siren stands as backup next to the main one in Excelsior, but today firefighters rely on pagers or cell phones. Newcomers to Excelsior may be puzzled or annoyed by the loud alarm three times per day (baffles have been raised to dull the noise for some neighbors), but many love this talking clock that reminds them of the time. Modern mealtimes are not as strict as those of the past, and the nine o'clock curfew only applies to kids twelve and under on weekdays. "As a parent I love the siren," says Natalie Hagemo. "When my kids were younger they knew when it was lunch or dinner time when they were out."

Fires swept away most of Lake Minnetonka's grandest hotels in spite of precautions and alarms set up to warn the guests. Even though efforts were made to control the dances at the Lafayette Club, the ballroom caught fire on June 18, 1922, and burned to the ground, killing two young women inside. Even as late as 1972, the bandstand pavilion in Excelsior, which had hosted the Rolling Stones, was intentionally burned to the ground. No one was caught.

An English Cottage

The Brooks House

Bushaway Road, the "most beautiful road" of Wayzata, extends onto a little spit of land into Lake Minnetonka and originally had a railroad bridge connecting the peninsula to the other side, making Gray's Bay more of a lake than a little cove of Wayzata Bay. The road is the most historic area of Wayzata and even houses a trapper's cabin that supposedly dates from before 1750 (which is unlikely because that would make it pre–Revolutionary War and nearly a hundred years older than the oldest house in Minnesota).

More fascinating is the Brooks House, a Tudor revival style home that seems like a transplanted English cottage in the middle of the north woods. It is easy to imagine Beatrix Potter concocting tales of Peter Rabbit in the gardens of this house. With its rough timbering and wrap-around roof, it looks like

Designed in 1919 by architect Harry Wild Jones and featuring a carriage house, a chauffeur's apartment, and a gardener's cottage, the Brooks House is a masterpiece of the Tudor revival style. Copyright Karen Melvin Photography.

a Shakespearean-era classic. A huge stone chimney evokes evenings sitting by the fire drinking chamomile tea as the rain and fog set in for the evening. Vines wiggle up the stucco by the multipane leaded windows and turn bright red and yellow in the fall.

In 1919, after summering many years in a cottage on Big Island, Minneapolis banker Dwight Brooks and his family built the house in the Locust Hills neighborhood. A carriage house and a caretaker's house in the same quaint style were erected closer to the road, and they entice drivers to peek at the main house, a bit hidden behind the trees, and wonder what sort of historical treasure it might be. Because Bushaway Road doubles as Highway 101, the Minnesota Department of Transportation has attempted to widen the road, which would require knocking down the historic Brooks carriage house. So far, local homeowners have succeeded in keeping at bay the ever-expanding asphalt and have preserved the classic feel of this enclave on the lake.

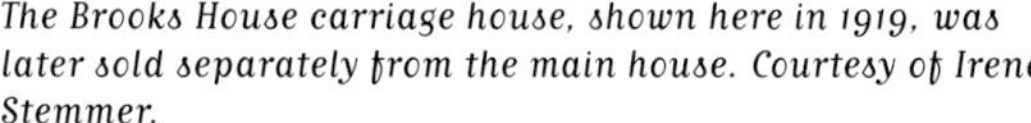

The Brooks House carriage house, shown here in 1919, was later sold separately from the main house. Courtesy of Irene Stemmer.

At Arthur Fruen's cabin retreat, built in 1927, a pair of charming boathouses are accessed by a fieldstone staircase that descends from the house above. Copyright Karen Melvin Photography.

From Screws to Swiss Chalets
The Fruen Cabin

William Fruen came to Minneapolis to make screws. Having learned the screw business in Boston, he set up a machine shop off Glenwood Avenue just east of Theodore Wirth Park in the Bryn Mawr neighborhood of Minneapolis. He soon converted his screw machinery to make waterwheel governors to protect Minneapolis mills from another explosion like the one that destroyed the downtown Washburn Mill, which famously blew up. Fruen's factory happened to have the best spring water in the city, and in 1884 he patented a "liquid drawing device" that would dispense a perfect cup of water for a penny. Jugs of artesian well water were lugged around town to offices and homes, and the company soon took up the now famous name Glenwood–Inglewood.

In the 1890s, Fruen experimented in new techniques of producing breakfast cereals, probably after hearing of the success of Pettijohn's Breakfast Food manufactured at Minnetonka Mills. He grew his experiments into the Fruen Cereal Factory at the same location and turned it over to his son Arthur in 1909. Arthur in turn used some of the profits to buy a choice piece of land on the southeastern point of Big Island to get away from the hustle of the city. High atop a hill covered with oak trees, he built what is arguably the most charming cabin on Lake Minnetonka. Many millionaires built elaborate houses to demonstrate their importance, but the Fruen cabin had no running water or electricity, and Arthur had to hop in a boat to cross the lake in his daily commute to Minneapolis.

Built in 1927, the Fruen House boasts a cozy sleeping loft upstairs and rustic wood built-ins. The stone steps and walls along the shore took four years to complete and required many trips over the frozen ice with loads of field stone. Apart from the large screened-in porches and the tree-covered deck overlooking the lake, the most prominent feature—from the lake, anyway—is the Swiss-style chalet and boathouse on the shore. Construction at the water's edge is now prohibited, so these green and red structures offer a glimpse of historic Minnetonka, when simple cottages lined the lake.

Craftsman "Cottage"

The Cargill House

When *Craftsman Magazine* published its widely popular plans for arts and crafts houses around the turn of the last century, the introduction usually included a socialist screed hailing the virtues of simple living and a return to high-quality, hand-built houses. According to architecture critic Eileen Boris, many of the arts and crafts artists "envisioned the 'cooperative commonwealth,' and promoters who popularized the ideas . . . turned these ideas into objects of consumption."

Ironically, James Flett Cargill, whose brother founded what is now the largest privately held company in the world, took these architectural ideas to heart and built a classic craftsman house overlooking Carson's Bay. Built in 1905, nearly thirty years before Governor Floyd B. Olson preached his vision of turning Minnesota into a cooperative commonwealth, the Cargill House embodies the arts and crafts aesthetic, thanks to the Chicago-based prairie school architect Hugh Garden. Frank Lloyd Wright's vision lives on here, since Garden borrowed some of Wright's prairie

Hugh Garden's prairie style home, built for James Flett Cargill in 1905, overlooks Carson's Bay and features generous porch space on three sides. Copyright Karen Melvin Photography.

school ideals: elegant wraparound porches, stone foundations, and an open veranda to take advantage of the striking surroundings.

At about the same time the Cargill House was built, arts and crafts idealist Gustav Stickley wrote that a "house that is built of stone where stones are in the fields, of brick where brick can be had reasonably, or of wood if the house is in a mountainous wooded region, will from the beginning belong to the landscape. And the result is not only harmony but economy." While some of the mansions on the lake seem distinctly out of place, the Cargill House fits into the landscape. Its one defining feature is the long straight roofline that echoes the horizon and, in this case, the lake. This feature, according to architecture critic Irving Pond, recalls "the spirit of the prairies of the great Middle West, which to [prairie school architects] embodies the essence of democracy." Thankfully, a landscape architect purchased the Cargill House in 1999 and carefully restored the home to its arts and crafts splendor after some remodeling had stripped it of some of its character.

Cottage Culture

When Lake Minnetonka Was a Summer Retreat

The hotel heyday on the lazy shores of Lake Minnetonka began in the 1870s and reached its peak twenty years later with the Hotel Del Otero and the Hotel Lafayette. Rich southerners ventured north to escape Yankee carpetbaggers and the South's heat, settling on the large wooden verandas overlooking the waves. At the same time, Minnesota's demographics were changing rapidly, as thousands of Scandinavians homesteaded in the state or set up shop in the city. Urban dwellers built cottages on Lake Minnetonka where they could spend their weekends lollygagging on wraparound porches far away from the filth of the muddy downtown roads filled with horses.

The E. W. Dyer House, with its long, wraparound front porch, epitomized the quaint cottages and lake homes built by early settlers around the lake. Courtesy of the Excelsior–Lake Minnetonka Historical Society.

Most of the Norwegian immigrants came from remote rural surroundings and cherished their mountain *hytta* (hut, cottage), which had to be spartan and isolated. Even today, Norwegians argue that these cottages should not be massive lake homes with modern luxuries; rather, they must be simple and rustic, a cabin set high in the hills or a fishing shack on stilts with the water lapping under its floorboards. The more remote, the better. Running water and electricity are modern complications. In search of wilderness, they built their bare-bones cabins on Lake Minnetonka.

Some "cottages" were more like castles. In 1891, Norwegian immigrant Olaf A. Searle built a home on Big Island that cost an estimated quarter of a million dollars. His fortunes sank soon afterward, and he was forced to give up his estate. Courtesy of Hennepin County Library Special Collections.

In the 1920s, on summer Fridays my Norwegian grandfather and Swedish grandmother would hop on a trolley on Hennepin Avenue in Minneapolis. It carried them to the docks of Excelsior or Deephaven, where the streetcar boats picked up passengers and dropped them off around the lake or at the ends of their docks. My newlywed grandparents shared a wooden cottage on Seton Lake, one of the many smaller bays that makes up Lake Minnetonka. Perched in the woods above the water, this arts and crafts cabin provided summertime relief in what was then a remote destination. Once Minnetonka became too pricey and too populated, most cottagegoers looked north; my grandparents bought land on the remote Whitefish chain of lakes near Brainerd, which has now also become the site of fancy summer homes.

Some original cottages have withstood the building boom around Minnetonka, but most have been torn down, and new buildings have gone up on their foundations, grandfathered-in to let them be built too close to the shore. Even those original cottages that remain often find their panoramic views of the lake obscured by new houses. Some cottage communities have resisted the pressure, such as Crane Island on the far side of the lake, which has been listed on the National Register of Historic Places. Dating back to 1907, when its first cabins were built on the shore around a central commons, this summer retreat still shows a simpler, historic side of the old Lake Minnetonka.

With the arrival of streetcars on the shores of Lake Minnetonka, the hoi polloi could now enjoy the pristine beaches and forests that had previously been reserved for the wealthy or adventurous. Courtesy of the Excelsior–Lake Minnetonka Historical Society.

5

Enter the Trolleys

Excelsior's Trolley Returns!

Take the Tram to Water Street

Once Thomas Lowry set up streetcar lines from White Bear Lake to Excelsior in 1905, my grandparents and others like them could shake off cramped city living to summer on the sunny shores of Lake Minnetonka. Elegant hotels encircled by open-air porches housed the wealthy—at least until the railroads stretched to the national parks in Wyoming and Montana. Then the wealthy tourists moved on. Just as James J. Hill's railway brought his guests right to the doorstep of the Hotel Lafayette, Thomas Lowry's streetcars conveniently deposited tourists in front of his Tonka Bay Hotel in 1907. Visitors could also opt for the more humble cottages that dotted the sandy shores of Lake Minnetonka, and from which they might take a ride on a steamboat to the Big Island bandstand to see Tommy Dorsey or Lawrence Welk.

The Twin Cities Rapid Transit Company (TCRT) built the first line to Minnetonka on the old Minneapolis, Lyndale, and Minnetonka rail bed. A single track opened in 1905, and another followed the next year. "Electric arc lights, suspended from the span wires, lighted the right of way from 34th Street, just east of Lake Calhoun, in Minneapolis, all the way to Excelsior," according to *Twin Cities by Trolley*. Another spur, the Deephaven line, opened in 1906 and ran on the old Chicago, Milwaukee, and St. Paul track for the Hotel St. Louis, which had declined in popularity.

Why did the streetcars disappear? The first threat to trolleys came from posh Victorian bicycling clubs, which insisted the cities spruce up the dirt roads for smooth pedaling. Cyclists were fed up with catching their tires in trolley tracks and sharing the road with screeching trams. Cities and towns debated whether roads should be paved with macadam, wood from the endless northern Minnesota forests, or metal from the Iron Range in northeastern Minnesota. Iron rails, however, allowed much higher speed than any such roads. TCRT even debuted double-decker trolleys, but they were deemed "cumbersome" and "unsafe at the high speeds reached on the run to Tonka," according to *Happenings around Deephaven*. Two such cars were built to

By the early twentieth century, the rail lines to and from the lake were well established. Here the double-decker Twin Cities Rapid Transit trolley zips down muddy Water Street in Excelsior, circa 1906. Courtesy of Hennepin County Library Special Collections.

be used in 1906 and 1907, but the top-heavy construction worried the drivers, especially at sixty miles per hour.

Streetcar traffic boomed, with 2 million passengers in 1907, 3.7 million by 1911, and 5.2 million by 1921, but by then decent roads for automobiles had been paved around the lake. Roger Stubbs recalled "one of the lakeshore millionaires rattl[ing] by in his new automobile, steered by a tiller in the early days before steering wheels," according to *Tales from Tonka*. "With the main street either dusty or muddy, no one was likely to exceed the eight miles-per-hour speed limit then." Lake Minnetonka has the dubious distinction of being the site of the state's first fatal automobile crash: in Cottagewood, where the road crossed the railroad tracks, two members of the famous Gluek family were mashed by a speeding train.

The real menace to the trolleys came from General Motors (GM), Standard Oil of California, Phillips Petroleum, Mack Trucks, and Firestone Tire and Rubber, who teamed up behind the front company National City Lines (NCL) to dismantle American cities' streetcars. NCL's president, Roy Fitzgerald, hailed from Eveleth, Minnesota, and led the battle to convert eighty cities from streetcars to buses by 1946. Many of the trolleys in Minneapolis were burned, and their tracks were ripped up so that reverting back to streetcars would be impossible. GM knew that public money, specifically the gas tax, would go toward improving roads and making the United States more reliant on the automobile.

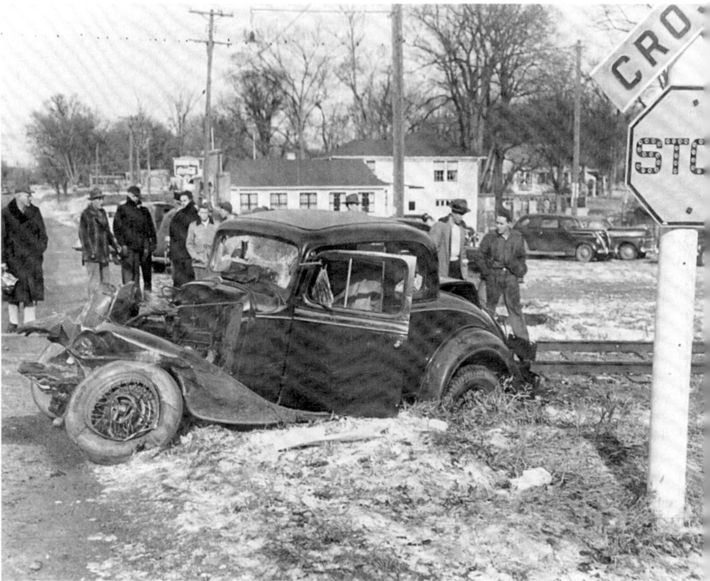

A casualty of the battle between trains and automobiles, this car lost in an encounter in 1946 at the Manitou Railroad Crossing in Excelsior. The first death from a train colliding with a car occurred in Cottagewood in 1908. Eventually cars won, and the railroad line was turned into a bike path. Courtesy of Hennepin County Library Special Collections.

By July 1926, streetcar usage had declined to Lake Minnetonka. In 1925 TCRT scuttled three of the so-called streetcar boats—which were designed to look like the trolleys and extended Lowry's trolley service from the end of the line in Excelsior over the water to Big Island—and in 1926 stopped service altogether. The downtown Minneapolis ticket office for TCRT closed

A couple escapes the city to relax on the shores of Big Island, circa 1906. Courtesy of Hennepin County Library Special Collections.

in 1928. A smaller office was opened in the bus station at First Avenue and Seventh Street. (It later became the nightclub First Avenue.) On August 11, 1932, headlines announced, "Tonka [Street] Car Makes Last Lake Run Early Today." Deephaven was stranded without public transportation, but Excelsior now had a bus line. Within twenty-seven months, all the streetcars had disappeared from the Twin Cities.

Nevertheless, nearly everyone remembers streetcars fondly. In Excelsior today, on weekends throughout the sunny summer months, tourists can imagine the past. On a small stretch of tramline, one can ride on a completely restored, canary-yellow streetcar with split-cane seats that brings back the old days of clanging trains.

Big Island's Boom and Bust
Bandstands and Minnetonka's Eiffel Tower

Lake Minnetonka had its first national splash when Hill's railroads connected well-to-do southerners to the grand hotels around the lake, making it the "Most Famous Lake of the Midwest," as brochures boasted. Big Island has always stood as the centerpiece of the lake, even when the lake and the lands around it were the home of the Dakota.

Before the island became a vacationers' paradise, half of it was owned by Olaf A. Searle. Searle dredged a channel to make his own new little island, Mahpiyata Island, which he attached to Big Island with a small bridge, and he erected a boathouse with a dock and a gazebo big enough for an entire orchestra. He built a fabulous mansion that rumor said cost upward of $250,000 in 1890 dollars. Searle earned his fortune selling real estate and working for banks, but after wild parties on the lake and with a wife who could not resist raiding his well-stocked wine cellar, his life slowly fell apart. He lost all his property, including the Big Island mansion. In the end, a friend discovered him destitute in downtown Minneapolis at Schiek's restaurant (before it was a strip club) and convinced him not to throw away his last $2,500, but the once-wealthy Searle died soon afterward in obscurity.

With the property on Big Island up for sale, TCRT took advantage of the real estate opportunity and in 1906 announced a contest to name a brand new amusement park that was to open at the far end of TCRT's streetcar line on Lake Minnetonka. All a rider from the cities needed for a day of fun at the park was the ticket price of a streetcar and streetcar boat. Already Wildwood Amusement Park was luring the likes of F. Scott Fitzgerald to live it up in White Bear Lake, where homeowners complained that their once-calm village had become a town of taverns.

Lowry, the "streetcar man," reassured the worried residents of Excelsior that an amusement park would only add to Lake Minnetonka's charm, pointing out

View from Big Island Park, Lake Minnetonka
COPYRIGHT BY SWEET, MPLS.

Picnickers came by the hundreds from Minneapolis to fabulous Big Island via the streetcar boats. The centerpiece of the island, seen here under construction, was the two-hundred-foot-tall water tower and lighthouse (thanks to underwater electrical cables), based on a campanile in Seville, Spain. Courtesy of the Excelsior–Lake Minnetonka Historical Society.

that his park would be far from town, on sixty-four acres he had purchased on Big Island. His grand plan called for shuffling tourists from his streetcars right to the island via streetcar boats painted in the same canary-yellow color scheme as the trolleys. Five trolleys an hour came from Minneapolis, and six streetcar boats and a ferry brought visitors to the island.

Letter writers waxed poetic with contest entries for the new name; suggestions included "Whooperup" and "Uneedagoodtime," according to James Ogland

in *Picturing Lake Minnetonka.* TCRT opted for the more sober, and obvious, "Big Island Park." Still, the publicity campaign worked, for fifteen thousand festivalgoers loaded onto the trams and streetcar boats on opening day to ride on the new rollercoaster, take the "Scenic Ride to Yellowstone," and see sites such as the Old Mill, a tunnel of love with photos illuminated on spooky cavernous walls. Other sites included a Merry Maze, a Laughing Gallery, and penny odeons, where visitors could see flip films. Tourists could wander through the aviary of exotic birds from Europe and beyond, and up to fifteen hundred spectators could watch New York musicians at the new Big Island Pavilion, erected in 1907 to accommodate the large crowds.

On balmy Saturdays in the summer, ten thousand visitors would pack the park to picnic at the mission-style pavilion and to stroll under the replica of a tower in Seville, Spain. The spire served as a water tower and lighthouse, which was fed electricity via an underwater cable. This two-hundred-foot-tall Electric Tower was the crown jewel of Big Island, serving as a beacon lighting up the night for tourists. Even though postcards bragged that it was "Minnetonka's Eiffel Tower," the square cement building, a replica of a Spanish tower, fit in with the mission-style architecture that was all the rage in arts and craft bungalows of the time.

From thrilling roller coasters to bathing beauties, the lake's "Picnic Wonderland," Excelsior Park, had it all—at least until the amusement park shut its doors in 1973. Collection of Chris Foote (www.minnesotaposters.com).

A Minneapolis Tribune *photographer shot this dizzying image from the heights of the Excelsior roller coaster in 1925. Contrary to popular belief, this roller coaster was not moved to the Valleyfair amusement park in Shakopee when the Lake Minnetonka park closed. Courtesy of Hennepin County Library Special Collections.*

Big Island Park lost four thousand dollars in 1907 and lost more revenue each year afterward. TCRT's other lake property, the Tonka Bay Hotel, made money only in its first year of operation. Big Island Park lasted just six summers before TCRT accountants recognized the financial sinkhole it had become. The metal from the Electric Tower was hauled into Deephaven and melted down to support the war effort. The dance hall and roller rink from the Lake Park Hotel were dismantled in the winter of 1918 and hauled by horses over the frozen lake to Excelsior. According to *Twin Cities by Trolley*, "Salvagers took down most of the park during World War I, and the final remnants were carted away in 1924."

The park's decline is attributed to a financial panic in 1907, which echoed an earlier recession in 1893. In addition, the forty-eight-hour workweek meant that although "some businesses closed at noon on Saturdays, . . . that still left Sunday as the only free day of the week," according to *Twin Cities by Trolley*. Paid vacation was only for the wealthy. On special holidays the park had thousands of visitors, but the short season could not sustain it.

The Big Island Amusement Park gave way to the Excelsior Amusement Park, which cost $250,000 and opened on May 30, 1925. Rides included the Whip, the Chair-o-Plane, a Ferris wheel, and the Electric Flying Skooters. The dance hall from the Tonka Bay Hotel for big-band concerts was called the Lakeview Park Pavilion, but it was soon renamed Big Reggie's Danceland and hosted such rockers as the Rolling Stones in 1964. Although Wayzata had its North Shore Pavilion and Parker's Lake had Parker's Lake Joy Club, those dance halls could not compare to the "largest dance floor in the Northwest" in Excelsior. Not everyone approved: an elderly church woman, quoted in *Tales from Tonka*, said, "Dances were the curse of the community."

Streetcar service continued to Excelsior until 1932, when buses brought the day-trippers. The Excelsior Amusement Park closed in 1973, but once again workers dismantled parts of it to be used elsewhere. Both the Scrambler and the carousel went to the Valleyfair amusement park in Shakopee, where fun seekers can still have a thrill on historic rides.

Christmas Lake

Home of Kris Kringle?

The name "Christmas Lake" suggests that this idyllic spot on the edge of Hennepin and Carver Counties might be a secret hideout of Santa Claus. Or it conjures up images of a giant yuletide parade, with sleighs pulled by reindeer and bearing elves tossing packages to bundled-up youngsters. Nope. Christmas Lake is known not for a spectacular wintertime procession of sleighs with jingle bells but, rather, for a Fourth of July parade of "float boats" on the pristine eighty-seven-

Christmas Lake was named to honor not Santa Claus but, rather, Charles W. Christmas, who hired the original surveyors of the surrounding land. Courtesy of the Minnesota Historical Society.

foot deep waters. A new parade motif is chosen each year, and judges rate the best-decorated boats—usually pontoons. "Rock-n-Roll" was the 2009 theme; the parade featured an Elvis sighting, smoke machines, skinny dippers, and even a "Jailhouse Rock" boat with ersatz prison bars holding "Bernie Madoff" and disgraced Chicago governor "Rod Blagojevich," guarded by kids with Super Soakers. Nor does the etymology of Christmas Lake have anything to do with December 25. The lake bears the name of Charles W. Christmas, who was elected the first surveyor of Hennepin County in 1852 and laid out the original map of Minneapolis.

Suddenly, these newly formed towns needed new names. Some used an anglicized version of a Dakota name. Wayzata is an example. The town "came into existence right in the center of Chief Shakopee's Indian village," according to *Minnetonka Story*. Still, the first name the immigrants gave it was "Garrison's," for Oscar Garrison, who settled the area and soon after sold out. Its name became "Freeport" for a while, and then "Wayzata City." According to *The Early Background of Minnetonka Beach*, Wayzata is "a phony derivative from the holy Dakota word *Waziah*, which was an aspect of the Great Mystery that purified the earth with winds" from the north. The pronunciation has changed from "Way-za-tay." Ironically, tourists who are new to the area often "mispronounce" the name as it was originally said.

The name "Mound" obviously derives from all the Indian mounds in the area. The origin of "Cottagewood" is also easy to understand. In fact, Samuel Gale, the advertising director for General Mills who built the Maplewood Inn in 1869 and who invented the radio jingle, platted the peninsula in 1875 and advertised it as a "fine location for summer cottages . . . within easy sailing or rowing distance of the railroad station . . . and directly in the line of the steamboat route from Wayzata to Excelsior." Other names tend to be more literary, such as "Deephaven," after the novel of the same name by New England author Sarah Orne Jewett, a favorite of early settler Hazen J. Burton. George Bertram, the real estate speculator from New York who with Hezekiah Brake established Excelsior, wanted a lofty name for his new town, one that would ring in the ears of potential customers for his new offerings on the south shore of Lake Minnetonka. He looked to Longfellow's poems and chose "Excelsior," meaning "onward, upward, higher!"

Perhaps a link to Santa Claus can be made for the unusual "Christmas Lake" because of all the early Scandinavian settlers in the area (both Norway and Finland claim to be the site of Father Christmas's "real" home in Lapland). An early settlement on the south side of Christmas Lake named itself Vinland, after the Icelandic/Norwegian words for "wine" and "land," because abundant wild grapes flourished in the summer there. Some claim that the historic Vinland detailed in the Icelandic sagas from the eleventh century, where

Vicious battles against moonshiners raged in Minnetonka. In 1925 Hennepin County sheriff Earle Brown made a public display of axing a still for bootleg liquor. Courtesy of the Minnesota Historical Society.

Vikings settled in the New World, could be in Newfoundland, Cape Cod, or even further inland (Shorewood, on the south side of the lake?). Why couldn't it be Christmas Lake? The Vinland on Christmas Lake was founded in 1898, the same year that Swedish immigrant Olof Ohman discovered the disputed Kensington Runestone, which claims that Norse visitors came to the middle of Minnesota in 1362. Maybe Santa came along and hid on the shores of Christmas Lake, where in winter it is colder than northern Norway.

Prohibition on Lake Minnetonka

"Blind Pigs" and Bootleg Liquor

Before the Civil War, many of the teetotalers along Lake Minnetonka were also strong Republican abolitionists, and they had seen their efforts to eradicate slavery succeed (and sometimes boil over into spats between the northerners and southerners on Lake Minnetonka). In the second decade of the twentieth century, teetotalers were often also pacifists who wanted no more wars in Europe, and the women among them were also often suffragists, who marched for the right to vote.

These do-gooders drew a line between decency and debauchery and let their neighbors know if they transgressed that line. One Sunday sermon at Calvary Memorial Chapel in Navarre just west of Wayzata was entitled "Why Every Tavern Keeper on Lake Minnetonka Ought to Go to Hell." The prohibitionists gained steam in western Minnesota as Congressman Andrew Volstead from Granite Falls sponsored the Volstead Act in October 1919 to fulfill the Eighteenth Amendment to the Constitution, which outlawed liquor. To skirt the law, doctors began prescribing alcohol, especially cognac, to reduce fevers. A running joke around the lake, according to *Tales from Tonka*, was that "Prohibition has made the swallow our national bird."

The teetotalers struck back, arguing, "The wets have no party symbol to compare with the drys' camel, unless, of course, they adopt the blind pig," a euphemism for a speakeasy. In 1923, an editorial in the *Western Guard* newspaper of Madison, Minnesota, praised the teetotalers' program: "The anti-saloon league is to be commended for its effort in proposing the passage of a law to prohibit doctors from prescribing liquor as medicine and ministers from using fermented wine at the communion table. Would that every minister of the gospel from now on enter this fight, and be on the dry side."

The battle of Prohibition played out more dramatically in St. Paul, where gangsters sipped moonshine in the Wabasha Street caves, and in Minneapolis, where Kid Cann and his syndicate gunned down interfering journalists. Minnetonka kept its reputation for fun as illegal watering holes popped up. One such was a speakeasy in the basement of Minneapolitan politician Martin Smaby on Priest Bay. It had a secret buzzer in a coat closet to let people in, and there were rumors that the up-and-coming Andrews Sisters would play a surprise concert there.

Ellen Wilson Meyer, who wrote extensively about the lake, described her father as "a Kansas Baptist so dry he rattled" and remembered that "many people were eager to break the law for a 'swig of hooch.'" As a young girl, she heard of the "blind pigs" and parties at speakeasies like Fat Emma's on St. Alban's Bay and Blind Julia's at Minnetonka Manor. Whisky might be hidden in a cabbage patch or even "buried in a snowdrift or sunk in a channel in the Lake. One time a fire in a Minnetonka Mills home exposed nine fifty-gallon drums of alcohol," according to *Tales from Tonka.* Near Meyer's house, the feds raided "Grover's old henhouse where he was living and distilling whiskey. . . . Beyond the kitchen were piles and piles of fermented 'mash' of various grains dumped from barrels. We picked our way over and under metal pipes for distillation that had been pounded, twisted and broken beyond redemption."

The story of the failure of Prohibition as most often told highlights the allure of the illegal speakeasies. Part of the missing story is how dangerous the moonshine could be. Charles Hicks, from Lake Minnetonka, hooked up with a bootlegger who brought hooch down from Canada. Before Hicks distributed the illicit liquor to his friends, he asked a chemist to test it to ensure its purity. "The chemist certainly made a convert out of me. It was terrible stuff, all doctored up," according to *Tales from Tonka.* He identified three separate poisonous substances in each of the bottles. "Bootleg liquor has revised the old saying about putting the cart before the horse," he said. "Now it's putting the quart before the hearse."

On March 14, 1933, well-known boatmaker Arthur Dyer proclaimed at a Deephaven Village Council meeting, "We should have someone man enough to close up the moonshine joints!" Prohibition was repealed on April 7 of that year; the council passed an ordinance to license the sale of beer, but not hard liquor. Prohibition and the temperance movement had failed dramatically, and soon the booze flowed again. As Charles Walker wrote four years after the repeal of the Eighteenth Amendment: "Statistics show that Minnesota drinks more beer in a year than Kansas does in a decade."

Even though the Volstead Act was overturned, the battle continued. In 1937, the teetotaling Deephaven council voted that "there should be neither direct relief nor work relief for anyone," after some on the village payroll had been spotted spending money on beer and liquor on the job. Prohibition was over, but the teetotalers in power still wanted to keep employees in line with the threat of holding back funds to punish supposedly deviant behavior. Almost a decade later, Deephaven was still dragging its feet on liberalizing liquor laws. On October 11, 1946, the council debated the merits of prohibition when a proposal was put for-

PLEASE VOTE NO
ON SUNDAY SALE OF LIQUOR
TUESDAY, SEPTEMBER 10
WHY?
BECAUSE SUNDAY IS
GOD'S DAY
A HOLY DAY
A TRAVEL DAY
A FAMILY DAY
A RELIGIOUS DAY
KEEP IT THAT WAY
BE SURE TO VOTE
WORK AND PRAY
Minnesota Good Government League, Inc.
Rev. Henry J. Soltau, State Director
Minneapolis, Minnesota
Women's Christian Temperance Union
Violet M. Geary, President
Minneapolis, Minnesota

Minnesota's blue laws, which stem from Prohibition, are still enforced today. This post-Prohibition flyer encourages the devout to rally against encroaching decadence. Courtesy of the Minnesota Historical Society.

ward for a municipal liquor store. In a villagewide vote on whether licenses were to be granted "for the sale of intoxicating liquors in the Village of Deephaven," there were 274 votes in favor of and 397 against allowing alcohol. On December 5, 1952, Dr. Lewis Reid requested permission to build a medical–dental building on Vine Hill Road, but the finished project also included a drugstore and a liquor store on the property. The Deephaven council was outraged over this "breach of faith," according to Mayor Schoell. And the Deephaven PTA united to proclaim a unanimous *no* to allowing the sale of alcohol. The tide was unstoppable, however, and by the end of 1952 the council let Deephaven become wet.

Jazz Age Wedding

A Gatsby-Like Bash without the Booze

Even during the bitter years of the Great Depression, Lake Minnetonka was a swinging place. F. Scott Fitzgerald took notes about the Roaring Twenties by imbibing with the country club set on White Bear Lake and becoming an honorary member of the Lafayette Club on Lake Minnetonka. He set *The Great Gatsby* on Long Island, and its narrator is a simple midwesterner, but its descriptions of debauchery could have come from Scott's personal experience of youthful abandon on the big waters west of the Twin Cities.

In 1929, Minneapolis was the boomtown of the

Even though the stock market crashed in 1929, a fancy (yet dry) Gatsby-esque wedding enlivened the shores of Lake Minnetonka in 1931. Photograph courtesy of Chuck Parten.

Northwest. John Philip Sousa came to town to conduct a march he wrote for the opening of the new Foshay Tower—but the twenty thousand dollar check he received from Foshay bounced as the market collapsed later that year. In spite of the market crash and Prohibition the Jazz Age lived on, with speakeasies pouring the booze and bootleggers happy to supply moonshine to big bashes.

A 1931 Gatsby-esque shindig on the shores of Lake Minnetonka at the estate of the parents of Chuck Parten was saved on 16 mm silent film. Parten's grandfather had purchased a large swath of land on the far side of the lake in Orono (which includes the North Arm, Stubbs Bay, and Maxwell Bay) for just $1.25 an acre in 1892. Years later, Parten's parents staged their wedding on this scenic site, and all the local VIPs attended.

The film capturing the Partens' upper-class summer wedding on Lake Minnetonka showed that cocktails were nonexistent and any champagne must have been off-camera. Either the cameraman chose to avoid implicating the newlyweds, or this is a true document devoid of the stereotypes of flappers flashing their

(Opposite) With the coming of World War I, no one spoke German anymore, and even children denounced the kaiser. Courtesy of the Minnesota Historical Society.

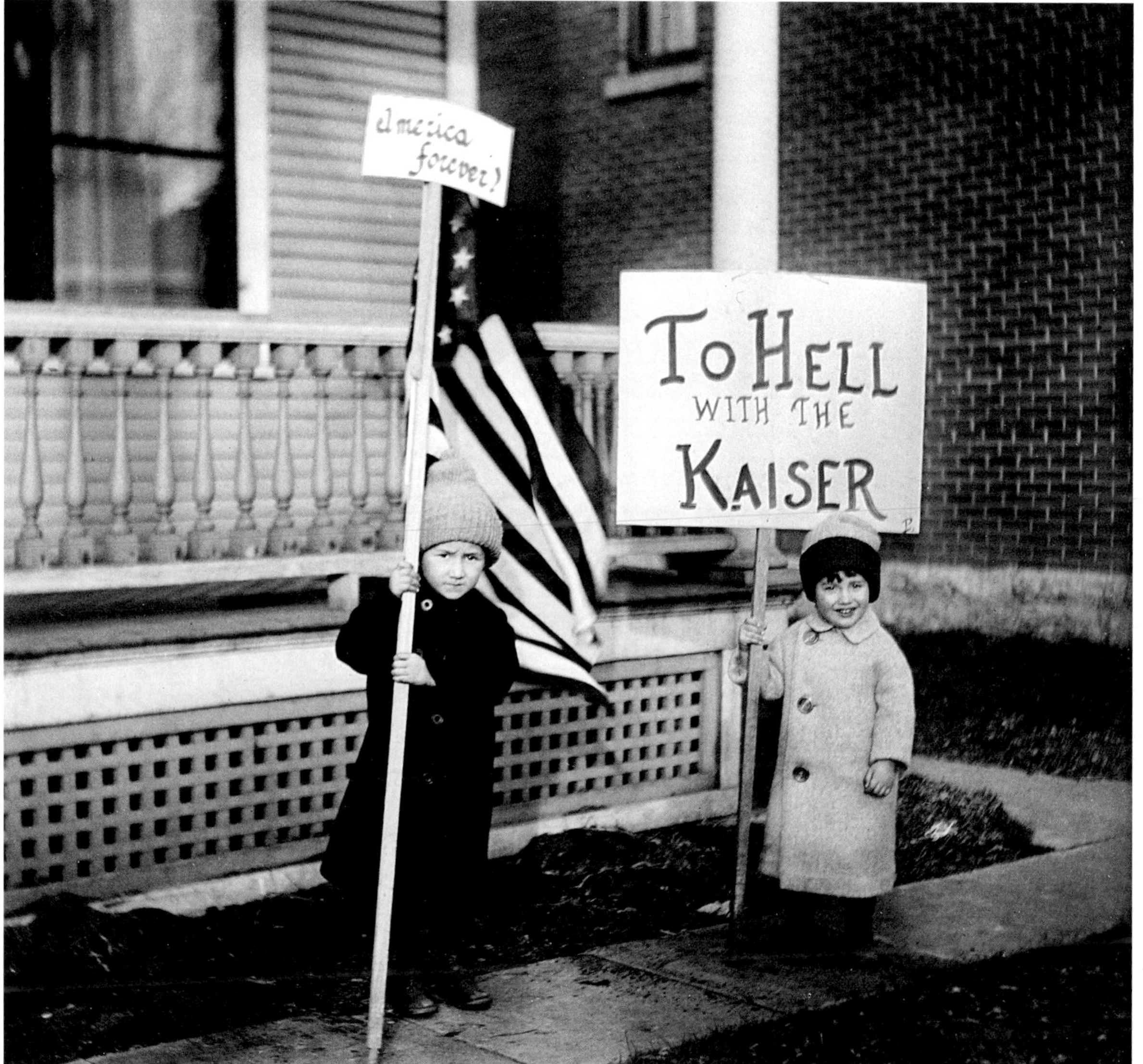
America forever!
To Hell
with the
Kaiser

ankles while performing the Charleston on tables. The film portrays a formal summer soiree. The men, their hair slicked back with pomade, wore wide-lapel black blazers with pressed white slacks. Women with bobbed hair and wearing dainty hats, white dresses, and fresh corsages chitchat demurely. Today (83 years later), the Parten family—the offspring from this elaborate garden wedding—still lives around Lake Minnetonka.

Hun Huskers and Austrian Knights

Lake Minnetonka during the Wars

Just as the Civil War caused divisions, so did World War I. On June 15, 1917, President Woodrow Wilson passed a law requiring all men between twenty-one and thirty-one years of age to report for duty. Soon, a group of 160 "Hun Huskers" from around Lake Minnetonka left for the front. Before World War I, a German or Austrian background had been considered noble and upstanding, especially in Minnesota. Now, suddenly, everyone was anti-German, even the Germans.

Up until that time, one of the most prominent men on Lake Minnetonka was Sir Charles Gibson, whose Hotel St. Louis attracted vacationing southerners to Lake Minnetonka's shores. Gibson had helped the king of Prussia establish his autocratic government. On December 16, 1882, the German emperor had awarded him the Commander's Cross of the Royal Prussian Crown, an honor usually bestowed on heads of state. The Emperor Franz Joseph had awarded him the title of Commander of the Knights of Austria.

Gibson spent his winters in Missouri, whose political delegation to Washington insisted that this double knight be award an ambassadorship to Germany, saying, "[The U.S.] diplomatic service . . . has been ornamental long enough. It has been the health resort long enough of millionaire dudes with the dyspepsia and fourth-rate poets clutching at an ode over a bottle of Burgundy," as quoted in the *New York Times* of April 18, 1885. The *Times* further poked fun at the Missourian knight and wrote that the U.S. government would only appoint "Sir Charles on behalf of hogs, cattle, sheep, grain, and vigorous manhood." Even if New York and Washington were not impressed, the southerners summering on Lake Minnetonka were.

World War I erased the good feelings toward Germans. On November 25, 1918, the Deephaven Village Council unanimously voted to change the Prussian imperial name of Hohenzollern Avenue to Sibley Avenue, for Minnesota's first governor (whose military attacks against the Native Americans in the U.S.–Dakota War of 1862 resulted in the largest mass execution in U.S. history and the exile of the Dakota to South Dakota and Nebraska). To fight the Germans on the home front and support the war effort, lake dwellers saved cooking fats. Residents saved peach stones; seven pounds of the pits were needed to make one gas mask. *Happenings around Deephaven* reported that each day of the week marked another local effort to defeat the Germans: "wheatless Mondays and Wednesdays, meatless Tuesdays, and porkless Thursdays and Saturdays. On gasless Sundays some people hitched horses to the front bumper of the family car, or stayed home and watched their war gardens grow."

World War II reinstated the strict conservation. The Deephaven Salvage Drive saved metal, silk stockings, rags, and newspapers and magazines, all bundled to be reused in some form. Eight-page ration books contained twenty-four prized coupons for necessities. In Deephaven alone, 1,300 residents registered for the highly valued sugar allotment stamps. The total number of automobiles allowed to be sold in all of Minnesota between March and May 1943 was 2,503. Because of the shoe shortage, residents cheered when a shoe stamp was added to the ration book on August 1, 1945: "Airplane stamp No. 4 in War Ration Book Three."

The Defense Program set up air sirens on public buildings around the lake in case of an attack. The government performed an air-raid drill on October 14, 1942, between 9:30 and 10 p.m., with a mandatory blackout. All electricity had to be shut off, all electric signs turned off, and all cars pulled over. Apparently, Lake Minnetonka was considered a possible target. According to *Happenings around Deephaven*, "A dozen or more Cabin Cruisers belonging to our Coast Guard cruised the lake waters [to sweep] them clear of hidden mines." For the time being, the Coast Guard found nothing: "Lake Minnetonka was declared safe for rowboats."

Sir Charles Gibson was known as the "Knight of the Lake" because of two prestigious awards, from the king of Prussia and the Austrian emperor. Hailing from Missouri, he founded the fabulous Hotel St. Louis to attract fellow southerners to Lake Minnetonka. Courtesy of the Minnesota Historical Society.

Just another day at the Chapman House Docks on Cook's Bay: rowboats are ready for fishermen to take anglers out for the catch of the day, sailboats can be rigged if the wind is willing, and small steamboats are available to transport pleasure seekers to Big Island. Courtesy of the Excelsior—Lake Minnetonka Historical Society.

6

Hitting the Water

Shipwrecks!

Beware the Exploding Steamboats

In 1854, William Lithgow earned the dubious distinction of being the first white man known to have drowned in Lake Minnetonka, when a thunderstorm whipped up and shipwrecked his sloop. But the most tragic story of a boat turned turtle happened off Starvation Point (now often called Brackett or Orono Point) on October 19, 1859. The family of Martin B. Stone had arrived in Minnetonka Mills and loaded all their household belongings, including a cast-iron kitchen stove, on a double-masted sailboat, the *White Swan*, to sail across the lake to settle. Loading at the Mills took the entire day, and by early evening the wind had picked up. Two hours later, they set sail when the lake had calmed down and the moon peeked through the clouds. When the sailboat veered around Starvation Point close to midnight, a stiff wind struck the boat, causing the cargo to shift dramatically, and the boat capsized in the dark.

The cargo floated around them or sank to the bottom. The three men tried to hang on to the keel of the boat in the frigid waters but eventually slipped beneath the waves. The mother and two girls lay on a featherbed atop the semisubmerged sail as it slowly took on water. One by one they slid under the waves, never to be seen again. One child floated away. A whitecap engulfed the other daughter. The only survivor was Robert McKenzie, a boy of seventeen, who watched the others wave goodbye as the featherbed slowly sank beneath the surface. The boy held tight for twelve hours as the wind and waves whipped against the keel. Around eleven in the morning, the double masts stuck against the bottom of the lake near Deephaven, and young McKenzie swam to shore. No houses were in sight, so the exhausted lad struggled along a footpath until he found the cabin of settlers named Bartow, who nursed the poor boy back to health.

In an age before lifejackets, nearly every summer saw some tragedy. On July 12, 1885, a terrible thunderstorm whipped up near Maplewood and struck the *Minnie Cook*. "Mr. Hardenbergh saw the disaster through his glasses, rowed there with two of his sons, and picked up the body of Mrs. Rand from among the

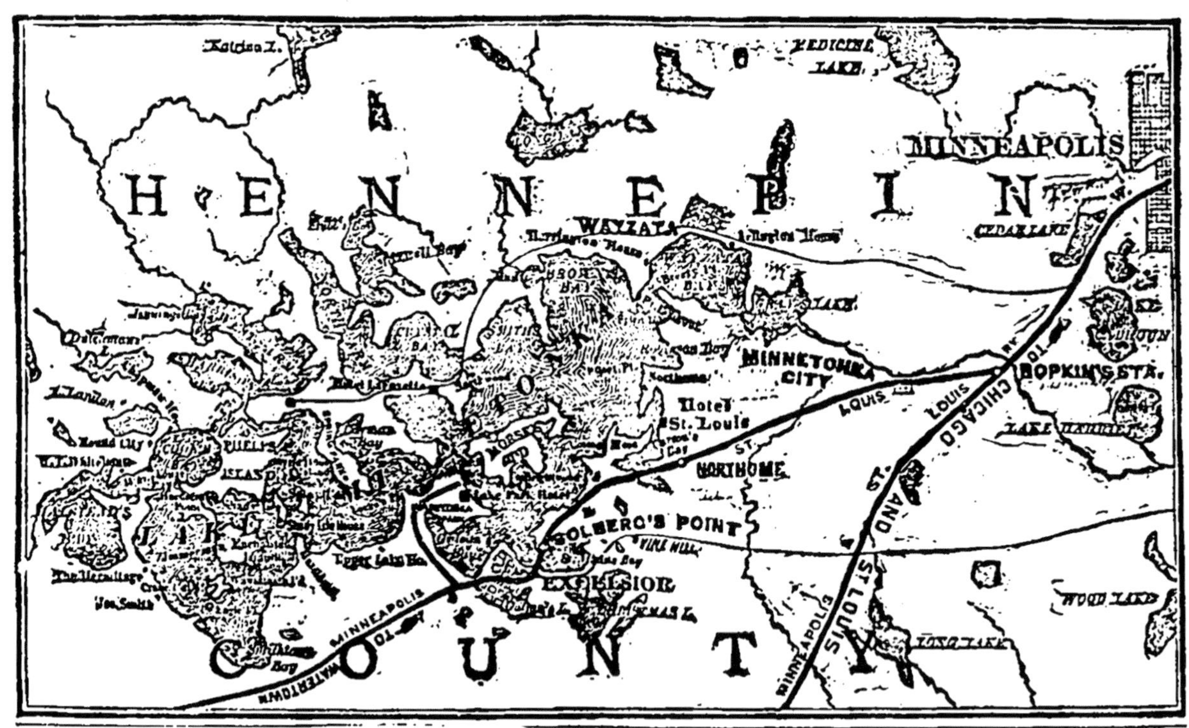

A SAD SEARCH.

The Work of Diving and Dragging for the Victims of Sunday's Disaster.

The Long, Painful Task Finally Completed at 7:15 O'clock Last Evening.

Harvey Rand and His Sister, Mrs. Coykendall, Clasped in Each Other's Arms.

Details of the Search as It Proceeded Through the Gloomy Day.

Affecting Scenes as the Bodies One by One Are Brought to the Surface.

Expressions of Grief and Sympathy Heard on Every Hand from All Classes.

Appropriate Resolutions Passed by the City Council at a Special Meeting.

Telegrams of Condolence Received from Many Quarters—Funeral Arrangements.

A tragic drowning occurred on Lake Minnetonka in July 1885, as described in this Minneapolis Tribune *clipping. Alonzo Rand and four members of his family all perished before searchers recovered their bodies.*

floating hats and cloaks. The body of the pilot, George McDonald, was fished up by the hand of his own father," according to *Once upon a Lake*. Ten people drowned, including five just from the family of A. C. Rand. The boat, on the other hand, was dragged to shore and refurbished. The *Minnie Cook* was back on the water within two weeks and almost sank again off Cottagewood.

Not only did boaters and sailors risk simply capsizing and being swallowed by the lake, but the whole boat could explode. The high-pressure steam engines, in particular the popular Ames Firebox Return-Flue Boilers, were the culprit. In the fall of 1876, Charles May set sail with his second steamboat, the *Katie May*, a luxurious boat with an enclosed cabin to protect the passengers from the elements. The cover could not protect them from the danger inside, however. The next summer, the captain of the *Katie May* demanded "full-speed ahead" leaving one of the docks in Robinson's Bay. Nothing happened, so the engineer pushed the motor even further. The boiler blew up with a violent bang, and the captain's and engineer's bodies were torn apart. The pilot nursed his broken leg, and three dead passengers were fished out of the bay. Despite the obvious defect in the *Katie May*'s boiler, no reforms were made to prevent further catastrophes. In fact, within a year the *Katie May*'s stern and bow had been restored and put together with an extra ten feet of midsection. The engine was back on board as well, but now the boat had a new name: *Saucy Kate*.

Two years later, the steamboat *May Queen* left the dock at Minnehaha Creek, only to explode a mere ten miles out, at Shady Island. Captain A. H. Rockwell took a bad blow to the stomach, but survived a few years before dying from the injury. W. F. Haynes, the engineer, was wrapped in oiled cotton to help his burns but later died. Even though ten passengers were badly hurt, the valuable and volatile engine was fished out of the lake, reassembled, and used on a steamboat on Lake Okoboji in Iowa. As Thelma Jones wrote about this dangerous age, "The frequent drownings only threw the gaiety into relief."

On July 1, as the management of the Hotel St. Louis was preparing for a festive Fourth of July celebration in 1880, Major George Halstead's steamboat *Mary* pulled up to the hotel's docks and promptly exploded. The shock wave knocked over even those on the beach. The blast caused a gruesome scene across the beach and well-trimmed yards; the hotel manager called on the African American staff to clean up the carnage in time for the Independence Day party. The journalist A. S. Dimond was injured in this dramatic blast, and the *St. Paul Globe* soon ran a series about "the Minnetonka murder," caused by a "cracked and rotten boiler and criminal incompetency." The *Globe* reported that "the explosion was the result of criminal inattention or carelessness." After that point, the Ames Firebox

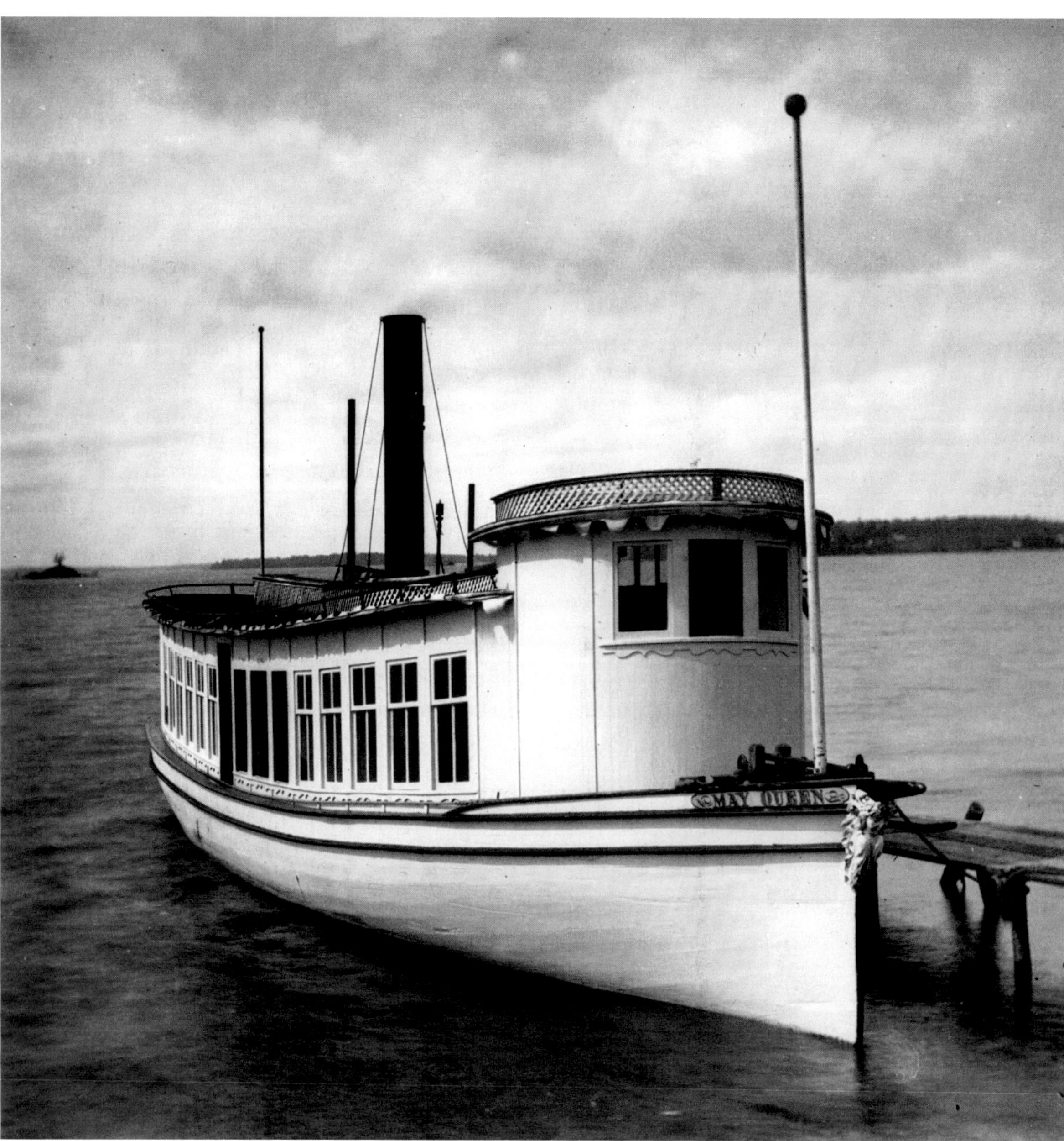
MAY QUEEN

Return-Flue Boilers were outlawed on the lake. Even so, the *Mary* was rebuilt before the end of the summer and was given new names to hide its past: the *Hiawatha*, the *Scandinavian*, and the *Star.*

Steamboat Races

The City of St. Louis *versus the* Belle of Minnetonka

W. D. Washburn's *City of St. Louis* made headlines as the largest boat on Lake Minnetonka and as the first inland steamboat to have electric lights. It could carry fifteen hundred passengers in luxury across the waters of this midwestern wonderworld. Washburn's rival James J. Hill would not be outdone, and he purchased a riverboat, the giant *Phil Sheridan*, which carried passengers up the Ohio and Mississippi Rivers to the Midwest, mostly from St. Louis to St. Paul. Hill was ashamed that he had missed a chance at having President Grant ride his boat on a visit to Lake Minnetonka, and he did not want to make that mistake again.

Steamboats had been a fixture on Minnetonka ever since 1860, when Reverend Charles Galpin rigged up the first one on the lake, the *Governor Ramsey*. A steam engine propelled the giant side-wheel to push the fifty-foot-long flat-bottomed boat. The *Ramsey*'s primary responsibility was delivering mail from Minnetonka Mills to Excelsior. Galpin expanded the capacity of the boat in 1867 with updated machinery and a romantic new name: *Lady of the Lake.*

The boilers on these boats were notoriously unreliable. As already noted, the *Ramsey*'s motor conked out during the 1862 Dakota War while ferrying settlers to safety. Deficiencies in design led to exploding boilers and many deaths, and in 1871 the *St. Paul Pioneer Press* called the two steamboats on Lake Minnetonka "murderous." Government agents had inspected both boats and condemned them with "an injunction upon the two ocean steamers." In spite of a series of articles on the subject by the paper, the boats ran anyway and passengers piled on board.

Cottagers and tourists needed these boats to get around before the age of the automobile. As quoted in *Tales from Tonka*, Mrs. Lindley fondly recalled being picked up right outside her summer home: "A flag was stuck on the end of the dock to signal the boat to stop. Sometimes the great *City of St. Louis*, or the even clumsier *Belle of Minnetonka*, would lumber in and make a difficult landing, requiring a quick jump aboard at a particular second, not always easy for the fat and elderly."

Some thought it folly to put a boat as enormous as the thousand-plus-passenger *City of St. Louis* on the lake. However, few could resist admiring the boat, which "looked like a wedding cake, all tiers dripping with white scroll work." On the two sides of the paddle boxes, artists carefully painted large murals of the

The May Queen, *seen here in 1876 in a photograph by William H. Illingworth, was lost to the lake when its boiler exploded soon after the boat left the dock at Minnehaha Creek. Courtesy of Hennepin County Library Special Collections.*

Lake Minnetonka attracted hundreds of tourists from St. Louis. In recognition, a grand hotel and this elegant steamboat took the name of the city. W. D. Washburn owned the City of St. Louis, *the first inland steamboat with electric lights. It could transport fifteen hundred passengers in complete luxury. Courtesy of the Minnesota Historical Society.*

Not wanting to be outdone by his rival W. D. Washburn, James J. Hill purchased a giant riverboat with thirty-foot paddle wheels and named it the Belle of Minnetonka. *The mammoth boat was double the size of the* City of St. Louis *and could hold more than three thousand passengers. Courtesy of the Excelsior–Lake Minnetonka Historical Society.*

St. Louis Bridge and Fort Snelling. The boat was built in Indiana, but the oak frame and pine body were assembled in Wayzata. A sixty-piece orchestra regularly performed in the dance hall, which was lined with windows and expensive mahogany veneer. "The real surprise came, however, when Captain Johnson snapped on the electric lights," according to *Minnetonka Story*. "Passengers gazed speechless at the blazing chandeliers." Electric lamps on an inland ship were a novelty.

Hill wanted to show up the *City of St. Louis* with an even grander boat. His deadline was the Fourth of July 1882 for the festivities at his just-opened Hotel Lafayette on Lake Minnetonka. The *Phil Sheridan* had won many speed records on the Mississippi; it was dismantled in La Crosse, Wisconsin, and shipped in sections to Wayzata, where workers sweated around the clock to make it lake-worthy. Mechanics prepped and oiled the pair of two-hundred-horsepower engines (a pittance by today's standards) that pushed the thirty-foot paddle wheels. The fire-engine-red smokestacks stood stark against the whitewashed boat, and electric lights would make the boat a beacon on the waters. Hill renamed his grand steamboat the *Belle of Minnetonka*.

On its maiden trip on the lake on July 3, 1882, painters and carpenters were still painting and pounding as the hull cut through the waves. From bow to stern, the *Belle* stretched 285 feet—nearly double the size of the *City of St. Louis* and obviously too large for the lake. Twenty-five hundred passengers could climb comfortably on board, but *The WPA Guide to Minnesota* claimed that 3,500 people fit on board. And in one instance, 3,360 passengers did squeeze on deck to watch a hyped-up rowing match between the Hanlon–Teemer crews.

Hill had made his Independence Day deadline, and his big boat became famous as the largest "and best steamboat on inland waters in the country." Most important, it was almost double the size of the rival *City of St. Louis*. The *Belle of Minnetonka* boasted both a dining room and a high-class restaurant and had forty cabins where guests could be lulled to sleep by the gentle waves. Two dance floors and a big band rocked the boat. "Twelve sets of square dancers could easily whirl on the deck at one time, and on the upper deck twenty sets could dance. The decks were propped up by two-by-fours spaced four feet apart, and the boat inspector looked the other way," according to *Once upon a Lake*.

A group of wealthy ladies were so smitten by this fabulous steamboat that they donated $650 worth of their silver utensils and plates to be sold to finance a bell for the *Belle*. The 1,100-pound bell was cast and raised atop the boat to announce its arrival around the lake.

The *Belle of Minnetonka* only sailed for a decade, and in 1892 it was left at the docks all summer. The once grand boat was dismantled, and a junk dealer bought the bell. In 1899, the people of Excelsior pooled their money to buy back the bell, for two hundred dollars, to be raised into the belfry of the town's new school. The bell rang across town for years, but in 1962 the tower was deemed unsafe. As the last remnant of the *Belle of Minnetonka*, the bell stands on a granite pedestal in front of the Excelsior Public Library.

Sailing Away

Lake Minnetonka Regattas and Yacht Clubs

Braving the waves and wind of Lake Minnetonka, captains and commodores rigged their boats to capture the gusts, soak in the sun, and catch the mist from the spray of the whitecaps. Sailing on the big lake carries a storied tradition dating back to the first regatta in 1882 and surviving strongly today, despite the big cigarette boats blasting by in no-wake zones.

Hoisting the mainsail and ducking under the swinging boom as the boat comes about carries a certain dangerous fascination as sailors push their boats to the limits and risk tipping or, worse, turning turtle. Currier and Ives lithographs of picturesque sailing scenes evoke the romance of being scooted across the water by the power of a blustery gale.

Lake Minnetonka has been regarded as a sailor's mecca, not because it has steady, easy winds but because it is difficult. In *Minnetonka Story*, Blanche Wilson writes of overhearing a soldier in Louisiana, fresh back from World War II, who sees a map of his grandfather's favorite lake and exclaims, "For gosh sakes! Lake Minnetonka, sure's thunder! Of all the times Granddad's told me about sailing her, I'd never seen a map of her. Look at all those darn bays. Bet the wind plays hide-and-seek 'round there in great shape—plenty of squalls, too."

That challenge is why sailors venture out on the water: to test their skill under adverse conditions. Today jet skis, pontoon boats, and oversized speedboats churn up waves and create odd whitecap patterns that leave sailors perplexed about incoming gusts that could otherwise be read on the water's surface. But even with these new obstacles, real sport lies in sailing. The first regatta on the lake dates back to 1882, the same year the Minnetonka Yacht Club was formed. When the lake was dredged, all the materials from the deep were dumped to form Lighthouse Island, a tiny man-made bit of land in St. Louis Bay near Deephaven Beach, the future home of one of the oldest yacht clubs in the country. In 1889, the sailors started building a gorgeous clubhouse, whose prairie-school-meets-pagoda porches overlooking the lake gave it a Far East feel. The unusual structure burned to the ground in 1943 and has since been replaced. The club had a hundred boats and about 275 members when it opened its doors in 1890.

That first regatta in 1882 saw fifteen boats hoisting their sails and setting out without good maps or much idea of how shallow the water could be. "Those first yachtsmen sailed with the most utter abandon and with completely reckless pleasure. The 'good sailors'

Lake Minnetonka's first sailing regatta took to the waves in 1882. The lake's many peninsulas and bays made for tricky maneuvering. Here a regatta of sailboats in 1940 sets off despite the threatening clouds. Courtesy of Westonka Historical Society, Mound.

were those who could carry the most sail without capsizing," according to Arthur Pegler, the father of conservative columnist Westbrook Pegler, quoted in *Minnetonka Story*. The sailing tradition began on Lake Minnetonka when three notable sailors came to the area: Hazen J. Burton, who had sailed on Cape Cod; H. C. McLeod, a boatmaker from Halifax, Canada; and William Peet, whose father had founded the Atlantic Yacht Club. The Minnetonka Yacht Club's first commodore, George Brackett, was one of the first cottagers on the lake and helped bring the age of sailing to this remote lake.

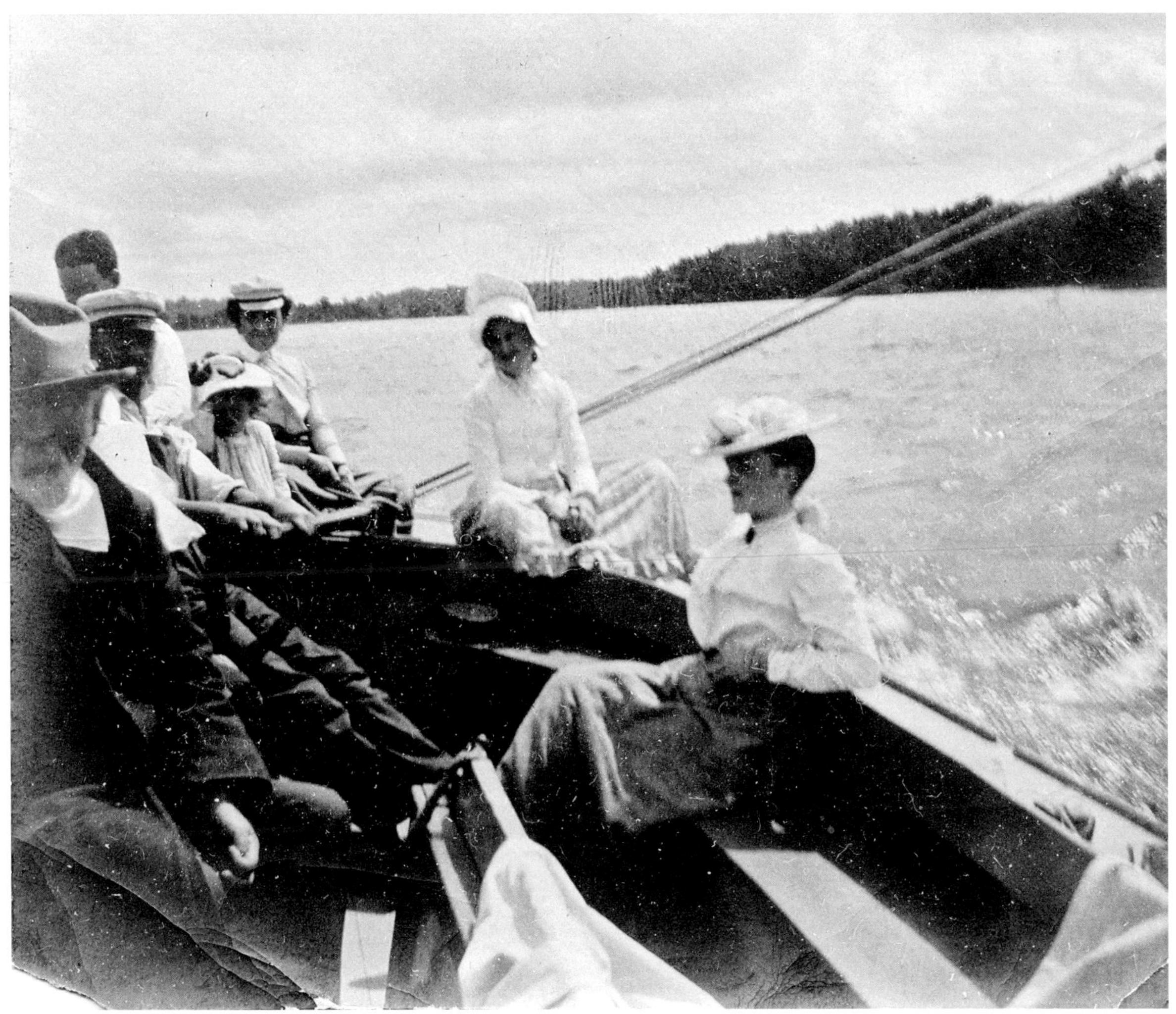

Relaxing on deck, the Tryson family harnesses the wind around 1890. Lake Minnetonka has long been considered a sailor's mecca. It was home to some of the earliest yacht clubs in the country and has a history of innovative sailboat design. Courtesy of the Excelsior–Lake Minnetonka Historical Society.

The innovative Onawa, *built along the shores of Lake Minnetonka, revolutionized the design of sailboats by ditching ballast, which inevitably slowed the boat. The* Onawa *rode higher in the water rather than pushing through the waves. Courtesy of the Excelsior–Lake Minnetonka Historical Society.*

The Excelsior Yacht Club was founded in 1883. In 1889, it united with the Minnetonka Yacht Club, so larger regattas could take place more regularly. During the earliest races, bags of ballast filled with sand or rocks kept the sailboats steady—a technique now considered quaint. New designs by a blind East Coast boat builder, John Herreshoff, arrived on Lake Minnetonka in the 1890s, but soon Minnetonka builders Ward Dyer and his son Arthur revolutionized sailing with their two-sailed *Onawa* and made the "sandbaggers" obsolete. The *Onawa* did not use ballast, so it could be more easily handled than other, clunky, boats. This two-sailed sloop "slipped *over* rather than *through* the water," according to reviews of the time, and was heralded as the eighth wonder of the modern world in 1893. Lake Minnetonka was suddenly in the news for its innovative, world-champion sailboats.

Across the Twin Cities, the White Bear Lake Yacht Club wanted to show the Minnetonka Yacht Club that they were not the only inland-lake sailors. A challenge of an annual regatta between the two clubs was announced in 1895, and a cocky skipper from the Minnetonka Yacht Club joked, "Well, if those White Bear folks really want to make us a present of a couple of silver cups, why all right, we will help them carry out their laudable desire. In fact, we'll take all the trophies they offer us." He even pitied the White Bear sailors since they would be humiliated in their own territory.

The upcoming regatta was splashed across newspapers, and the trolleys were full of visitors to White Bear Lake, where they gathered on lawn chairs and hammocks on green lawns next to the blue lake. The white sails were unfurled, and boats tacked back and forth for position on the way to the buoys that marked the starting line. A pistol shot rang out announcing that the regatta had begun as the crowd cheered in delight. A visiting Nebraskan could not believe all the hype. "Race? You sure ain't callin' *that* a race! Why, a race is where somebody does somethin'. Land sakes, all of them sailors air a-doin' is jes' a-settin' still and a-lettin' the wind blow 'em along," according to *Minnetonka Story*. In spite of the world champion *Onawa*, the Minnetonka Yacht Club was soundly defeated three years running.

For more than 125 years, sailing regattas have run numerous times during the warm summer months—usually Wednesday evenings and over the weekends. Both the Wayzata Yacht Club (formed in 1965) and the Minnetonka Yacht Club offer the opportunity for new sailors to crew in a regatta and to find out if they like the thrill of the big boats or prefer the safety of a pontoon. Or as Captain George Hopkins, one of the earliest sailors on the lake, said decades ago, "We've been havin' 'em [regattas] since 1882. Sailboats came in long before the big boats and big hotels went. . . . But sailboats are goin' to stay."

Ice Yachting

The Fastest Way to Travel in the 1890s

Hard-core sailors on Lake Minnetonka could not wait until the warm summer breezes filled their sails. Instead they took a cue from the bundled-up New York yachtsmen who built their ice boats beginning in the late 1790s to skate over the frozen ice on the Hudson River. These ice yachts were the fastest vehicles of their era and famously zipped past steaming locomotives chugging along the shores of the river. Because of Bernoulli's principle of aerodynamic pressure, the ice boats often traveled at three times the speed of the wind, sometimes more than eighty miles per hour, and the ice provided almost no resistance.

In the 1890s, some of the first ice yachts cruised the wide expanse of Lake Pepin on the Mississippi River, and the Pepin Ice Yacht Club of Wisconsin challenged the Lake City Ice Yacht Club (where Ralph Samuelson would invent water skiing in 1922). The Minnetonka Ice Yacht Club was incorporated on September 23, 1899, and within two years had 167 members. Beginning with its seventeen ice boats, which ranged from twenty-eight feet to forty-nine feet long, the club soon joined the race for the J. B. Hudson cup, which marked the championship of the ice-racing world in the Northwest. The Minnetonka club purchased ice yachts from the Hudson River club in New York and added them to its fleet, for a total of thirty-five ice boats. Some of these boats could handle up to eight people, who would have to shift their weight constantly to balance the schooner.

Ice conditions varied widely, and only a trace of snow is permissible, which often meant the races were run early in the year when the ice was thin. A typical course for an ice race was at least twice around a five-mile triangle. Pine trees were posted at the turning points because they were easily visible against the white backdrop. The final finish line or goal had a large flag.

In the 1890s a historic race took place on Lake Minnetonka, with the Lake Pepin team challenging Minnetonka. The race began with a crew pushing the boat to get up to speed and then the crew, usually two persons, hopped aboard. Boats such as the heavy *Cyclone* from Lake Pepin had already reached eighty miles per hour in races, and others, such as the *Phoebe*, a "jack-rabbit" boat, were made very light with silk sails. A couple of newsies from Minneapolis had built a homemade boat, the *What-Not*. Another was the *Nancy* run by a young man, George Bassett, and his seventeen-year-old sister Nan, for whom the boat was named.

During the tie-breaking race, George and Nan pushed the boat from the starting line, but he slipped on the ice and the boat zipped away without him, leaving only his little sister Nan to steer. Even though she had never handled the boat alone, she controlled the sails and took advantage of her light weight to fly

Holding their ice yachts in place, sailors wait for the timekeeper to give the signal. This photograph is from 1904, when the fastest means of transportation in the world was an iceboat. One went 110 miles per hour from Wayzata to Excelsior. Courtesy of Hennepin County Library Special Collections.

The Lake City Ice Yacht Club often cruised across the expanse of Lake Pepin. The Minnetonka Ice Yacht Club incorporated in 1899 and soon had 167 members and thirty-five boats to challenge its rival. Courtesy of the Minnesota Historical Society.

This rare photograph shows both the Minnetonka Yacht Club (on the right) *and the Minnetonka Ice Yacht Club* (on the left). *Both structures burned down, the latter in 1904 and the former in 1943. Courtesy of the Excelsior–Lake Minnetonka Historical Society.*

through the course. With gusts nearly tipping the boat, she held on to win the race for Minnetonka. Even the Lake Pepin team congratulated her as the first woman to win an ice yacht race.

Theodore Wetmore, the "father of ice-yachting in the West," took the title of commodore and by 1899 had helped incorporate the new club, as part of the Minnetonka Yacht Club, on little Tahtu (Bug) Island, also in St. Louis Bay. This salty old sailor had the fastest ice yacht on the lake, the *North Star.* One day, he zipped back and forth outside Excelsior challenging the only other ice boat that could come close: the *Red Dragon.* The cowardly *Red Dragon* stayed home, so Wetmore and his cronies stopped on the ice in front of Excelsior to claim their win by forfeit. The commodore forgot to anchor his ice yacht, and as they stood on the ice, a gust of wind filled the sails. The *North Star* skated away and crashed into a nearby pavilion, reducing the boat to kindling.

In spite of occasional calamities, the Minnetonka Ice Yacht Club can claim the fastest speeds ever reached on the lake. According to *Happenings around Deephaven,* "Ward Burton once covered the 6¼ miles between Excelsior and Wayzata in a record 3 minutes 37 seconds, averaging better than 100 miles an hour!"

Although the original building for the Minnetonka Ice Yacht Club burned to the ground on January 14, 1904, and was never rebuilt, ice boating continues on Lake Minnetonka during the winter months. The club merged with the Minnetonka Yacht Club. When asked if this sport is safe, the Minnesota Ice Sailing Association wrote, "Nope, not a chance. Iceboating is an inherently dangerous sport; anybody suggesting it's safe is lying. In fact if you do it long enough, it's sure to either kill, cripple or maim you."

The Tattooed Countess Survives the Titanic

A French-Minnesota Renaissance on Lake Minnetonka

When Walter Douglas retired at fifty years old, he and his wife Mahala built their twenty-seven-room estate on Lake Minnetonka where the elegant Hotel St. Louis had once stood. Douglas had made his fortune in Minneapolis in linseed oil in a company that became the giant Archer Daniels Midland; it did not hurt that he inherited millions from his father, who helped found Quaker Oats.

Mahala's poetic aspirations are reflected in the house, as she and her husband Walter Donald Douglas eponymously named the new chateau "Waldon" (Wal–Don), perhaps as an homage to (or a spoof of) Henry David Thoreau's masterpiece about a pokey little pond back east. Over the years the name of the house and environs has reverted to "Walden." The newly built French Renaissance mansion in Deephaven needed proper bureaus and buffets to entertain the elite, so Walter and Mahala set off on a lengthy European tour to shop for furnishings and hobnob with the Lost Generation in Paris. Mahala was an aspiring writer and admired the expatriates and bustling French culture, which she hoped to transplant in part to her native Midwest in the form of a "Minnesota Renaissance," beginning with her house.

After her husband went down with the Titanic, *Mahala Douglas returned to her estate at Waldon (later Walden) and hosted elegant parties with prominent guests, including Gertrude Stein and other literary figures. Photograph courtesy of Brucemore / National Trust for Historic Preservation.*

Once the couple had acquired appropriate furniture, they loaded everything on the world's largest luxury passenger steamer, the RMS *Titanic*, at Cherbourg, France, and prepared for their triumphant return to Lake Minnetonka. But on its maiden voyage the *Titanic* famously struck a giant iceberg in the North Atlantic on April 14, 1912, and was completely submerged within two and a half hours. Douglas made sure his wife and her Swiss French maid Berthe Leroy were comfy on a lifeboat; he froze to death in the frigid saltwater. After hearing of the way Douglas had helped women and children onto the lifeboats before he perished, Judge Weatherby from Mississippi, who knew Douglas from the judge's frequent trips to the lake, said, "A man who had lived in such a spot on your lake would do a thing like that. He'd already found out what heaven was like," according to an interview in *Minnetonka Story*.

The RMS *Carpathia* picked up Mahala and brought her and her maid to New York, and she went home to Deephaven without her husband. She never married again, turning down many proposals. She became the muse for Carl Van Vechten's book *The Tattooed Countess* because of her high-class literary lifestyle and was soon nicknamed "the countess." Inspired by Parisian life, she hosted salons at her lakeside mansion and entertained Gertrude Stein and her lover, Alice B. Toklas, when they made a second grand tour to America in 1934. Walden even inspired President Calvin Coolidge. He sent an agent on May 13, 1927, to investigate whether it would be a suitable summer home for the president. He liked it but decided on the Black Hills instead.

Mahala's elegant mansion, decorated inside with rare blue orchids, sheltered this famous survivor of the

Titanic who wrote a haunting poem about the sinking of that floating behemoth. Here is a section from Mahala Douglas's poem "Titanic":

> . . . Silently the prow sinks deeper,
> As if some Titan's hand,
> Inexorable as Fate,
> Were drawing the great ship down to her death.
>
> Slowly, slowly, with hardly a ripple
> Of that velvet sea,
> She sinks out of sight . . .

Raise the Minnehaha!

Burning Boats and Sunken Streetcars

Far below the waves of Lake Minnetonka lay six steamboats from the early part of last century—like Spanish galleons in freshwater. For more than fifty years they lay preserved at the bottom, visited only by the occasional northern pike. Then one day in 1979, a local diver discovered one of these yellow steamships amid the mud and seaweed of the deep. Now loungers around the lake in the summer cannot help but notice the flashy yellow antique steamship with a triangular red flag proclaiming *Minnehaha* and a smokestack puffing away into the blue sky.

But who originally built this boat? Lori Cherland-McCune discovered the answer when her recently deceased mother passed on the family scrapbooks and photo albums with many old snapshots of the Moore Boat Works in Wayzata, which her great-grandfather had founded. Fascinated by this history, she has researched her family's past and its links to the early days of the lake. Cherland-McCune has now published *Royal C. Moore: The Man Who Built the Streetcar Boats*, with numerous photos of Lake Minnetonka's bygone days.

R. C. Moore hailed from Lake Champlain in upstate New York and moved to Minnesota at nineteen years of age. Already having built rowboats since he was fourteen, Moore fell in with Dingle Boat Works in St. Paul and soon plied his craft along White Bear Lake. Lake Minnetonka soon lured Moore to its waters, where he and Gustavus Johnson opened their own boatyard on Wayzata's north shore in 1879.

With three large buildings to construct boats, Moore's business was booming until the all-wood structures caught fire in 1902. All three buildings were destroyed. The Wayzata fire department could not save the boat works, but Moore's employees somehow managed to salvage all the finished wooden vessels inside, including twenty rowboats and ten sailboats.

Moore planned on rebuilding his workshops immediately in Wayzata, but Excelsior tried to tempt him to the south side of the lake. Moore's business could mean jobs for nearly a hundred men during the peak summer season. The village of Excelsior plotted a

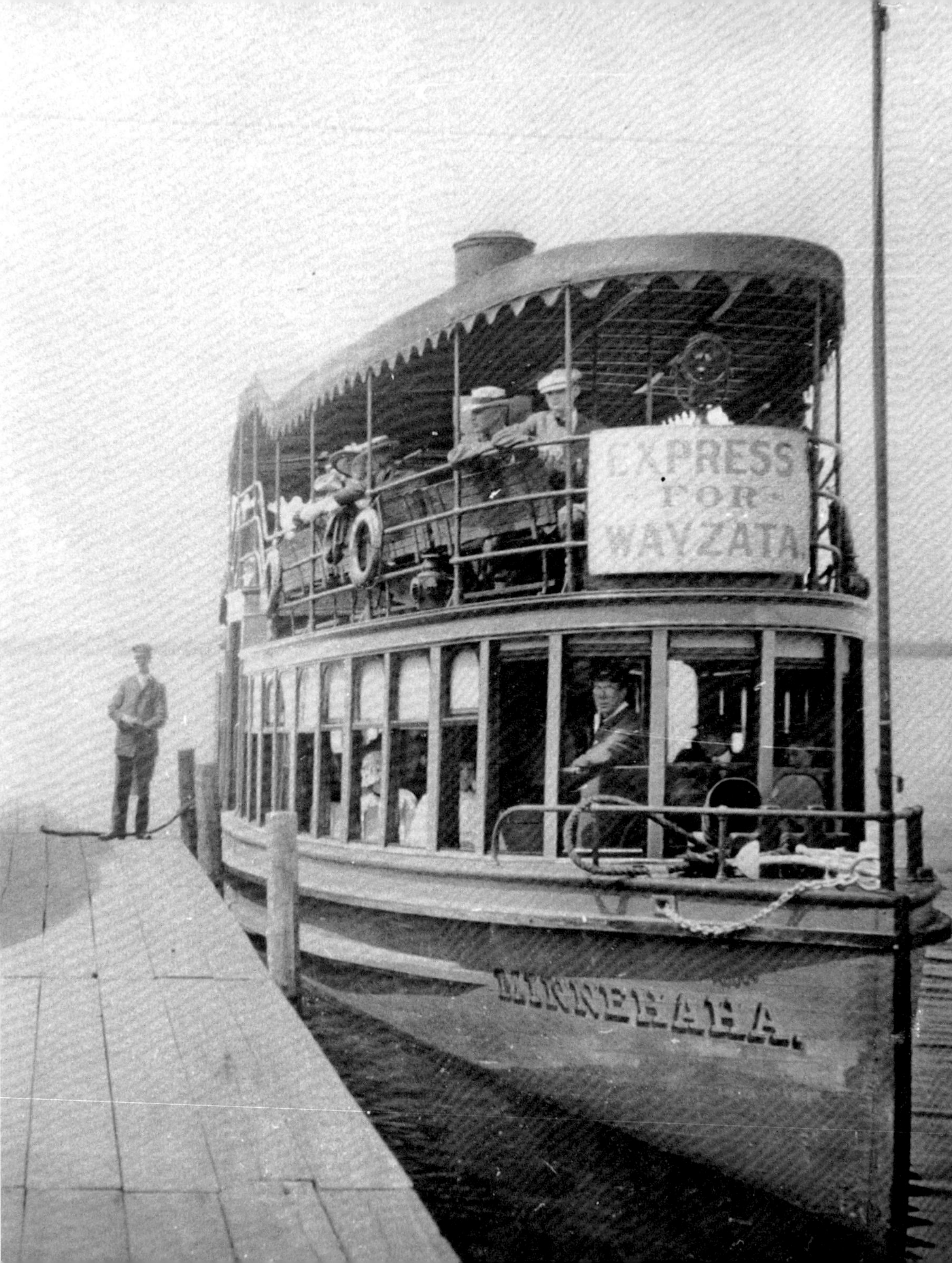
EXPRESS
FOR
WAYZATA
MINNEHAHA.

stretch of land along the western edge of Gideon's Bay for the new boat works. In the end, Moore opted to stay in Wayzata, where he built essentially the same plan he had for Excelsior. In spite of losing nearly all his building materials, blueprints, and tools, Moore was producing new boats within weeks of the blaze.

One era was ending on Lake Minnetonka, that of the railroad boom bringing wealthy, often southern, guests to grand tourist hotels with large verandas overlooking the lake. Trolley cars were the new rage, linking Lake Minnetonka to the Twin Cities with lines extending all the way to Stillwater on the St. Croix River. Thomas Lowry, the "streetcar man," brought the masses to Minnetonka aboard TCRT trolleys, but once there these new visitors needed a speedy way to cross the lake.

Lowry looked to some of the established boat manufacturers for a slick new design rather than using the cumbersome steamboats weighed down with hundreds of visitors. His TCRT had already bought up several of the paddle-wheel boats already on the lake to transport passengers to Big Island—the *Minneapolis*, the *St. Paul*, and the *Minnetonka*. TCRT painted these double-side-wheeler steamboats the same canary yellow as the trolleys so that passengers could not miss

Thomas Lowry's Twin Cities Rapid Transit Company launched the Minnehaha *in 1906 but scuttled it twenty years later when business waned. After fifty-four years at the bottom of the lake, the boat was raised and restored to steam another day. Courtesy of the Excelsior–Lake Minnetonka Historical Society.*

the transfer that came with their twenty-five cent streetcar ticket, which also covered the ferry trip.

Even though Lake Minnetonka had been full of steamboat ferries hauling tourists and residents to cabins and the big hotels, more visitors demanded passage to the swinging scene at Big Island Park. Lowry dreamed of efficient transportation that would run on a regular schedule rather than just servicing the tourist industry. In 1905, he sent his vice president to scout out other such boats back east. The executive gathered ideas from the speedy ferryboats on the Hudson River in New York to base the design for eight to ten new "Express Boats" for Lake Minnetonka.

Moore was tapped to design and build these new "streetcar boats." According to *Twin Cities by Trolley*, the idea was to make what was essentially a floating streetcar. "TCRT designers took streetcar bodies and modified them to conform to the contour of a ship's hull." Workers sawed the ribs in Wayzata and shipped them to the much larger streetcar shop of the Twin Cities Rapid Transit at Thirty-First Street and Nicollet Avenue in Minneapolis for assembly. These seventy-foot-long boats could hold 135 commuters. The lower decks were sheltered, and their upper decks, with thirteen benches, offered a wide but windy view; TCRT eventually mounted a canopy on top to protect the passengers. The steam engine would propel them around the lake thanks to the combustion power of more than six tons of coal a week.

As the streetcar boats neared completion in 1906, Moore realized he must have docking stations for these "yellow jackets," as the streetcar boats were affectionately known. TCRT built a second dock at Wayzata that extended sixty feet out into the lake to safely board passengers. TCRT launched just six streetcar boats in 1906. Their names evoke the area: *Como, White Bear, Hopkins, Harriet, Stillwater,* and, of course, *Minnehaha. Excelsior* was added to the fleet in 1914. For just ten cents, visitors could hop on board one of these boats to travel over the waves, and for twenty-five cents the fare would include streetcar travel to anywhere along the lines.

In her book, Cherland-McCune claims, "A seventh nearly identical TCRT streetcar boat was built with the express boats' designer and builder [Moore] conspicuously absent." None of the original plans for Moore's famous streetcar boats survives—they would have come in handy when the Minnesota Transportation Museum restored one—perhaps because of a spat between Moore Boat Works and TCRT that went clear up to the Minnesota Supreme Court.

"Keep your hands outside of the engine!" warns the captain on the restored *Minnehaha*. "Safety regulations are different today than in 1906." In fact, traveling on the beautiful *Minnehaha* feels like traveling in a time machine back to old-time Lake Minnetonka when John Philip Sousa might have played at the Big Island Dance Pavilion. Imagine: for just fifty cents, a day-tripper could have a round-trip ticket on the streetcars from Minneapolis, a connection with the steamboats in Excelsior, admission to the rides, and then a tour of the lake with stops at Orono, Wayzata, Spring Lake, or a lake cabin (as long as there was a dock). The neighbors complained furiously about the big-band noise wafting across the lake from the dance hall. To make matters more lively, the Excelsior Amusement Park was opened in 1925 with the Whip, the Chair-o-Plane ride, the Caterpillar, a Ferris wheel, and Electric Flying Skooters.

Thanks to Lowry, the tracks had been laid in 1905 stretching from White Bear Lake to Excelsior. Lowry bought out the enormous 1,100-room Tonka Bay Hotel and the White House Hotel on Lake Minnetonka as travelers from all over the world came to enjoy the splendors of the lake—and, he hoped, to buy some real estate.

Lowry had overextended his reach. The amusement park was too ambitious, and Big Island's glory days began to wane. In 1912, as a final hurrah, the *Minneapolis* steamboat was doused with tar, pitch, and oil and set aflame in the middle of the lake as hundreds of spectators gathered nearby on boats or along the shoreline. Many of the other steamboats were scuttled, sunk in the deep waters where swimmers now take a dip from anchored boats.

By 1932 the line to Lake Minnetonka was closed. The dance pavilion was burned to the ground by an arsonist in 1973. The carousel and the Scrambler were moved to Valleyfair, and condos were built in their place, blocking the lake view. The streetcar boats were scuttled one by one and sent to rest at the bottom of the lake. The *Minnehaha*, which had been built in 1906, was sunk in 1926 and spent fifty-four years under water.

The recent history of the *Minnehaha* begins with the nearly heroic tale of diver Jerry Provost's discovering the sunken vessel in sixty feet of water in 1979. In 1980 a salvage crew led by Bill Niccum raised the *Minnehaha* to the surface after groups of divers attached eight airbags that could lift two thousand pounds each. A decade later, the Minnesota Transportation Museum began a complete restoration of the ship so it could steam another day. Five hundred thousand dollars and eighty thousand (mostly volunteer) hours over six years restored the *Minnehaha* to its past glory, including a nearly identical steam engine dating from 1946.

The one boat that had initially escaped the ax, the *Hopkins*, was finally doomed to join its sisters in 1948. The day before the streetcar boat was scheduled to be sent to its final resting place, someone boarded the *Hopkins* and stole the steering wheel. That wheel was the final touch to the restoration of the *Minnehaha* to help the steamboat navigate the waters of Lake Minnetonka and give boaters today an idea of Excelsior's heyday.

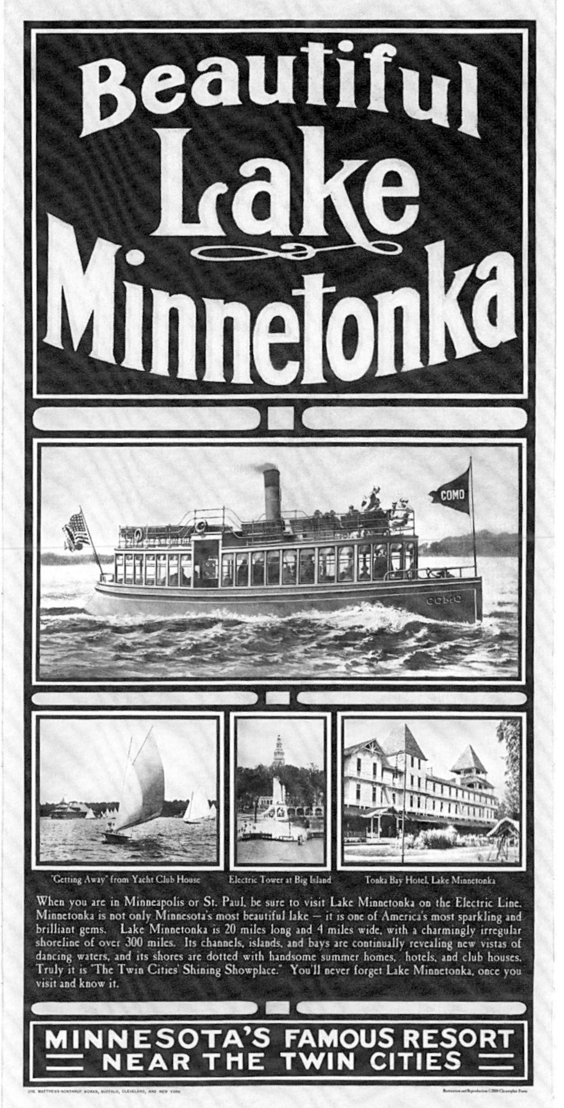

Twin Cities Rapid Transit specialized in more than trolleys: the company expanded into streetcar boats, the Tonka Bay Hotel, and real estate sales. Potential clients were brought to their destinations on an expansive transportation network. Collection of Chris Foote (www.minnesotaposters.com).

Long before insurance companies deemed high dives dangerous, these girls staying at Lyman Lodge plunge into the crystal waters of the lake circa 1925. Courtesy of the Minnesota Historical Society.

7
Work Hard, Play Harder

"A Honeymooners' Paradise"
Walking on Water

Poets, artists, and musicians have always romanticized Lake Minnetonka. Longfellow waxed poetic about Minnehaha Falls in 1855 in *The Song of Hiawatha*, but he never visited Minnesota. In the same vein, Charles Wakefield Cadman wrote the song "From the Land of the Sky-Blue Waters" in 1909 (later adopted as the Hamm's Beer jingle), including Indian tom-toms to complete the atmosphere. The most famous song about the lake had to be Thurlow Lieurance's "By the Waters of Minnetonka: An Indian Love Song," heard on every jukebox in the country in 1926:

> Moon Deer, how near
> your soul divine
> Sun Deer, No fear
> in heart of mine.
> Skies blue o'er you,
> Look down in love;
> Waves bright give light
> As on they move.
> Hear thou my vow
> To live, to die.
> Moon Deer
> Thee near, Beneath this sky.

Newspapers trumpeted the lake as being even better than the clichéd Niagara Falls for lovers. The *Kansas City Star* wrote in the 1890s that Lake Minnetonka was a "honeymooners' paradise." The book *Once upon a Lake* describes the feel in the 1880s: "It was a lovely life, that of the eighties. Some of it was debonair and all of it was gay."

Many came for the sports of sailing, fishing, and tennis on grass courts. Roller-skating took the area by storm in the late 1870s: "Parlor skates have at last reached Minneapolis," according to the *Minnetonka Tourist* of 1877; "J. H. Fenton, of New York, has leased a hall and announces a reception on the 18th" for a skating party. Tonka Bay and other areas on the lake had roller rinks.

Other crazes included bloomers, made popular by Amelia Jenks Bloomer, marking a liberated woman. Abbie Wakefield, one of the first women to attend the

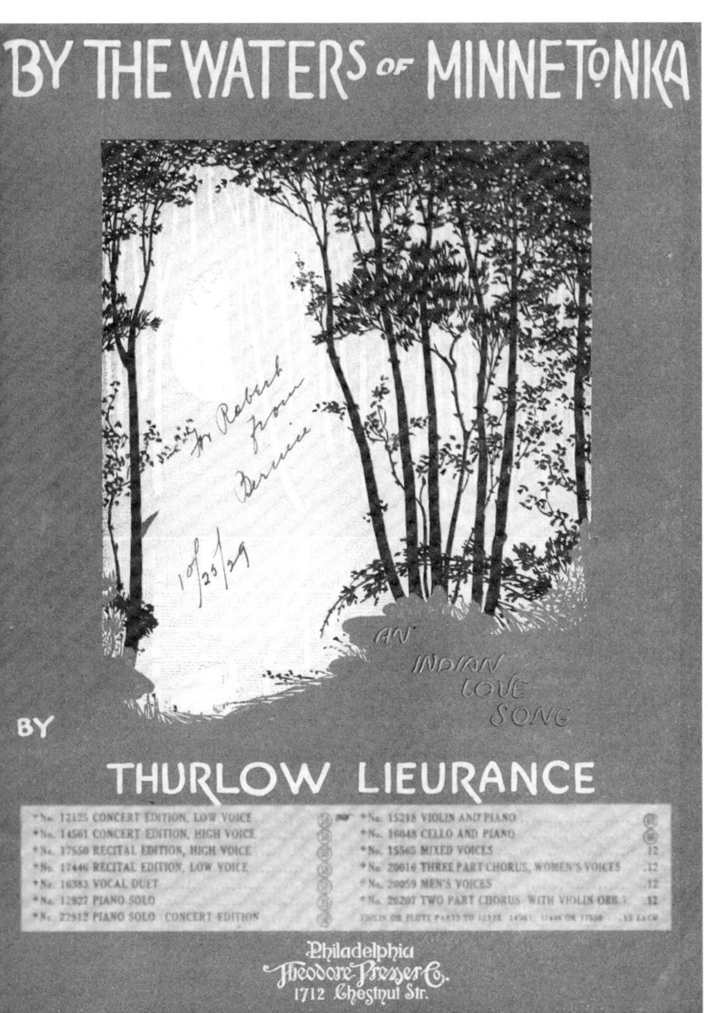

Thurlow Lieurance's "By the Waters of Minnetonka" did more to promote the lake than anything else. Everyone from Glenn Miller to Desi Arnaz and Lucille Ball covered the song about a mythical Indian romance in the spirit of Longfellow's "Song of Hiawatha." Courtesy of the Hennepin History Museum.

University of Minnesota in the 1870s, proudly wore bloomers and long trousers, much to the shock of her peers. When the Nineteenth Amendment passed, giving women the right to vote in 1920, no one was surprised that she was the first in line to vote. Wayzata had no voting booths, so she called the fire department to bring her to the voting booths at Minnetonka Mills. After all, this was an emergency.

Most women wore hoop skirts and other uncomfortable fashions that prevailed in the 1870s. Corsets were the rage, but doctors predicted "gland trouble, liver complaint and death." However, "the laced-up ladies paid no attention." Before bikinis and sexy swimsuits, both women and men kept covered even in the water. Nellie B. Wright told author Blanche Wilson about the early days on Lake Minnetonka: "It was a secluded spot, so folks didn't need bathing suits. The women wore Mother Hubbards and the men used everyday pants. . . . Swimming was done dog fashion, and nobody'd ever heard of diving."

One man in Excelsior avoided getting wet altogether and looked back to Leonardo da Vinci's "water shoes." His version of the Italian's invention was essentially a pair of long wooden boards strapped on his feet; they had zinc fins underneath so he would not just tumble into the drink. In 1880, he walked on water all the way from Excelsior to Wayzata. While his feat made the papers, some joked that it would have been much easier and quicker to just walk all around the twisting shoreline.

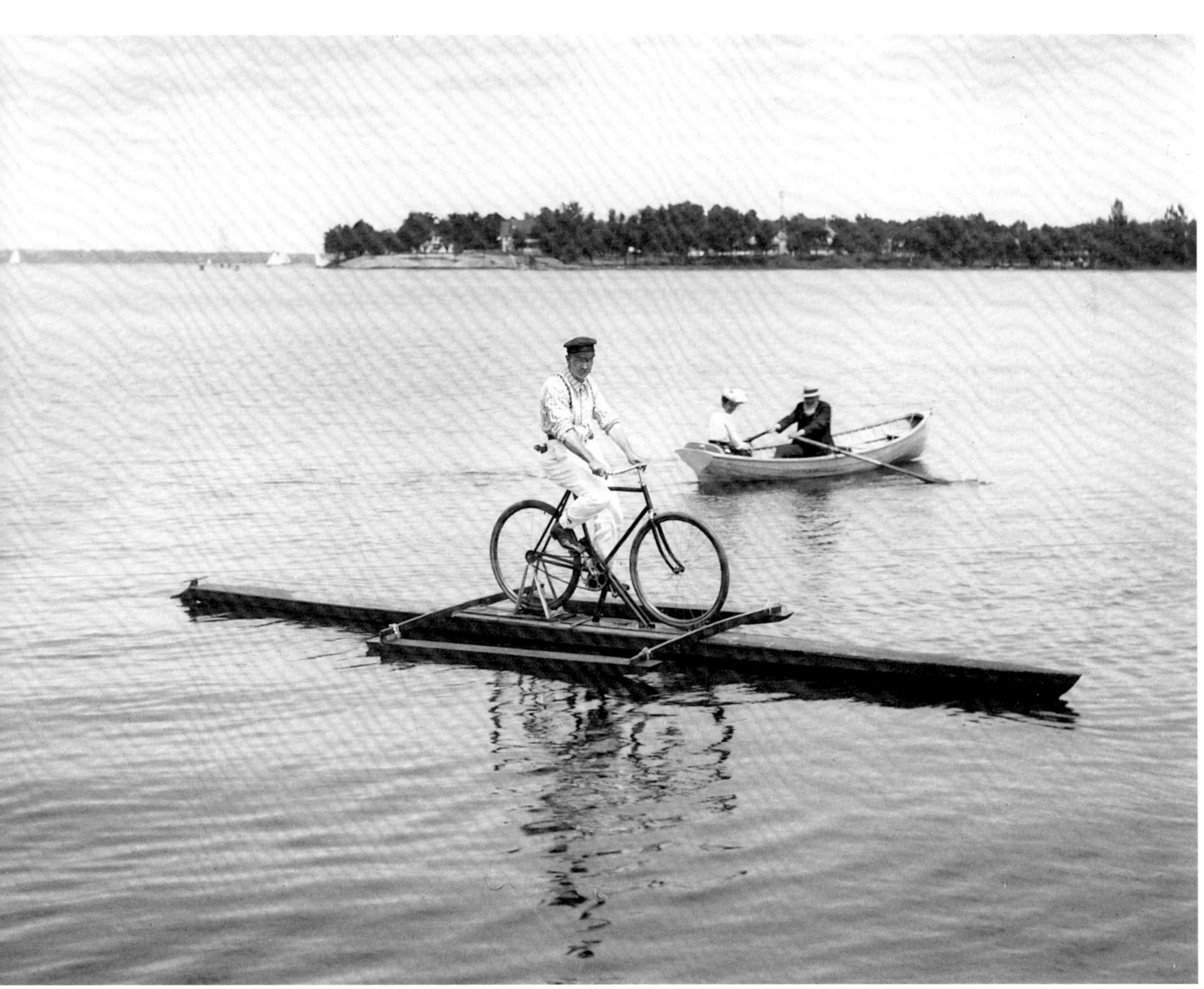

Lake Minnetonka has always been a showcase for waterborne inventions. This enterprising stuntman fitted his bicycle to a pontoon in 1905 and hoped waves would not dump him and his dapper outfit in the drink. Courtesy of the Minnesota Historical Society.

The goal of all such shenanigans was purely to get attention, and the towns around the lake took notice. Some of the entertainments available were benign and family oriented, such as those at Wayzata's picnic grounds west of town: there was a croquet pitch, a dancing stage, and a "victualizing stand" that offered fresh ginger pop. Others seem cruel by today's standards, such as Excelsior's display in 1880 of an Eskimo girl, who had been brought to town so visitors could come and observe her, as if she were some sort of animal. Deephaven went high class in 1905 when it was visited by a Shakespearean troupe consisting of Sir Philip Ben Greet and his English Company of Woodland Players. At a natural outdoor amphitheater near the tennis courts, they performed *As You Like It* and *A Midsummer Night's Dream* under the stars.

By far the preferred entertainment, however, was dancing. In 1873, the Excelsior Commons boasted an elevated stage where locals could dance cheek to cheek, but some of the more prudent in the area viewed the whole spectacle "as pretty disgusting since it gave aid and comfort to those males who had an eye for a shapely ankle," according to *Once upon a Lake.* Many of the antidancing crowd were probably the prohibitionists, who frowned on this bawdy merrymaking, which they feared might be stirred by demon drink.

The dancing could not be stopped. In 1912, "a wave of the 'Bunny Hug' and the 'Turkey Trot' swept the dance halls of the nation," according to *The Early Background of Minnetonka Beach.* That same year, a committee of the Board of Governors of the Lafayette met "to restrict as far as possible the introduction of new and objectionable dances at the club house." In the end, efforts to control the foxtrots at the Lafayette Club proved unsuccessful. The ballroom caught fire on June 18, 1922, and burned to the ground, killing two young women inside. Surely the Victorian prudes had predicted this kind of catastrophe.

Tough Tonka Toys

A Six-Ton Elephant on an Eight-Pound Truck

Formed in a rundown schoolhouse along Lake Minnetonka, Mound Metalcraft made garden tools immediately after World War II but soon turned to toy trucks as a side project, and Tonka Toys was born. The name stems from the metropolitan area's largest body of water, Lake Minnetonka, and the "Tonka" part, from the Dakota word meaning "big," rolls satisfyingly off the tongue. The original oval logo had lapping waves in homage to the Big Water right outside the company's doors.

Riding on the baby boom, this little company soon moved into a huge new factory (now the Balboa Building in downtown Mound) and soon earned Mound the nickname "Trucking Capital of the World" for all the little vehicles sold worldwide. Tonka's yellow

Most local elementary schools visited the fantastic Tonka Toy factory in Mound as a regular field trip. I remember my school outing to this fantasyland, with every toy I had ever wanted just out of reach. Courtesy of Westonka Historical Society, Mound.

Tonka Toys advertisements featured another Minnesota native, the Jolly Green Giant. All this miniature machinery was perfect for digging in the sand along the shore. Collection of George T. Kitchen.

dump trucks were mini-monster-trucks before those massive beasts with oversized wheels ever existed.

In the mid-1970s, our elementary school class of third graders from Groveland School ventured to the far side of the big lake to tour this magical factory—like Santa's workshop specializing in metal trucks that even an elephant couldn't crush; such toys would be an anomaly now in our age of ubiquitous plastic. Inside this fantasyland, conveyor belts transported the fire-engine-red pickup trucks, the robin's-egg-blue tow trucks, and the pearly white airplanes overhead and through trap doors in the wall to be sent to toy stores across the country. How we wanted to snatch some of those toys and sneak them out in our backpacks! Would anyone ever notice? Our teachers told us to keep our hands to ourselves—just like Willy Wonka warned disobedient rascals not to touch—or we could get caught in the cogs, flattened out, and turned into a toy truck.

Alas, in 1982 much of the manufacturing was moved first to Texas and eventually to China, and the company was bought out by Hasbro. The old schoolhouse has since been torn down, but the Westonka Historical Society in Mound dreams of reviving these memories with a Tonka Toys Museum near the lake for which the toys were named.

(Opposite) In 1926, long before leaving Lake Minnetonka to answer the call of Hollywood, the Andrews Sisters posed on the dock at Mound beach with their parents, Olga and Peter. Collection of Robert Boyer.

Andrews Sisters' Mound

The Boogie-Woogie Trio of Lake Minnetonka

Peter Andreos traveled from sunny Greece to snowy Minneapolis and opened the Pure Food Café in Minneapolis with his new bride, a Norwegian Lutheran named Olga Sollie. To fit in with these northern Europeans, Peter changed his surname to "Andrews." The couple had three harmonious daughters, Maxene, Patty and LaVerne. Their mother taught them to carry a tune, even though their father sometimes scowled at the idea that their sing-alongs would take them far from home. From 1920 to 1924, the family lived in Mound, where Olga's brothers also lived and ran a grocery store. To earn cash to go roller-skating, the sisters would set pins at the bowling alley in Mound, when they were not trying to impersonate the melodious Boswell Sisters of Bing Crosby's radio show. LaVerne also played piano accompaniment to earn the sisters fancy dancing lessons at the Clausen School of Dance downtown.

In 1931, Larry Rich and his big band traveled through town with RKO Radio Pictures in search of the next big talent from the heartland, so the sisters signed up to sing "On the Sunny Side of the Street." The judges unanimously awarded them first prize (despite competition from ventriloquist Edgar Bergen, father of Candice Bergen). They soon sang regularly on Minneapolis radio station WCCO, performed at the Orpheum Theatre on Hennepin Avenue, and even performed with the Glenn Miller Orchestra. They accompanied Rich on tour, but they earned a measly dollar a day split three ways. Still, performing in front of huge audiences honed their talents and expanded their fan base. The girls' singing kept the family afloat during the bust times of the Depression as their father, now convinced, drove them from town to town, venue to venue.

The Andrews Sisters became the voice of America during World War II and sang their upbeat tunes to sometimes dispirited GIs on numerous USO tours. Often playing four or five shows a day, the prolific Andrews Sisters climbed the charts—achieving more top-ten hits than Elvis or the Beatles—and acted in more than fifteen films. Even though they had hit the big time, the trio often ventured back to the shores of Lake Minnetonka in their fancy cars for a brief summer vacation with their uncles. Today, the Andrews Sisters Trail in Mound commemorates the local girls who made good. Although the Andrewses' house and store still stand, they have been transformed since the sisters' melodies filled the air.

Frank Lloyd Wright's Minnetonka Malfeasance

The Architect's "Immoral Acts" on the Lake

Frank Lloyd Wright made Spring Green, Wisconsin, and Oak Park, Illinois, famous with his prairie school houses that meshed the landscape with his long horizontal lines and Japanese-cum-craftsman designs.

Lake Minnetonka, however, had a less cordial relationship with America's most famous architect. Wright's familiarity with the lake began with one of his last great residential projects, the Francis Little House in Deephaven. In 1908, Chicago investment banker Francis Little and his wife Mary commissioned architect Frank Lloyd Wright to build a house in Deephaven on a spot overlooking the lake. Wright's prairie school aesthetic took advantage of the surrounding countryside for this, his first house in Minnesota, and he designed the house to fit into the landscape.

Soon after Wright took the commission, he traveled first to Europe and then to Japan and delayed construction of the house. Fortunately, Francis Little and his family still had a house in the Kenwood neighborhood of Minneapolis, but they were frustrated with the delay. Rather than switch architects, Little had a small cottage built in the prairie school style on the property so that the family could take advantage of the lake while they waited for Wright, who took three summers to finish the house. Even when the enormous house was finished in 1915, the Littles considered it just a "summer-retreat cottage," and it was not even winterized until 1951.

Wright put banks of windows all along the water side of the house so the Littles could have a panoramic view of Lake Minnetonka. Mary Little objected to all the small window panes, which Wright had designed especially for the house, since she preferred larger picture windows. The Little House had the typical prairie school characteristic of long horizontal roof lines—250 feet in this case—to parallel the horizon and the lake below. The open floor plan flowed from room to room, as Wright was influenced by Japanese design and by the Asian idea of feng shui. One of the rooms was a small concert hall specifically for Mary Little, a virtuoso pianist who had studied under Franz Liszt in Cologne, Germany. The gorgeous music room, fifty-five feet long and thirty-five feet wide, had sixty-five stained-glass windows.

Wright's turbulent personal affairs made his soap-opera life fodder for the tabloids and recently inspired novelist T. C. Boyle's book *The Women* about Wright's three wives plus soul mate. Wright's first wife refused to grant him a divorce when he met his true love, Mamah Cheney, in Oak Park. The couple escaped to Fiesole, Italy, which caused most American firms to avoid working with him, as an "immoral" architect. Wright eventually built his prairie school workshop, Taliesin, in Spring Green, Wisconsin, but while he was away, a servant set it aflame and murdered Mamah, her two children, and four workers with an ax.

Wright married again, to Miriam Noel, but that marriage unraveled because of his new wife's morphine addiction. Before getting divorced, he shacked up with married Montenegrin dancer Olgivanna "Olga" Hinzenburg on the shores of Lake Minnetonka to work on his autobiography. The lovebirds' spouses were not amused. Wright's wife charged him with infidelity, and Olga's husband with "alienation of affections."

After Francis Little's enormous "summer-retreat cottage" was torn down, the remnants of the building were scattered to various museums. The living room is on permanent display at the Metropolitan Museum of Art in New York. Copyright 2014 Metropolitan Museum of Art / Frank Lloyd Wright Foundation, Scottsdale, Arizona / Art Resource, NY / Artists Rights Society (ARS), NY.

Wright evaded court orders from both Milwaukee and Chicago to explain his actions and used the alias "Mr. Richardson" to live incognito at a little cottage in Wildhurst on Lake Minnetonka with Olga and her two young children. The newly enacted Mann Act forbidding "white slavery," named for Illinois Republican congressman James Robert Mann, banned interstate transport of females for "immoral purposes." Hennepin county deputy sheriffs nabbed Wright as he was exiting his porch door on October 20, 1926.

"Is this my country and is this what I have worked for?" Wright said to the *Minneapolis Tribune* the next day from the Hennepin County jail. "Can't I be left alone? Everyone I see, except those I love, reminds me of the hog that trampled down the corn it couldn't eat." Wright's wife eventually gave him the divorce, and he married Olga, his third and last wife.

Perhaps fed up with this puritanical state, Wright built only a dozen houses in Minnesota, relatively few considering that he was born just across the river in Richland Center, Wisconsin. He was the most famous architect in America; his houses have become tourist sites, and his turbulent lifestyle has become legend.

During the 1960s and '70s, teardown mania struck, and Minnesota would never be the same. Minneapolis's beautiful brick buildings and mansions were leveled, and Lake Minnetonka was not spared. Old houses were torn down along Lake Minnetonka to make way for McMansions, and architectural gems that did not fit current tastes sometimes succumbed to the wrecking ball. The Littles had since passed their house to new owners, the Stevensons, who were fed up with the idiosyncrasies of a Frank Lloyd Wright house, including built-in furniture that could not be moved and inevitable drafts and water problems.

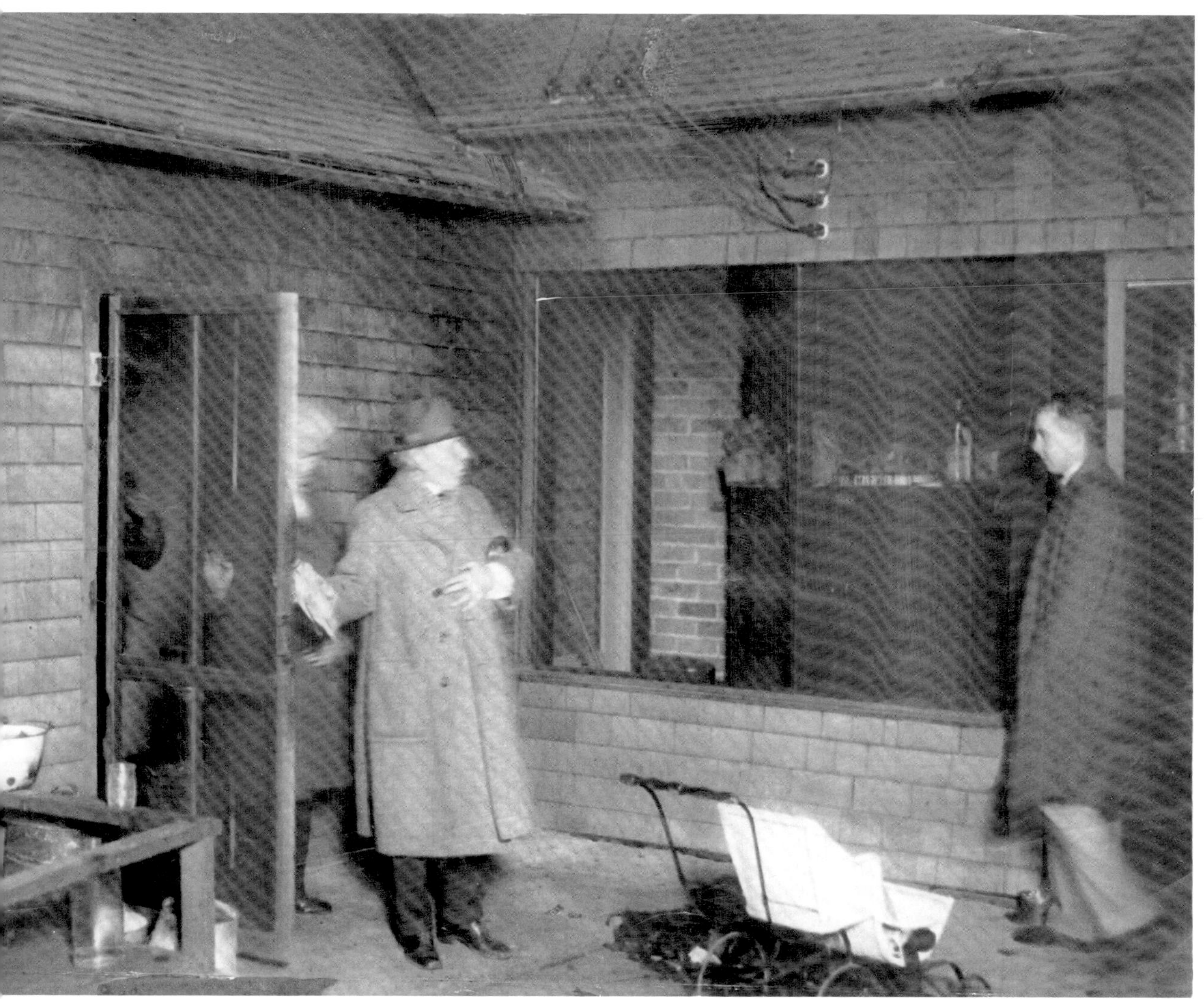

While still married to his second wife, Frank Lloyd Wright came to Lake Minnetonka with a married woman and was arrested by the Hennepin County deputy sheriff for "white slavery." Courtesy Hennepin County Library Special Collections.

Wright had been dead for more than a decade and had come to be considered one of America's greatest architects. The idea of destroying this house, a perfect specimen of his prairie school phase, was blasphemy to his fans. A group of enthusiasts contacted the Metropolitan Museum of Art in New York to see if it could save this midwestern masterpiece. The museum salvaged parts of the house so the Stevensons could build a more modern house that suited them.

In 1982, the living room from the Little House was installed at the Metropolitan Museum of Art, where it overlooks a grand view of Central Park rather than the lake. Also that year, the museum sold a hallway from the house to the Minneapolis Institute of Arts, where it is proudly displayed on the third floor. The Allentown Art Museum in Pennsylvania purchased the library from the house. Wright aficionados now must travel to three cities to visit the best architectural site of Lake Minnetonka and to witness Wright's vision of connecting to the land through architecture.

Rolling Stones Invade Excelsior!

"You Can't Always Get What You Want"

Beatlemania and the British Invasion shocked the United States when the mop-headed Mods landed at Met Stadium, on the only leg of their tour that did not sell out. The bad boys of rock, the Rolling Stones, followed in 1964 with a sporadic tour at mostly out-of-the-way venues—including Danceland at Excelsior Amusement Park on June 12, where the Beach Boys had just staged a sellout show. The management of Big Reggie's Danceland booked the bands and figured that the fame and infamy of the Stones would pack the place in spite of jacked-up ticket prices and almost no publicity. But it was not to be. On his television show, Dean Martin had just referred to this "caveman quintet" as a bunch of "orangutangs." Besides, who would want the mass hysteria of screaming teenagers along quiet Lake Minnetonka?

Only about 283 fans paid to see the future superstars, most of them after the admission price had been slashed halfway through the evening. When a student from Minnetonka High yelled to singer Mick Jagger, "Who do you guys think you are? The Beatles?," Jagger looked down at him and uttered in his thick English accent, "Son, we're going to make you forget all about the Beatles."

As the possibly apocryphal tale goes, the next morning, Jagger went down to the Excelsior drugstore to get a prescription filled. He was standing in line with Jimmy "Mr. Jimmy" Hutmaker, who looked pretty ill. When Hutmaker could not get cherries in his Coke at Bacon Drug, he turned to Jagger and said the now-famous line "You can't always get what you want."

This story has been more or less accepted (only Mick can confirm it, as Mr. Jimmy died in 2007), but

The British Invasion conquered Big Reggie's Danceland at Excelsior Amusement Park when the Rolling Stones took over on June 12, 1964. Courtesy of the Excelsior–Lake Minnetonka Historical Society.

multiple interpretations of the song persist. Was the "Mr. Jimmy" of the song in fact Jimi Hendrix, Excelsior's Jimmy Hutmaker, or the Stones' producer Jimmy Miller, who ended up playing drums on the song? Is it Chelsea Drugstore (a nickname for a hip pub on King's Road in London) or Excelsior ('celsior) Drugstore (Bacon Drug with its soda fountain)? Is the song about Jagger's girlfriend at the time, Marianne Faithfull?

Danceland in Excelsior did survive the British Invasion, at least until the wrecking ball closed the Excelsior Amusement Park in 1973. The Chelsea Drugstore in England has shut its doors and a McDonald's has sprung up on its site, a sad tombstone for Swinging London and a sign of the arrival of the American invasion. Bacon Drug and its soda fountain have since closed. But at least Excelsior has managed to keep fast food franchises on the edge of town.

Bonnie Raitt's Minnetonka Moment

Her First Recording on Enchanted Island

Bonnie Raitt's blues career, including ten Grammies, began on Lake Minnetonka at an old summer camp on Enchanted Island. The camp setting made her feel at home because she had performed as a kid at a remote summer camp in the Adirondack Mountains, much as Bob Dylan (then Robert Zimmerman) did when he lugged along his guitar to a Jewish camp in Wisconsin.

Bonnie Raitt had not intended to be a blues musician; instead, she went to the all-girls Radcliffe College in Cambridge before it merged with Harvard. She took a semester off to play her soulful folk music around Boston with the likes of Howlin' Wolf and other blues musicians. Soon scouts were sitting in on her shows, and Warner Brothers offered her a contract. Along with her brother Steve, Bonnie hooked up with a who's who of musicians from the West Bank of Minneapolis to record her debut and eponymous album *Bonnie Raitt*, released in 1971. Dave Ray of the Twin Cities trio Koerner, Ray, and Glover was the sound engineer along with Sylvia Ray. Willie Murphy, who still plays piano regularly in Minneapolis, produced the record, and his band, Willie and the Bees, provided the backup for the album.

To keep the rough, spontaneous feel of her shows, Bonnie Raitt chose to use the old summer camp rather than a slick urban studio for the "live" four-track recordings. All the musicians could stay in the house and porch and they recorded in the old barn. "I was going to go out there because it was a big party out on the lake," remembers Fred Case, a music aficionado who lived in the famous Sign House on the West Bank, "but there was so much going on with music in the cities at the time."

Dr. Demento, who grew up in Minneapolis and knew many of the musicians at the sessions, had already left town by the time of the recording to work for Raitt's label, Warner Brothers, in Burbank, California. He wrote about her first album for a trade magazine to help promote the record and recalled fondly that he was able to get tickets to one of her first shows supporting the LP recorded on the shores of Minnetonka: "She opened for J. J. Cale at the venerable Ash Grove folk club [in Los Angeles]."

Raitt continued her Minnesota connections over the years, playing on *A Prairie Home Companion* in particular. Her bittersweet performances at the Minnesota State Fair include a tribute to guitarist Stevie Ray Vaughan the day after he died in a helicopter crash in Wisconsin. She credited him with helping her get clean from drugs, and she flew out right after the concert to attend his funeral with many other blues musicians. Raitt has performed occasionally at the Minnesota State Fair Grandstand and dedicated a heartfelt performance to her brother Steve, who played music for years in the Twin Cities and played on that first record on Enchanted Island.

At an old summer camp on Enchanted Island, Bonnie Raitt gathered musicians from Minneapolis and beyond for her first album. The ensemble, which included blues greats Junior Wells and A. C. Reed, posed for a photograph, which graces the back of the album cover. Collection of Richard Tvedten.

Lake Minnetonka has long been a vacationers' paradise. This steamer drops visitors at a dock so they can scurry up to a campsite. Courtesy of the Excelsior–Lake Minnetonka Historical Society.

Afterword

WHAT WILL THE FUTURE BRING for Lake Minnetonka? I keep coming back to the lake and discovering new stories and new innovation as the area reinvents itself.

My grandparents long ago, in the 1940s, gave up their Seton Lake cottage near the main lake and built a little cabin on the remote Whitefish chain of lakes north of Brainerd. Lake Minnetonka has been built up with million-dollar mansions, and the same cycle is occurring around northern lakes. Some of the railroad overpasses I used for bridge jumping when I was young have been torn down, and James J. Hill's railway legacy is less and less visible.

Most of Minnetonka's quaint cottages have been torn down, replaced by giant McMansions bulging over the original foundations. Fortunately, some visionaries recognize the charm of these classic cabins and have renovated them and kept the magic. Remnants survive, such as the Cottagewood Store, which has miraculously endured thanks to neighborhood involvement, and the Wayzata train depot—"the best on the line."

Bacon Drug, Mick Jagger's supposed inspiration for "You Can't Always Get What You Want," is not serving up "cherry red" and won't until an entrepreneur puts a classic drugstore, with a soda fountain, back in the building that still stands there. Considering the town of Excelsior's dedication to local businesses and its determination not to let chain stores ruin historic Water Street, perhaps a resurrected Bacon Drug is possible.

Giant steamboats such as the *City of St. Louis* and the *Belle of Minnetonka* are long gone, replaced by costly speedboats with engines more powerful than those of the old paddle-wheel boats that carried thousands of passengers. The decadence of the past survives in such scandals as the notorious Minnesota Vikings "Love Boat" party on the lake in 2005, but this is hardly the norm of activities on the lake. As a snub to such debauchery, the restored streetcar boat *Minnehaha* braves the wakes thrown up by speedy cigarette boats and persists as a testament to those dedicated to preserving the lake's fascinating history, even if it means dredging it up from the muck dozens of feet under the surface. What other treasures are preserved on the bottom of the lake, waiting to be rediscovered and lovingly revived?

Even the Excelsior trolley is back, making regular runs on summer weekends—perhaps the area will preserve its charm after all. Although the bucolic Commons still opens the town to the lake, the amusement park is never coming back, not least because condominiums now fill that space. Big Island's grandeur is nothing but overgrown ruins. The dozens of grand hotels around the lake have either been demolished or have ended up in ashes. No hotels line the lake now, and a new proposal to build a replica was shot down. Would a copy of a classic old hotel with wide verandas just be a cheesy imitation?

Frank Lloyd Wright's breathtakingly beautiful house in Deephaven was stupidly torn down, but have we learned our lesson to preserve the old? Perhaps not. The guesthouse by today's great architect Frank Gehry was moved seventy miles south to Owatonna, but at least it was not destroyed. Ralph Rapson's fabulous modernist house for the Pillsburys was razed in 1997. Will we recognize the value of these amazing architectural gems, or will we keep making the same mistakes? Perhaps new marvelous houses will rise from the ashes of the past, just as the elegant old hotels made way for the mansions of the Jazz Age.

Telling these tales about the lake's history matters because only through them can we know our past. Some of these stories are rife with embellishments and half-truths, such as the Dakota legends that we can't confirm, but should we stop telling them? Although reenacting supposed Native American rituals in groups such as Indian Guides may leave many shaking their heads, at least such activities may ignite interest in those early years, even if we may never know the exact truth. The French voyageurs and the early settlers certainly exaggerated their experiences for better effect, but does that mean they aren't good stories? Always keep in mind what the storyteller hopes to gain and why the tale is being told.

These stories and others of the past need to be told; I had to dig to discover them in books and in the collections of historical societies. Only once we know the depth of our local history can we halt the wrecking ball and appreciate the bounty of what was and what will be. ❧

For Further Reading

Andrews, Maxene, and Bill Gilbert. *Over Here, Over There.* New York: Zebra Books, 1993.

Atwater, Isaac, and John H. Stevens, eds. *History of Minneapolis and Hennepin County.* New York: Munsell, 1895.

Berthel, Mary W. *Horns of Thunder: The Life and Times of James M. Goodhue.* St. Paul: Minnesota Historical Society Press, 1948.

Bost, Theodore, and Sophie Bost. *A Frontier Family in Minnesota: Letters of Theodore and Sophie Bost, 1851–1920.* Minneapolis: University of Minnesota Press, 1981.

Brake, Hezekiah. *On Two Continents: Along Life's Experience.* Topeka, Kans.: Crane, 1896.

Brooks, Frona M. "How Nan Raced." In *Purpose and Success.* Boston: Perry Mason, 1899.

Brown, Charles W. *My Ditty Bag.* Boston: Small, Maynard, 1925.

Canton, Rolf. *Minnesotans in the Movies.* Minneapolis: Nodin Press, 2007.

Carley, Kenneth. *The Sioux Uprising of 1862.* St. Paul: Minnesota Historical Society Press, 1976.

Cherland-McCune, Lori. *Royal C. Moore: The Man Who Built the Streetcar Boats.* Edina, Minn.: Beaver's Pond Press, 2013.

Dahl, Borghild. *A Minnetonka Summer.* New York: E. P. Dutton, 1960.

Deloria, Philip J. *Playing Indian.* New Haven, Conn.: Yale University Press, 1998.

Diers, John W., and Aaron Isaacs. *Twin Cities by Trolley: The Streetcar Era in Minneapolis and St. Paul.* Minneapolis: University of Minnesota Press, 2007.

Dillman, Daisy Ellen. *100 Years in Excelsior.* Minneapolis: Holden Printing Company, 1953.

Dimond, Alfred. *The Magic Northland: An Illustrated Guide to the Great Northwest.* Minneapolis: Hoppin, Palmer, and Dimond, 1881.

Douglas, Marjorie Myers. *Barefoot on Crane Island.* St. Paul: Minnesota Historical Society Press, 1998.

Dregni, Eric. *Midwest Marvels: Roadside Attractions across Iowa, Minnesota, the Dakotas, and Wisconsin.* Minneapolis: University of Minnesota Press, 2006.

———. *Minnesota Marvels: Roadside Attractions in the Land of Lakes.* Minneapolis: University of Minnesota Press, 2001.

———. *Vikings in the Attic: In Search of Nordic America.* Minneapolis: University of Minnesota Press, 2011.

———. *Weird Minnesota.* New York: Sterling Press, 2006.

Du Bois, W. E. B. *Darkwater.* New York: Harcourt, Brace, and Howe, 1920.

Eaton, Leonard K. *Landscape Artist in America: The Life and Work of Jens Jensen.* Chicago: University of Chicago Press, 1964.

Ellet, Elizabeth Fries. *Summer Rambles in the West.* New York: J. C. Riker, 1853.

Featherstonhaugh, George W. *A Canoe Voyage up the Minnay Sotor.* London: Richard Bentley, 1847.

Folwell, William. *A History of Minnesota.* St. Paul: Minnesota Historical Society, 1922.

Gray, James. *The University of Minnesota, 1851–1951.* Minneapolis: University of Minnesota Press, 1951.

Hammel, Bette. *Legendary Homes of Lake Minnetonka.* St. Paul: Minnesota Historical Society Press, 2009.

Innli, Kjell, ed. *The Norwegian Kitchen.* Kristiansun, Norway: Svein Gran KOM Forlag, 1994.

Janik, Erika. *Apple: A Global History.* London: Reaktion Books, 2011.

Jones, Thelma. *Once upon a Lake.* Minneapolis: Ross and Haines, 1957.

Koutsky, Kathryn, and Linda Koutsky. *Minnesota Vacation Days.* St. Paul: Minnesota Historical Society Press, 2006.

Lanegran, David. *The Lake District of Minneapolis.* Minneapolis: University of Minnesota Press, 2004.

Larson, Paul Clifford. *A Place at the Lake.* Afton, Minn.: Afton Historical Society Press, 1998.

Leipold, Darel J. *A Historical Review of the Picturesque Lake Minnetonka Area.* Excelsior, Minn.: Minnetonka State Bank, 1981.

Meyer, Ellen Wilson. *Happenings around Deephaven: The First Hundred Years.* Wayzata, Minn.: Excelsior–Lake Minnetonka Historical Society, 1978.

———. *Tales from Tonka: Stories of People around Lake Minnetonka.* Excelsior, Minn.: Excelsior–Lake Minnetonka Historical Society, 1993.

Millett, Larry. *Lost Twin Cities.* St. Paul: Minnesota Historical Society Press, 1992.

Morledge, Phillip J. *The Many Legends of Jesse James.* Sheffield, England: PJM Publishing, 2009.

Mowry, H. W. *Guide and Directory of Lake Minnetonka.* Excelsior, Minn.: Lake Minnetonka Print House, 1884.

Ogland, James. *Picturing Lake Minnetonka.* St. Paul: Minnesota Historical Society Press, 2001.

Parkman, Francis. *The Old Regime in Canada.* Boston: Little, Brown, 1899.

Potter, Merle. *101 Best Stories of Minnesota.* Minneapolis: Harrison and Smith, 1931.

Richards, Bergmann. *The Early Background of Minnetonka Beach.* Minneapolis: Hennepin County Historical Society, 1957.

Rockvam, Tom. *The Andrews Sisters and Their 100-Year Connection to Lake Minnetonka and Mound.* Mound, Minn.: Tom Rockvam Publications, 2008.

Sforza, John. *Swing It!* Lexington: University Press of Kentucky, 2000.

Snelling, William Joseph. *Tales of the Northwest.* 1830. Minneapolis: University of Minnesota, 1936.

Stickley, Gustav. *Craftsman Homes: Architecture and Furnishings of the American Arts and Crafts Movement.* New York: Dover, 1979.

Stiles, T. J. *Jesse James: Last Rebel of the Civil War.* New York: Random House, 2003.

Stokker, Kathleen. *Remedies and Rituals: Folk Medicine in Norway and the New Land.* St. Paul: Minnesota Historical Society Press, 2007.

Thibault, Isabel. *My Island: Memories of a Childhood on Gale's Island.* Excelsior, Minn.: Excelsior–Lake Minnetonka Historical Society, 1978.

Walker, Charles Rumford. *American City: A Rank and File History of Minneapolis.* Minneapolis: University of Minnesota Press, 2005.

Wilson, Angela. *What Does Justice Look Like? The Struggle for Liberation in Dakota Homeland.* St. Paul: Living Justice Press, 2008.

Wilson, Blanche. *Minnetonka Story.* Minneapolis: Ross and Haines, 1950.

Winchell, Newton H. *The Aborigines of Minnesota.* St. Paul: Pioneer, for the Minnesota Historical Society, 1911.

Wingerd, Mary Lethert. *North Country: The Making of Minnesota.* Minneapolis: University of Minnesota Press, 2010.

Yeatman, Ted P. *Frank and Jesse James: The Story behind the Legend.* Nashville, Tenn.: Cumberland House Publishing, 2003.

Eric Dregni is associate professor of English at Concordia University in St. Paul. He is the author of many books, including *Minnesota Marvels* (2001), *Midwest Marvels* (2006), *In Cod We Trust: Living the Norwegian Dream* (2008), *Never Trust a Thin Cook and Other Lessons from Italy's Culinary Capital* (2009), and *Vikings in the Attic: In Search of Nordic America* (2011), all published by the University of Minnesota Press. During the summer, he is dean of Lago del Bosco, the Italian Concordia Language Village in northern Minnesota. He lives in Minneapolis.

STUBBS BAY
MAXWELL BAY
ORONO
ORONO PT.
NORTH ARM
WEST ARM
MARKVILLE
CRYSTAL BAY
HARRISONS BAY
HOTEL DEL OTERO
LAFAYETTE CLUB
MINNETONKA BEACH
ARCOLA
SPRING PARK
LAKE LANGDON
MOUND CITY
SPRINGPARK BAY
LAFAYETTE BAY
COOKS BAY
ISLE VIEW
CARMANS BAY
CASCO
NARROWS
GALE I.
SPRAY I.
PHELPS BAY
TONKA BAY HOTEL
ENCHANTED I.
SHADY ISLE
HALSTEDS BAY
GIDEONS BAY
BIRCH BLUFF
EDGEWOOD
CRANE I.
DUNLAP I.
WOODSIDE
DOCK STATION
ZUMBRA HEIGHTS
SMITHTOWN BAY
EXCELSIOR
LAKE VIRGINIA
LAKE MINNEWASHTA
LAKE ZUMBRA